CW00554728

SPITFIRE SQUADRON

First published in 1990
by Air Research Publications
34 Elm Road, New Malden,
Surrey KT3 3HD
Great Britain
© Dilip Sarkar 1990

"Spitfire!" First published by
John Murray (Publishers) in 1942

All rights reserved. No part
of this publication may be
reproduced, stored in a retrieval
system, or transmitted in any
form or by any means without
prior permission in writing
from the publisher.
ISBN 1 871187 09 5

Typeset by Arioma Editorial Services
Gloucester House,
High Street, Borth,
Dyfed SY24 5HZ
Printed and bound in Great Britain
by L.P. Printing Services Limited
Burgess Hill, W.Sussex.

SPITFIRE SQUADRON

The story of No. 19 Squadron 1939 - 1941

by

Dilip Sarkar

AIR RESEARCH PUBLICATIONS

"Spitfire Squadron" is dedicated to the memory of Squadron Leader Brian James Edward Lane, D.F.C., R.A.F., one of the Second World War's unsung heroes.

276182

Moray District Council
Department of Libraries

940. 544

Part One

SPITFIRE

The Experiences of a Fighter Pilot
By Squadron-Leader B.J.Ellan

CONTENTS

Dedication   5

Foreword   7

Introduction   8

Acknowledgements   10

Fifty Years On   11

Bibliography   14

Part 1 "Spitfire!", S/Ldr. B.J. Ellan D.F.C   15

Part 2 "Spitfire Squadron", Dilip Sarkar   95

Chapter One   97

Chapter Two   117

Chapter Three   140

Chapter Four   165

Chapter Five   173

Appendix I
Service record of S/Ldr. B.J.E. Lane, D.F.C.   183

Appendix II Casualties.
Sustained by No.19 Sqn.
Sept '39 – June '41   184

Appendix III Claims.
Submitted by pilots of No.19 Sqn.
Sept '39 – June '41   187

Index to RAF personnel   191

Photo section   between pages 96 and 97

FOREWORD

by Dr Alfred Price FRHistS

One of the finest first – person accounts on the air fighting during the Battle of Britain period was a small book entitled *Spitfire!, the Experiences of a Fighter Pilot,* which appeared in 1942.

Spitfire! was not, and was never meant to be, a carefully considered work of history. It was written shortly after the Battle and the author, free from the doubts and controversies that would emerge later, provided a rare insight into the events of that momentous period as they appeared to the front – line fighter pilots involved in them. This was a story of men forced to live one day at a time, men to whom death and destruction were ever – present companions.

During the early years of the war the need to maintain the security of information on military matters was all important, and it was forbidden to link the names of Royal Air Force pilots with published descriptions of their exploits. The author of *Spitfire!* was Squadron Leader Brian J. Lane, commander of No. 19 Squadron from September 1940 to June 1941. We shall never know with what degree of reluctance Lane resorted to the pen name "B.J. Ellan", but the shallow subterfuge cannot have deceived anyone who knew him. Sadly, Brian Lane was killed in action in December 1942. His book has remained out of print for nearly half a century, the small number of copies surviving being much prized by aviation aficionados.

When I first heard of the plan to re – issue Brian Lane's book I was delighted. As we near the fiftieth anniversary of the Battle of Britain we shall see a vast number of books on the subject. Some will be good, others will be less so. The shortest possible list of books on the battle that are worth reading must include that by Brian Lane. I was also pleased when I heard that Dilip Sarkar, a capable and enthusiastic researcher, had made a study of Lane's service career and the actions in which he took part. The additional information on Lane and on No.19 Squadron comprises the final part of the book, and provides the historical background that Lane's own account lacked. I wish this book well, and hope that it will gain the sucess it deserves.

7

INTRODUCTION

A number of events occured which, unintentionally, led to the researching and writing of "Spitfire Squadron". Firstly, on September 21st, 1940, official photographers descended on Fowlmere Airfield and recorded on Kodachrome the pilots and Spitfires of No.19 (Fighter) Squadron. By that date the Battle of Britain had already reached its climax but was still being fought fiercely on a daily basis. The Duxford Sector, of which Fowlmere was a part, had operated the "Big Wing" of several fighter squadrons during the battle, led by Squadron Leader Douglas Bader, which had first gone into action on September 7th. By the time of the photographers' visit, the wing squadrons had been engaged with the enemy on many occasions, and had performed regular standing patrols as a matter of course. A fighter pilot faced a long and arduous day in the summer of 1940; deprivation of sleep soon lead to a state of exhaustion, but with the added strain of combat, the pilots were under tremendous pressure. Amongst the official photographs taken at Fowlmere were a number showing the pilots of No.19 Squadron in various poses. Many of these photographs have since been used to illustrate numerous books on the summer's conflict, and have been given general captions such as "Spitfire pilots at rest", or similar, neither the squadron or the individual pilots being identified. One of their number always caught my eye, a slim, dark haired young man, exhausted, his face clearly showing the strain of battle. His name was Squadron Leader Brian James Edward Lane, and by the time of the Battle of Britain he had already been awarded the Distinguished Flying Cross.

My research into the history of one particular Spitfire, R6644, took three years to complete, and comprised of identifying and tracing the pilots who had once flown that machine. One was Arthur Frank Vokes, from Erdington in Birmingham, who had flown the fighter whilst a pupil at No.5 Operational Training Unit, Aston Down, in June 1940. Later the same month he reported to No.19 Squadron, with whom he remained until his death in a flying accident on September 5th, 1941. Being an only son, and after the death of his parents, the few surviving relics of his life, such as his pilot's flying log book, letters, personal papers, medals and photographs, were passed around distant relatives. They eventually came into the care of the Malvern Spitfire Team, an aviation historical society of which I am secretary. Amongst these items was a book called "Spitfire!", written by Squadron Leader "B.J. Ellan DFC", whom I immediately identified as Brian Lane. I read the book, and Arthur Vokes's papers, with fascination and decided to commence my own research into the life of Squadron Leader Lane.

I was sad to discover that, having become an "ace" in the dangerous skies of 1940, twenty – five year old Brian Lane had been killed in action in 1942 on his first operational sortie following staff appointments at home and abroad. His body was never found. Left behind was a young widow, Eileen, who was also to die prematurely, of cancer, in 1967. As my research progressed, it appeared that Squadron Leader Lane was a pilot and leader of exceptional qualities, one of the unsung heroes of the first half of the Second World War.

Furthermore, a Spitfire from an operational training unit which crashed not far from my Malvern home in 1942, P9546, had served with No.19 Squadron during the Battle of Britain. During my research into that fighter's history I had discovered that P9546 was the regular mount of Flight Sergeant George Unwin. I seemed to be being drawn inexorably towards No.19 Squadron in my researches, so I decided that I would gather as much information as possible regarding the squadron's exploits from roughly the time Brian Lane joined the squadron in September 1939 until he left in June 1941. My intention was then to continue the story by researching his death in action, ultimately, I hoped, identifying the German pilot responsible.

In connection with this work I traced the majority of No.19 Squadron's surviving former pilots from the period, all of whom offered whole hearted support for my project; I feel privileged to have met some of them and corresponded with the rest. Their enthusiasm has really made the project a success, and has certainly made mine an extremely enjoyable task. Several things came across to me as a result of the research into the survivors' experiences and recollections, not least being their high regard of Brian Lane. As my material grew, I decided that the project would culminate in the book you are now about to read. I hope that as a result of this work Brian Lane's qualities will receive public recognition, and that my story of No.19 Squadron's exploits during this tumultuous period of history has recorded for posterity the extraordinary deeds of a group of mere youngsters, aged between their late teens and mid twenties.

My only regret is that I have been unable to trace any surviving members of Squadron Leader Lane's family. I feel sure that his late parents and wife would have been proud to read this tribute, although mere words can be no recompense for the loss of a son or husband. Some solace it may be, however, that his courage has inspired a young man, born twenty – one years after the Battle of Britain was fought, to write this book, and that the deeds of the "Few" during that Indian summer, now fifty years ago, performed against a backdrop of vapour trails and gunsmoke, still commands the world's utmost respect and admiration.

DILIP SARKAR, MALVERN, OCTOBER 1989.

ACKNOWLEDGEMENTS

A number of people have helped me in my research for this book. I would firstly like to thank the following former No.19 Squadron pilots who enthusiastically supported me: –

Air Vice – Marshal M.D. Lyne CB, AFC, RAF (Ret'd)
Air Commodore J.B. Coward AFC, RAF (Ret'd)
Group Captain G.L. Sinclair DFC, RAF (Ret'd),
Wing Commander G.C. Unwin DSO, DFM & Bar, RAF (Ret'd)
Wing Commander B.J. Jennings AFC, DFM, RAF (Ret'd)
Wing Commander D.G.S.R. Cox DFC, RAF (Ret'd)
Wing Commander P.I. Howard – Williams DFC, RAF (Ret'd)
Wing Commander F.N. Brinsden RAF (Ret'd)
Flight Lieutenant W. Cunningham DFC, RAF (Ret'd)
Flight Lieutenant A.N. MacGregor AE & Bar, RAF (Ret'd)
Flight Lieutenant K. Wilkinson RAF (Ret'd)

I would also like to thank: Mr J.M. Pinkham, Mr R.C. Steere, Air Vice Marshal F.D.S. Scott – Malden, Wing Commander J.B. Wray, Mr Grant McIntyre of John Murray (Publishers) Ltd, Mr F.A. Connelly, Mr Owen Fargus, Royal Netherlands Embassy, Imperial War Museum, the Keeper and Staff of the Public Record Office, Wing Commander N.P.W. Hancock DFC RAF (Ret'd) of the Battle of Britain Fighter Association, Group Captain David Green, of the "Spitfire Society", Mrs Margaret James, Mrs Edna Murray, historians Dr Alfred Price, Chrstopher F. Shores, John Foreman, Winfried Bock, Alan White, Andrew Long, and Mr Richard King of MoD AHB. Mr Gilbert Davies of Victor Studios, Hay – on – Wye, for photographic work, Mr Ernie Hardy for assisting with Public Record Office research and for invaluable encouragement, Frank Gee, Mr John Lumsden and Mrs D. Green for passing into my possession the personal belongings of the late Flight Lieutenant Arthur Vokes, and my fellow members of the Malvern Spitfire Team.

I would particularly like to thank Simon W. Parry for his guidance regarding the publication and production of this book.

Last, but certainly not least, I must thank my wife, Maria, without whose support I could neither research or write.

FIFTY YEARS ON

When writing *"Spitfire!"*, Squadron Leader Lane was considerably hampered by the official wartime censor. For obvious reasons, he was unable to identify any squadron, airfield or personality – even the author had to use the pseudonym "B.J.Ellan". To clarify matters for the reader, the following is a list identifying those personalities and locations in their order of mention in *"Spitfire!"*. All personnel are of No.19 Squadron unless otherwise stated.

DRAMATIS PERSONAE

"Mac"	Squadron Leader Eric McNab (No.266 Squadron).
"E.J."	Believed to be Squadron Leader Jameson (No.266 Squadron).
Wilf	Flight Lieutenant Wilfred Clouston.
F/Sgt S.	Flight Sergeant Harry Steere.
John	Flying Officer G.W. "Johnnie" Petre.
Michael	Pilot Officer Michael Lyne.
S/Ldr L.	Squadron Leader James Leathart (No.54 Squadron).
F/Sgt U	Flight Sergeant George "Grumpy" Unwin.
Eric/"B"	Flying Officer Eric Ball.
Watty	Pilot Officer Watson.
Sgt P.	Sergeant Jack Potter.
"G"	Flying Officer Gordon Sinclair.
Sgt I.	Sergeant Irwin.
Frankie	Flying Officer Frank Brinsden.
Sgt J.	Sergeant Bernard "Jimmy" Jennings.
S/Ldr M.	Squadron Leader "Tubby" Mermagen (No.222 Squadron).
S/Ldr H.	Squadron Leader Robin Hood (No.41 Squadron).
Cras	Flying Officer J.H.E. Craster. No.19 Squadron Intelligence Officer.
Leonard	Flying Officer Leonard Alan Haines.
Woody	Group Captain Woodhall, station commander Duxford.
S/Ldr P.	Squadron Leader Phillip "Tommy" Pinkham.
Jock	Pilot Officer Wallace Cunningham.
"F"	Flight Lieutenant Walter "Farmer" Lawson.
Sgt P. (Czech)	Sergeant Plzak.

11

Russell   Flying Officer J.Russell Budd, adjutant.
S/Ldr B.   Squadron Leader Douglas Bader.
Dolly (Czech)   Pilot Officer Frantizek Dolezal.
The Admiral   Sub – Lieutenant Arthur Giles Blake.
Sgt R.   Sergeant Roden.
Sgt C.   Sergeant Charnock.
"H" (Czech)   Pilot Officer Hradil.
Arthur   Pilot Officer Arthur Vokes.
"L"   Unidentified C.O. of Hurricane Squadron, spring
                       1941.

LOCATIONS

new squadron forming at "N"   No.266   Squadron   forming   at
                               Northolt.
aerodrome at "M"   Manston airfield, Kent.
beach at "D"   Deal.
airfield at "R"   Rochford airfield.
airfield at "C"   Coltishall airfield.
airfield at "H"   Hornchurch airfield.

FIFTY YEARS ON

It must also be remembered that in addition to the censor prohibiting the true identity of the personnel named in *"Spitfire!"* from being included, Squadron Leader Lane was also unable to furnish the reader with any technical details of the squadron's aircraft. Fortunately, fifty years on, I faced no such restrictions in relating my story of No.19 Squadron, the majority of contempory offical documentation now being freely available at the Public Record Office, London, to all those with a valid readers ticket. Furthermore, those former pilots who have been kind enough to relate their personal experiences of various incidents have been able to do so freely and honestly. For example, whilst in *"Spitfire!"* Squadron Leader Lane mentions stoppages in connection with his armament, I can relate the fact that No.19 Squadron were the only unit in Fighter Command to operate the Spitfire Mk Ib armed with two Hispano Suiza 20 mm cannon during the Battle of Britain, the remaining squadrons being equipped with the standard Browning .303 machine gun armed Spitfire Mk Ia. Using the file 'Trials of cannon armed Spitfires' (Air 16/42) at the Public Record Office, I was able to study No.19 Squadron's experiences with the unreliable Mk Ib in some detail. Certainly Squadron Leader Lane would not have been allowed to include in *"Spitfire!"* that the cannon armed Spitfires suffered so many stoppages that the pilots

12

all but refused to continue flying them in combat, the Mk Ib's being replaced by the standard Mk Ia in early September 1940. During the Battle of Britain No.19 Squadron flew as part of the "Big Wing" based at Duxford, led by Squadron Leader Douglas Bader; again, although mentioning the Wing in passing, Lane could certainly not discuss the tactical thinking behind such a formation and less so the controversy surrounding the "Big Wing" and alleged friction between the commanders of 11 and 12 Groups. *"Spitfire!"* was written largely as a propaganda exercise and was never meant to be an historical appreciation of 1940. Fortunately *"Spitfire Squadron"* can expand upon the theme, and place *"Spitfire!"* into its historical context.

It is also interesting to note some of the phrases and language used in *"Spitfire!"*, giving insight into society fifty years ago. For example, Lane talks about the squadron's ground crews "working like niggers", a comment which would not be well received in the multi – racial and cosmipolitan society of today. It is doubtful whether phrases like the "mindless Hun" would be used in books written today, be they autobiographies by those who were there or books such as *"Spitfire Squadron"*. One must remember that when Brian Lane wrote *"Spitfire!"*. Britain was locked in a conflict of arms with Nazi Germany which could only end in total defeat for one or the other power.

BIBLIOGRAPHY

In the research for this book I consulted the following files at the Public Record Office, which can be inspected by anyone with a valid reader's ticket: –

	P.R.O.Reference
No.19 Squadron Operations Record Book	– Air 27/252
No.19 Squadron Combat Reports	– Air 50/10
Squadron Leader Lane's log books	– Air 4/58
No.61 Operational Training Unit Operations Record Book	– Air 29/685
No.609 Squadron Operations Record Book	– Air 27/2102
No.167 Squadron Operations Record Book	– Air 27/1092
No.611 Squadron Operations Record Book	– Air 27/2109
No.616 Squadron Operations Record Book	– Air 27/2126
No.242 Squadron Operations Record Book	– Air 27/1471
No.310 Squadron Operations Record Book	– Air 27/1680
Trials of cannon armed Spitfires	– Air 16/142

The below listed books were invaluable, and are suggested further reading: –

Hitler & the Rise of the Nazis, D.M. Phillips, Edward Arnold (Publishers) Ltd. 1968.
Fight for the Sky, Douglas Bader, Sidgwick & Jackson Ltd. 1973.
Reach for the Sky, Paul Brickhill, Fontana, 1954.
Aces High, Christopher Shores & Clive Williams, Neville Spearman Ltd.
The Second World War, A.J.P. Taylor, Hamish Hamilton Ltd. 1975.
The Battle of Britain, Len Deighton, Jonathon Cape Ltd. 1980.
Action Stations 3, David Smith, Patrick Stephens Ltd. 1981.
Spitfire at War, by Alfred Price, Ian Allan Ltd. 1980.
Spitfire at War: 2, by Alfred Price, Ian Allan Ltd. 1985.
Battle of Britain: The Forgotten Months, John Foreman, Air Research Publications, 1988.
The Battle of Britain Then & Now, Mk V Edition, edited by Winston Ramsey, Battle of Britain Prints International Ltd. 1989.
The Blitz Then & Now Volume One, edited by Winston Ramsey, Battle of Britain Prints International Ltd. 1987.
The Blitz Then & Now Volume Two, edited by Winston Ramsey, Battle of Britain Prints International Ltd. 1988.
Spitfire the History, Eric Morgan & Edward Shacklady, Key Publishing Ltd. 1987.
German Fighters over England, Bryan Phillpott, Patrick Stephens Ltd. 1979.

Part One

SPITFIRE!

The Experiences of a Fighter Pilot
By Squadron-Leader B.J.Ellan

AUTHOR'S NOTE

THE title of this book no doubt tells you what it is about. The name "Spitfire" first became a household word during the "Blitz" of last year, but before this these wonderful aircraft had given us valiant service at Dunkirk.

In this book I have set down the experiences of a pilot in a fighter squadron – myself. I have been with the squadron since the beginning of the war, first as a flight commander and later as C.O., and I never wish to meet a grander bunch of blokes. We went all through Dunkirk and the "Blitz" which followed a couple of months later, and in telling my story I have tried to answer the question of the man in the street : "What is it like up there?" and to give you an idea of what a fighter pilot feels and thinks as he fights up there in the blue.

To any members of the squadron who may read this book, I hope I have not left out any of their pet exploits, but if I have I hope they will bear with me and remember that I have had to write in odd moments after "release," etc., and under the difficulty of carrying on with the job in hand at the same time.

"So few," Mr. Churchill said – but no debt here as he would have you believe ; rather few so lucky to be able to get on with the job whilst less fortunate folk looked on and waited their chance. I think he was really referring to our mess bills, anyway !

In conclusion, I should like to pay tribute to the men who design and build our fighting aircraft. Our successes are their successes, for it is they who have placed in our hands the finest aircraft and equipment in the world.

To them we owe a special debt of gratitude.

HOW TO SHOOT A LINE

Shooting a line doesn't necessarily refer to shooting Huns, although sometimes it is much the same thing! By writing this book I am shooting a line, in other words, talking about myself and what I have done. Usually, however, a line is a semi — deliberate exaggeration of a humorous nature, a tall story about yourself, if you like. If you write a book or get your name in the paper that is a ginormous line, the strange word being evolved from Gigantic and enormous.

Some people shoot lines unconsciously all the time, that is, they swank, and everybody soon becomes browned off with them, i.e., fed up. The lad who swanks is looked upon as a poor type, whilst a popular chap is a good type. There is a lot more general slang, but I won't trouble you with it since you won't find it in the chapters which follow. Instead. I'll deal with the technical terms which may prove difficult to understand.

First take the aerodrome. This is occasionally referred to as the drome, but more usually as the deck. Deck also means terra firma in general. As opposed to dry land, the sea is called the drink.

The correct term for an aeroplane is an aircraft or in slang a kite. To run over the kite, first let's take the undercarriage, invariably referred to as the undercart. Then there are the flaps, which are hinged portions of the wing near the trailing (rear) edge, which act as brakes and reduce the landing speed of the aircraft.

An aircraft stalls when it has insufficient forward speed for the wings to maintain their lift. If you skim a flat stone over the water, it skims until its speed drops and then sinks or stalls. It is very much the same with an aircraft. The flaps reduce the stalling speed. For instance, a Spitfire stalls with flaps up at 69 m.p.h., and with flaps down at 63 m.p.h. Not an awful lot of difference, you may think, but it makes a world of difference in landing, and you would never get into a small aerodrome if you didn't use the flaps.

I have used the word wings several times above, but the technical term is mainplanes, as opposed to the tailplane. The cockpit is called the office and the control column just the stick. Rudder bias refers to the trimming tab on the rudder. By winding the bias control one way or the other moves the tab and gives port or starboard bias. The elevators on the tailplane have a similar device on them. These are necessary, as the trim of an aircraft varies with its speed and altitude. The trimmers relieve the pilot of the strain of pressing on the stick or rudder bar all the time.

Another thing you'll find in the office is the R/T control. R/T is the wireless equipment, consisting of a transmitter and receiver with a three – way switch control, Transmit – Off – Receive.

Now let's take off. Once airborne, i.e., off the ground, you retract the undercart, shut the lid, i.e., close the hood, and put the prop or fan into coarse pitch, which on an aircraft is much the same thing as changing gear on a car. (By the way, the prop is never called a propeller. The correct term is airscrew if you don't use the slang words.)

Now supposing you meet some Huns and manage to get on the tail of one of them. If he isn't a very experienced pilot, or if the machine is not very manoeuvrable or well armed, he is easy meat or cold meat. You press the firing button and give him a squirt.

If you are unlucky enough to get shot down yourself, you bale out, step out, or take to the silk. If you land in the drink you are wearing a Mae West, which is a life – saving waistcoat which gives you curves in the right places! A parachute is called a brolly or a jumpsack.

Well, now you know, and if I were to say that I nearly lost my prop today, I wouldn't mean that it fell off but, that I nearly stalled (stopped) the engine, which would have been a bad show, wouldn't it?

CHAPTER I

LUCK

I am told that I was born with a silver spoon in my mouth, which they say is a sign of luck. I have certainly been lucky all my life.

When the Hun was plagued with his vile disease a generation ago I could not lend a hand to cure him, my sole activity in this direction being when my nurse showed me what she called a Zeppelin and I blew a very immature raspberry at it. It was probably just one of our own blimps, at that.

In 1939, when the plague seized Europe again, I had another tale to tell. My luck was in.

* * * * *

But first of all I must go back a bit to the year 1935, when my story really begins. I was then employed by a big electrical firm, my job being to supervise a dozen or so girls turning out hundreds of electric bulbs. Quite a responsible position for an eighteen – year – old. It was always rather a mystery to me how I got it! However, the experience stood me in good stead. I learned a lot about human nature (and women!) if not much about the manufacture of lamps.

I was not really surprised when one day the powers – that – be informed me that the period of my employment coincided with a decline in their profits, and that if I would kindly leave them they could get along better without me. I complied with this request and went home to my lamenting parents with the additional news that I wanted to try for the R.A.F., which was then in course of expansion.

To want was one thing, to get there another. I filled in and sent off form after form, asking every conceivable sort of question, and then sat back and waited. Nothing happened for a bit, so I started to make a nuisance of myself at Adastral House. So that they shouldn't forget me there I paid such frequent visits that the sergeant at the door began to greet me like an old friend and was always ready with a facetious remark.

But at last I received a notification to report to the Selection Board. I imagine a microbe on a slide under a microscope feels much the same way as I did before the Board, but apparently they liked the look of me, for they passed me on to the doctors. A week after came a letter to say I had been accepted and telling me to report to the Elementary Flying School at H........

Then followed two months of bliss, for me but not for my instructor, a gentle giant with the most amazing capacity for beer of anyone I have ever met. He could drink any two men under the table with ease, but no matter how much beer he absorbed, it never seemed to have the least effect on him. He always turned up bright and cheerful in the morning, which was more than I could say for myself sometimes, and nothing ever seemed to disturb him, not even my flying. I remember once going up with him to do aerobatics. He started to show me a slow roll when half – way through came a muffled oath down the speaking tube and the aircraft did a most amazing manoeuvre, coming out right way up. I heard the instructor laugh, and then he said, "I've forgotten to do up the ruddy straps!"

Shortly after I went solo luck was on one occasion hard put to it to save me, but it held. I was doing circuits and bumps and feeling like a young god, as one does at this period of training, when I was rudely disturbed by the terrifying sight of another aircraft heading straight at me, mere yards away. I never stop being amazed at the speed at which the human brain can work in an emergency, and somehow I and the other pilot just about avoided the fatal collision. I say just about, because we did hit each other, the under – carriage of my kite knocking most of the other chap's rudder off. If there had been two instructors in the aircraft instead of two beginners, they would both have been killed for sure, but God looks after drunks and fools, and we lived to fly another day.

The instructors were very kind to us about this incident. Apart from telling us to say our prayers twice that night they left it at that. My own instructor, who was away at the time, merely remarked when he returned that he always missed all the fun! The most long – suffering folk in the world, instructors, and the finest psychologists. A harsh word or a raspberry at the time would probably have upset our nerves.

After two months we completed the course, and with fifty hours flying to each pupil's credit, twenty – five solo and twenty – five dual, we were sent to a Service Flying Training School at W..... to complete our training on Service type aircraft.

Here again we found the finest instructors and training in the world, and we were passed out and posted to squadrons. I had applied to go to a fighter squadron, and had been trained on Furies to this end, so I was tremendously pleased when I found I had been posted to a Gauntlet squadron, the Gauntlet being the latest fighter in the Service and one of the most wonderful aircraft ever built. It was almost the last of the biplane fighters and a perfect joy to handle.

Some months with this squadron, during which time I received training in operational flying, and then I answered the call for volunteers to go to a new squadron which was forming at N....... The first person I saw when I arrived there was an old school friend, Jackie, who had been at St. Paul's with me. He was to be my flight commander for the two and a half happy years I spent with the squadron. Our first C.O. was Mac, a Canadian and one of the best, who was one of the finest pilots in the Service. He later took over one of the flights and E.J. succeeded him. I am sure we were the happiest squadron going, for E. J. was a perfect C.O. I never heard him annoyed with anyone, and he never needed to be, for we would all do anything for him, and in addition he had a fine sense of humour which never deserted him.

Time passed, and after the crisis of September, 1938, the squadron was re – equipped with Hurricanes. A grand kite, the Hurricane, and one which was to do magnificent service in the near future. March, 1939, came and went. Mussolini took Albania. August, and the drums of war were beating. Hitler screamed his piece over Danzig, and then it came — war! Now in their true perspective we saw those years of training and flying, that unending stream of new pilots, those mock war operations, they were not just a game or the means of a livelihood, but experience now to be tested to the utmost in the grim new reality of war.

We quickly fell into the new routine, standing by all day and half the night, waiting for a blow that did not come. A few days after war was declared I was posted to my present squadron as a flight commander, and although I didn't want to leave a very happy squadron, still a change does everyone good and I soon settled down among another grand bunch of blokes, this time flying Spitfires.

CHAPTER II

FIRST BLOOD

It was a queer war. Everybody said so. The experts said it was going to be a war of attrition. Maybe that was their word for it, but it was still a queer war.

The Luftwaffe's expected blows on this island did not fall. Goering contented himself instead with raids by single aircraft against the convoys round the coasts. So for month after month we patrolled the shipping, no doubt frightening away many Huns but never so much as catching sight of one.

One day in October, however, excitement ran high in the squadron. "B" Flight were on patrol over a large convoy off the East Coast when the excited voice of Wilf, the flight commander, came back over the R/T saying he had sighted what he thought must be a raider. He was right, it was a raider, but alas for him the Navy put up a barrage which turned the Hun back and he was cheated of his prey. When the flight came back the remarks of the pilots about the Senior Service were neither respectful nor complimentary!

The winter came on and activity grew less and less. With the spring, however, single Huns began coming over in larger numbers for the purpose of making attacks on shipping or to carry out high flying reconnaissance work. Our luck in "A" Flight seemed to be right out, for it was "B" Flight which drew first blood. On the 11th May, 1940, Wilf with a section of "B" Flight was sent up after a reconnaissance machine over the East Coast. They intercepted him and saw it was a Ju88 at about 20,000 feet. The section formed line astern and turned into the attack. The Hun saw them coming and put his nose down, going hell for leather towards a layer of cloud at about 5,000 feet. Wilf and F/Sgt. S..... each managed to give him a squirt, and then he was into the cloud. A game of hide and seek followed, and Wilf told John, who was flying No. 3 in the formation, to go beneath the cloud layer in case the Hun should come out below.

As luck would have it, this was what actually happened, and John was able to deliver a good attack, closing to about fifty yards and giving the Hun all he had got. The Hun disappeared in the clouds again and the Spitfires returned to the aerodrome. John came in a few minutes later than the others, touched down and came to rest in the middle of the aerodrome with his engine stopped. We all went out to him to see what was up, and although he personally was all right he had a bullet hole in his oil – tank and several more in the wings and nose. The German rear gunner had put in some good shooting and John had come back from thirty miles out to sea with no oil pressure at all. He had only just managed to make the aerodrome before his engine seized up.

This was the first action in which the squadron was engaged, or as Michael, our Adjutant, put it in the Squadron diary, "The first shots to be fired in anger by the Squadron in the World War of 1939." A few days later came the news that the crew of a Ju88 had been picked up in the North Sea. The rear gunner claimed to have shot down one Spitfire – he was nearly right!

Just about this time we heard that the squadron was to move to France at short notice, the first Spitfires to be sent overseas. This meant terrific activity for us all in order to be ready for the great day, but the great day never came. Thanks to somebody's foresight "up top" we never went to France but moved south instead to relieve a squadron down there, and incidentally to take part in the Dunkirk evacuation. Although events were moving rapidly, King Leopold had not yet given in and I don't think any of us fully realised what was so soon to happen around that onetime peaceful gateway to the Continent.

It was at five o'clock in the evening of May 25th that the squadron took off and headed south into the gathering dusk. Nature herself might have been warning us with that grey sky that all was not well and that a stern task lay ahead of us.

As we circled our new station and glided down towards the ground past the innumerable balloons of London's barrage, each standing out blackly against the sombre grey of the sky, it was already getting dark. The sections landed and taxied in to their dispersal points and their pilots climbed out. As they stood silently about waiting for the others to come in, a curl of smoke rose here and there from a cigarette. Apart from the cracking noise of the cooling exhausts, and an occasional remark in quiet tones, the only sound was the distant drone of a tractor bringing a tanker out to refuel the silent aircraft. It was very peaceful that evening of early summer, though so few miles away on the other side of the Channel hell was going on.

Having seen the aircraft refuelled and ready for the morrow, we walked up to the mess, the sergeants giving us a quiet "Good night" as they left us to go to their own quarters. As we got nearer to the mess we could hear rounds of laughter and talking floating out across the lawns to disturb the silence. As we went in, our eyes blinking a protest against the sudden light, all was noise.

Snatches of conversation hit our ears. "I gave him a squirt and he broke up and went straight in........", "Bill should be back soon. I saw him put it down on the beach and get out, so he's O.K.....," " ......went into the drink. A destroyer picked me up – lucky for me it was going the right way," this from a pilot disguised as a seaman in a blue sweater, trousers and monkey jacket, which the Navy had given him when he was rescued.

I wandered off to the bar to get a drink. A rather dishevelled officer stood there with a glass in his hand talking to the barman. He turned as I came in. "Good Lord!" "Well, I'm damned!" It was Ian, who had been at F.T.S. with me. I hadn't seen him for years. He had left the Air Force and gone back to America some time back, but here he was again, once more in uniform.

We had a lot to talk about and I found that he had just returned from France. He had been shot down out there but had managed to get back to his aerodrome – only to find that his squadron had left for England. After sundry adventures he managed to elude the Germans, get to the coast and find a boat to bring him over. But except for the clothes he stood up in and a French tin hat he had taken from a poilu who would never need it again, he had lost everything he possessed. He was very proud of the tin hat. "Rather distinctive, what!" he said.

After supper the C.O. called us together in the writing room, and introduced the C.O. of one of the other squadrons on the station who gave us some tips on the sort of thing we might now expect to get. It was while we were thus engaged that an orderly interrupted the talk by calling S/Ldr. L...... to the phone. When he came back he told us, "They wanted an aircraft to go over to Dunkirk and drop an important message. But the weather's too thick, never have found it in the dark; I told them so."

The long shadow of Dunkirk had fallen across our path, and tomorrow would come the reality. It was now getting late, so we gradually drifted off to bed. We had to be up in the morning in time to take off on patrol at seven o'clock. I don't know about the others, but I slept like a log.

CHAPTER III

DUNKIRK – FIRST PATROL

Save for a layer of hazy cloud high up in the sky, through which the sun shone mistily, the next morning dawned bright and clear. We ate our breakfasts in silence, and not much of it at that. Eggs and bacon don't sit too well on an excited stomach.

Smoking, talking, fourteen pilots assembled on the tarmac wondering who would be the unlucky two who would have to stay behind. We had brought twelve aircraft with us, and two extra pilots had come down by road the previous night. The section leaders alone looked quite happy, for they knew they were definite starters. For fairness we drew names out of a hat and face after face lighted up as its owner's name was called. In my flight the unlucky one was F/Sgt. U....., and he stood looking at me with a hurt expression on his face, for all the world like a dog who has been told he can't come for a walk. I went over to try and console him, but he just shook his head sadly and said, "Well I'm damned, sir!"

I couldn't help it, I burst out laughing, while the other pilots shot humorous remarks at him.

"Go on, Grumpy, you'll live to fight another day!"

......"Don't get too drunk while we're away!"

And that was why, from that time on, one flight sergeant was called Grumpy.

We, the lucky ones, got into our aircraft and started up, the fitters fussing round the cockpits polishing mirrors and windscreens which were already spotless. A pat on the shoulder – "Good luck, sir. See 'em off good and proper!" – and they jumped down to guide their pilots out onto the aerodrome.

As we turned into wind and opened up, I noticed a lonely figure walking slowly back along the tarmac – it was Grumpy!

The C.O. was leading the squadron with a section of "A" Flight, myself with a section on his right, Wilf with one of "B" Flight on his left and Eric, with a section, above and behind us all, the rearguard and lookout section.

We set course for Calais and climbed away south towards the thickening clouds over the French coast. Our instructions were to patrol Calais – Dunkirk at 17,000 feet. As we went higher and higher we kept running into straggling wisps of cloud, thin misty stuff which shone dazzlingly white in the light of the sun above.

25

Spitfire

Below, the earth showed through as a dark mass, the Channel a slate grey ribbon with the reflected sun showing like a streak of silver paint down its middle.

We crossed the English coast at Dover. Ahead rose up a great black pall of smoke from Calais, drifting out in a long trail across the water. To the left another inky column showed the position of Dunkirk. There was something infinitely sad and terrible about that towering mass of smoke. I cannot describe just how I felt as I gazed fascinated on the dreadful scene, but I know that a surge of hatred for the Hun and all his filthy doings swept over me, and I felt that no mercy must be shown to a people who are a disgrace to humanity.

As these thoughts were racing through my mind, the C.O. turned and we flew up the coast towards Dunkirk. We were at 18,000 feet, just below the layer of high cloud and, turning at the other end of the patrol line, we gradually lost height towards Calais. Suddenly, from behind a bank of cloud, appeared twenty-one Ju87 dive bombers, heading out to sea over Calais and looking like some sort of strange bird, with their big spatted undercarriages and upswept wings. We turned in behind them and closed to the attack.

The Huns flew on unheeding, apparently suffering from the delusion that we were their own fighter escort, until the leading section of Spitfires opened fire. Panic then swept the enemy formation. They split up in all directions, hotly pursued by nine Spitfires, while Eric & Co. kept watch behind us. I picked out one dive bomber and got on his tail, staying there as he twisted and turned this way and that, trying to avoid the eight streaks of tracer from my guns. Finally he pulled up and stalled, rolled over, and then plunged headlong towards the sea out of control.

I felt happy! I had often wondered what it would be like really to shoot at an aircraft and bring it down. Now I knew, and it was definitely exhilarating! I turned to try and take stock of how the fight was progressing. Two other Stukas were spinning down, and several Spitfires were wheeling about over Calais looking for more targets. I soon found one for myself, a Stuka just starting his dive on to the town. I plunged after him firing at long range in the hope of putting him off. I saw him release his bomb, and then he was away as fast as he could go, heading east over the trees. I had turned and climbed up over the town again when Eric's voice came over the R/T: "Fighters, fighters!" A pause, then, "My God, there are hundreds of them!" This was an exaggeration, but there were about fifty, and I couldn't help smiling at his tone of voice.

There weren't many Stukas left now, but Eric turned and tried to hold off the German fighters, Me109s, while we completed the rout. But before we could complete this job the 109s were down on us. A burst of tracer came over my left wing and I turned violently as a grey painted shape with black crosses on it flashed past. I saw the pink blur of the pilot's face turned towards me as he passed, and then another darker shape, only yards in front of my airscrew, flashed after him. It was a Spitfire after that 109.

To my left I saw Watty, hot on the tail of a Hun. As I watched, I saw another Me109 get on Watty's tail. I switched on my transmitter and yelled a warning to him, at the same time turning to try and cut the second Hun off. Even as I did so I saw a flash on the Spitfire as a cannon shell hit it. The Spitfire went into a steep dive, smoke pouring from the engine. I circled and saw a white puff as a parachute blossomed out far below.

The noise of the machine – gun fire behind me suddenly reminded me that I was still in the game, and I found that three Messerschmitts were honouring me with their undivided attention. An awful feeling gripped the pit of my stomach. I knew I had very little ammunition left, probably only enough for one burst, and three to one wasn't so funny. I pulled round in a tight turn, the aircraft shuddering just above the stall. I knew I could out turn the 109s, but I had very little petrol to play with now as well as being short of ammunition, and obviously it was time to go home!

The leading 109 was firing short bursts every now and then, his tracer going behind me as he strove to get his sights ahead far enough to hit me. I remember I was cursing at the top of my voice. I was in a jam, I was frightened, and I was furious with those Huns for making me frightened. Something had to be done and done quickly. I tightened the turn still more. The aircraft flicked as she stalled. I rolled over on my back and out into the reverse turn, a trick I had learnt back at F.T.S. This manoeuvre temporarily got me away from the Huns and I dived hell for leather towards the sea, flattening out as near the water as I could and then opening the throttle wide.

I was beginning to breathe again when rat – tat – tat behind me and a tracer appeared over the cockpit, the bullets churning up a patch of foam in the water a hundred yards ahead. It was then that I remembered the automatic boost cut – out, a device giving maximum power from the engine for use in emergency. I pushed the lever down and felt the surge of power from the Merlin in front of me as the aircraft accelerated. Twisting and turning, I managed to keep clear of the Hun bullets, very nearly hitting the water several times while doing so. One of the 109s had evidently climbed up to one side and now came diving in at me from the beam. I turned towards him and gave him the last of my ammunition at point – blank range. I think he went straight in, for as I drew well away with my superior speed I could see only two Messerschmitts behind me.

At last I saw the white cliffs of Dover, never a more welcome sight than now, and feeling sick and rather limp I throttled back, climbed up to clear the cliffs and flew on to the aerodrome.

As I circled, putting everything out before coming in to land, I noticed three other Spitfires already on the ground refuelling. I had barely touched down when another appeared from the south, roared low over the aerodrome, and came in. My crew came running out to meet me as I taxied in, caught the wing – tips and guided me up to the tanker.

With a sigh of relief I switched off and climbed stiffly out of the cockpit whilst an army of armourers fell on the aircraft and reloaded the guns at top speed. A crowd of airmen and pilots surrounded me, questions were shot at me right and left. Before I could collect my wits and answer, the Intelligence Officer pushed his way through, handed me the green Combat Report form, and guided me to the tailplane. "Come on! the report first, please. You can talk to the chaps afterwards." Slowly I tried to sort out all the thoughts racing through my head and remember the sequence of events.

"How many did you get, first? I want the final score."

"I got a Ju87 and I'm pretty certain I got a 109 as well."

"Good show." he said, and made a note in his little book.

At last I had finished writing out my report and more pilots had returned. After a while no more came in and ten pilots trooped back to the mess, smoking and talking for all they were worth.

"I saw one of our kites spinning down. Nobody stepped out."

"I saw Watty go down, but he got out." Eventually we decided it was the C.O. we had seen spinning. Sgt. P...... had seen that the pilot who baled out was wearing black overalls. Watty had been in black overalls, the C.O. in white. Rather sadly we reached the mess, to flop down somewhat exhausted in an armchair, have a well – earned drink and count the score. Seven Ju87s and three 109s certain, and one Me109 probably destroyed. Not bad for the first show.

Our casualties were the C.O. and Watty missing, and Eric unserviceable with a crease across his forehead made by one of those Me109s and a flesh wound in his arm.

"I thought I was dead," he said amidst roars of laughter. "Then I saw some more tracer coming past me, so I came to the conclusion I must still be alive."

A very near thing, but with an Me109 to his credit he was more than quits.

CHAPTER IV

MORE PATROLS

In the meantime the N.C.O.s and crews were working like niggers, patching bullet – holes and checking everything over, to get the aircraft serviceable for the next patrol. I had only two bullet – holes in the wings of my kite, and two strikes on the tail, where bullets had been deflected. Those Huns must have been damned bad shots! But some of the other aircraft were worse off than mine, one of the other sections having seventeen holes in the fuselage.

By lunch – time we had mustered seven aircraft, and soon after we managed to get nine serviceable. A quick lunch and we were down on the tarmac again. As acting C.O. I was leading the squadron this time, and nine Spitfires taxied out and took off, the thundering roar of the Merlins reverberating across the 'drome.

We circled and climbed away south – east, the sun shining and glinting on our wings. It was a lovely afternoon. Several layers of cloud hung across the sky, the lowest being at about 9,000 feet. As we neared the French coast, I decided to patrol below the bottom layer, as it was obvious that any bombers knocking about would be flying below it in order to see their target; and at the same time it afforded us protection against a surprise attack from above.

We flew up and down that stretch of coast which was to become so familiar to us. Half an hour passed, and still nothing happened, though we scanned the ground below eagerly for bomb bursts and the sky above for enemy aircraft. Suddenly came a shout from the look – out man: "Eight 109s right above!"

We had come out into a clear patch just north of Calais and the Huns had evidently emerged from the clouds now behind us. I looked round but could see nothing.

"Where are they? I can't see them!"

"Right above us. About a thousand feet. Look out, they've seen us, they're coming down!"

I pulled round in a steep turn to the right, the rest of the squadron spreading out in line astern behind me. By this time we were over a convenient patch of cloud, and as I circled I saw a Spitfire dive into the cloud with a 109 on its tail. It was G......., who was leading his section. I turned to follow, but the Hun pulled up clear of the clouds and climbed away inland. I opened the throttle wide and climbed after him, keeping a good look – out

29

behind in case anything was after me. The sky was clear of aircraft. Half a minute before there had been seventeen aircraft within that small clear patch. Now, in the miraculous manner which defeats the logic of the eye, there was only that Hun and myself.

I was overtaking fast, just below and behind him. He obviously had no idea I was there. Carefully I manoeuvred my sights onto him and then slightly ahead, to get the deflection. Then I let him have it. It must have given him the shock of his life if he knew anything about it at all. His aircraft lurched, fell over almost on its back and went screaming vertically down. I half rolled and followed him, in case he was shamming, although I knew I had got him with that one carefully aimed burst. Down, down I went, watching for him to pull out, but he never did. I suddenly realised that I was perilously low myself, and doing a fair rate of knots as well. I had lost sight of my Hun, and realised he must have hit the ground by now, for he had been well below me and still in a vertical dive.

I pulled back on the stick and felt my head droop forward. At the same time everything went purple and then black in front of my eyes as I "blacked out". I came round again, climbed out to sea and made once more towards the clouds. Looking at my watch I noticed that only about three minutes had elapsed since the beginning of the fight. It had felt like a quarter of an hour at least.

I wondered how the rest of the chaps had got on. The English coast slipped by underneath me. Ahead the tower of Canterbury Cathedral shone in the sun and the Estuary glinted beyond. I came to M....... aerodrome, circling to see if anybody had landed there to refuel. Yes, there was a Spitfire just landing. I dived and flew low across the aerodrome, noting the letters on the fuselage as I flashed by. It was one of ours. A glance at my petrol gauge showed that my fuel was getting low, so I came in and taxied up to where the other Spitfire was parked. As I switched off, G.......walked over to me. He was swearing like a trooper.

"What's the matter with you?" I demanded.

"Did you see that little swine on my tail? Well, he got young B....... I saw him spinning."

"Blast him," I said. "Well, I got him, anyway, so we're quits. He climbed up after you went into that cloud, and I tailed him. He never knew what hit him and went straight in. Did you get anything yourself?"

"Yes, I got one of them after I came out of the cloud. A flamer."

"Good show. That's two, anyway."

Another Spitfire came in and taxied towards us. Out stepped

young B....... We looked at him as though he were a ghost.

"Didn't you go into a spin when that Hun had a crack at you?" asked G......

"Oh, yes, but I came out and everybody had disappeared, so I came back."

G...... and I looked at each other. "I wish you wouldn't give people such frights," said G........"I thought he'd got you."

One by one more Spitfires came in. I got on the phone to our own station to see if anybody had turned up there. None had, which meant two were missing, Michael and Sgt. I.......

But after the aircraft had been refuelled and we had been up to the mess for a cup of tea, we flew back to our own squadron and found that news had come through that Michael had parked down on the beach at D...... with a bullet in his knee. Sgt. I....... was still missing, though.

The following day was dull, with huge banks of grey cumulus cloud cutting off the sun. But in the afternoon it cleared, and the evening turned to perfect summer weather, without a cloud in the sky, as we took off after tea. The Operations Room had rung through to tell us that there would be "hell over Dunkirk this evening" and it was with a tremendous feeling of excitement that we climbed up over the aerodrome and settled down on the now familiar course over the Thames for Dunkirk. Once past the Estuary we could already see, miles away, the huge black column of smoke from the burning oil – tanks, rearing up rearing up nightmare fashion into the quiet evening sky.

Soon we were out over the sea and in a few minutes came to Dunkirk, turning eastward to run up the coast to Nieuport past those rolling yellow sand – dunes and beaches on which a chapter of Britain's history was beginning to be enacted.

The sea far below shone blue and gold under the westering sun. Above us was the deep blue dome of the heavens. Anxiously we scanned it, looking for the tell – tale glint of the sun on a pair of wings which would show us the enemy was above. Suddenly, just off the south mole of Dunkirk harbour below, appeared three white circles in the water near a tanker which was lying off – shore. Bombs! Frantically I searched the sky to the right of us, trying to see the aircraft which had dropped them. It was the barrage put up by our anti – aircraft batteries which showed me his position. There was only one enemy aircraft.

Thinking it might be a decoy, I called up Wilf on the R/T and told him to stay on patrol while I took a section after the Hun. I turned away to give chase, but I think the Hun must have seen us, for he immediately turned inland, pursued by bursts of Ack – Ack. We crossed the coast diving slightly, as our quarry was below us.

Gradually we overtook him, to find the enemy aircraft was an Hs126. As we neared him he began to turn and twist this way and that, the sun catching the dark green camouflage and the black crosses on his wings. I came up with him rather fast over Ypres and gave him a short burst as he turned back underneath me. Although he had a far slower aircraft he used his manoeuvrability to escape our fire and fought us off magnificently, and after another burst I lost him as he dived away behind me. Feeling that we shouldn't really be playing with a Henschel miles inside Belgium when we were supposed to be guarding the Dunkirk beaches, I called up the section to rejoin formation. Frankie, my No.2, was soon beside me making faces, as apparently he had found the Hun again, but Grumpy was not to be seen. The two of us dived down and tore back at twenty feet over the peaceful Belgium countryside. I tried to spot signs of either Germans or our own troops, but not a soul could be seen. Cattle browsing in the fields seemed to be the only living things in a deserted landscape. We passed over farms and villages all equally deserted, and then the dunes of the coast showed in front of us. As we flashed over the beaches and out to sea I saw hundreds of khaki – clad figures on the front and among the dunes waving to us as we went by. Under the huge black pall of smoke that hung over the town and drifted slowly out to sea it was almost like full night.

Out of reach of any German guns we climbed up again trying to find the rest of the squadron. I called Grumpy and heard him answer faintly. He was telling me his position, but I could not quite get what he said, though I did hear his triumphant voice repeating, "I got him, I got him!"

Later on I had his story. When that Henschel had seen Frankie and me reform and turn back, he had thought himself safe, whereupon Grumpy, sitting unsuspected above him in the sun, had dived on him and sent him crashing into a field with his engine on fire.

But to go back a little, we still continued our patrol, having fetched up with two aircraft of "B" Flight, but at last I called up the others and said we were going home, and we turned north – west towards our supper. As we came to the aerodrome in the dusk and sank down to Mother Earth the balloons of London seemed to be made of gold and silver. The weather was still beautiful and calm.

Soon after the rest of the squadron arrived. They had been lucky. Wilf, searching the sky for a target and wondering where I had got to, suddenly espied a Dornier just ahead and above him. He attacked and the Dornier burst into flames, plunging like a comet down into the blue water below. A few minutes later he saw two more, and a section between them sent down one of these on his last long dive to the sea. The ear – splitting "blue note" of his over – revving engines must have sounded like music to the weary troops on the sands, ending abruptly as he hit the water far below in a huge cascade of white foam.

The other Dornier, the third, had suffered a similar fate at the hands of Sgt. J........., and then, petrol getting low and no more Huns being in sight, they had followed us back.

I pounced on Grumpy after we landed. "Why didn't you join up when I told you to?" I demanded.

"I must have had my R/T switched off, sir!" he said with a sly grin.

"You're a damned liar," I said, unable to suppress a smile. "You know perfectly well you heard me call up." His grin just got a bit wider. I added: "It was a good show, your getting him like that, but you obey orders in future."

He was still grinning as we said "Good night," before parting to go up to our respective messes.

CHAPTER V

FIRST WING PATROL

Up to now we had encountered two big snags. In the first place we were operating at the limit of our operational range – we could only stay on Patrol for a maximum time of one hour and – secondly we were almost always out numbered.

The latter disadvantage was temporarily overcome on the following day, May 28th, when the three Spitfire squadrons on the station took off together and patrolled as a wing. The Huns were now beginning to escort their bombers more strongly and the idea was that the leading squadron of the wing should take on the bombers whilst the other two tackled the fighter escort.

This was the first time we had tried operating as a wing, and on this first patrol we met with quite a fair measure of success. The weather was dull, with big masses of thundery – looking cloud covering the sky, the base varying from 5,000 to about 10,000 feet. We hadn't been on patrol long when the leading squadron dived away through a fantastic ravine in the mountainous black clouds and disappeared from view. Although we gave chase we weren't able to find them again, but we found something else instead.

As we emerged from the valley between the towering clouds into an open space I suddenly espied, just above and in front of us, about sixty Me109s and a dozen Spitfires in a tremendous dogfight. Climbing as fast as I could, and keeping clear of the fight, I circled round the edge of this cloud arena until I had reached the height of the combatants. The squadron behind me then broke up and dived into the fight. As I went in I saw five more 109s come diving out of a tunnel high up in the black cloud on my right, and then another. By this time I was well into the battle, and as a Hun crossed my nose I turned after him and closed in on his tail. Glancing in my mirror I saw coming round in a turn behind me another 109. "I'll have to be quick getting the one in front," I thought, "before his pal gets on my tail."

I got my sights on and pressed the firing button. My guns fired, but only very slowly and spasmodically. I swore as another glance in the mirror showed me Hun No.2 just on my tail. Then I half rolled and let my aircraft plummet down in the ensuing dive until the clock showed 400 m.p.h. Slowly I eased back on the stick, feeling my eyelids and head grow heavy with the pressure that was pressing me down in my seat. But now I was out of the dive and soaring up and up, the black wall of cloud in front of me dropping out of sight below the nose of the aircraft as it reached the vertical. I tilted my head back to watch the clouds on the opposite side come slowly down to meet the nose as the aircraft came over on its back at the top of the loop Then I eased the stick forward and to the right and rolled out right way up.

This had brought me out to one side of the dogfight and at the same height, and I cruised around trying to find the cause of the gun trouble. I looked at my air gauge, which showed the pressure in the compressed air bottle operating the guns, and it read 80 lbs. I swore again. No wonder the guns wouldn't fire properly. I wondered if I had been hit; a bullet might have struck a pipeline, causing a leak.

However, I turned into the fight again to have another squirt and see what happened. A 109 saw me coming and turned to meet me. Tracer appeared from his guns and passed just underneath my starboard wing. Not a bad shot, as I was a rather awkward target from his position. I turned hard to the left as we passed and slowly began to come round on his tail. He suddenly came out of his turn and gave me a fleeting shot, but as I pressed the button there was a single crack and a single bullet sped on its way.

"That's a fat lot of good," I thought, seeing the Hun rolling away out of sight below me. I pressed the button again but nothing happened at all. There didn't seem much point in sticking around in the middle of so many Huns with guns that didn't work, so I dived down into the clouds and flattened out below them at 2,000 feet. Looking at my watch I saw that only five minutes had elapsed since we first sighted the Huns.

Suddenly coming towards me I saw three twin – engined aircraft. If these were Heinkels I was going to look an awful twirp. But as I got nearer I saw they were Ansons and heaved a sigh of relief. The worthy Coastal Command pilots, however, apparently did not recognise me so easily for they turned in line astern into a tight circle. I rocked my wings and circled round them. They still appeared suspicious, but eventually straightened up and continued on their way whilst I steered for home.

As I climbed out of the cockpit my crew came up.

"Did you get anything, sir?"

"Not a ruddy thing," I said in disgust. There's no air in the bottle, it must be leaking." I added. "I only fired about twenty rounds before the guns petered out." Grimacing their disappointment the men started in to check the air system.

I was one of the first down, but one by one the others came in until all had returned! Good show, no one missing! I wandered round talking to the others as they climbed out. F/S. S...... and Grumpy claimed one each, both flamers. Several of the others thought they had got one but they couldn't claim as they did not see what had happened to their opponent. As Wilf put it, "There wasn't time to see anything. I just fired when something came into my sights and then turned like hell as something fired at me! What a party! It seemed amazing that everybody had come back from that fight. I had a word with Grumpy and S...... Grumpy was grinning happily, but S... only made a face.

"What's the matter?" I said.

"I got one in flames and the poor swine got stuck half – way out of the cockpit. Rotten sight." And he turned away to light a cigarette.

Back in the mess we learned how the other squadrons had fared. Two pilots were missing but the next day, one of them returned. He had parked down on the beach at Dunkirk and had got back on a destroyer. He reported that he had seen two 109s come down in flames and two more go straight into the sea. The leading squadron had sighted some Dorniers and given chase, when we had lost them in the clouds.

That evening the weather cleared and after dinner I was strolling in the garden in front of the mess when Wilf, standing on the lawn, called me over. "What does that remind you of?" he asked, pointing above his head. I looked up and saw a cloud of gnats milling about in the evening air for all the world like that dogfight in the morning.

We both laughed.

Next day the two other squadrons went to another station and were relieved by two more squadrons, both of which had at one time or another been on the same station with us. They both had grand C.O.s in S/Ldr. M..... and S/Ldr. H......... We were now the veteran squadron on the station, and after one or two wing patrols during the course of which nothing was seen, it was decided that we should lead the wing to try and change the luck. For two fruitless days it seemed as though we were still going to be unlucky, but on June 1st things really happened.

CHAPTER VI

DAWN PATROL

On June 1st the wing was on the dawn patrol. Still full of sleep we rolled out of bed at 3.15 a.m. and staggered downstairs to the anteroom for tea and biscuits. Then down to the tarmac to the rising and falling thunder of noise as fitters ran up the engines, to the sight of dim aircraft, shown up by the blue flames from the exhausts which stabbed the half light. Still dazed with sleep I climbed into the cockpit, tested the oxygen supply and the R/T and then taxied out to the far end of the aerodrome and turned into wind, there to sit yawning whilst the other aircraft warmed up around me. Thumbs up from each section leader; and I waved my hand over my head, the signal to take off, and opened up.

A throbbing roar all around cut off the outside world as we sped across the aerodrome. The bumps from the undercart became less and less, until with a final bump we beat gravity and the green blur of grass slipped way beneath us. My right hand dropped to the undercart control, moved it back, and then felt for the pump. A few seconds later two faint thuds told me the wheels were up, and with a confirming glance at the cockpit indicator I reached behind me and pulled the hood shut. Changing hands on the stick, I closed the radiator and put the airscrew into course pitch, throttling back to cruising revs., and then glanced at the rev. counter, boost and oil gauges to make sure that every thing was O.K.

As I turned left round the 'drome I glanced in the mirror to see the rest of the squadron formed up behind me. Three circuits and the other two squadrons were in position, S/Ldr. M......, Tubby to everybody, immediately behind us and Robin, (S/Ldr. H.......) bringing up the rear with his squadron.

I straightened up and climbed away towards Dunkirk and the rising sun, circling as we left the English coast to pick up a fourth squadron of Spitfires from another aerodrome which had a rendezvous with us. Then out over the North Sea, forty – eight Spitfires looking for trouble!

When we reached the Belgian coast I turned left to run up to Nieuport, past the packed beaches looking oddly like Blackpool or Margate on a Bank Holiday, past the hundreds of small craft lying offshore to ferry those heroic troops to the bigger vessels standing farther out. Every kind of craft was represented there, Thames barges, lighters, rowing boats, lifeboats, in fact anything that would float. Stretching back towards the cliffs of England was an unending stream of ships, some taking precious loads from the hell beneath us now to the comparative peace and safety of our island, others returning in the opposite direction, back to the inferno to save some more of that undefeatable little army.

From 5,000 feet we watched the drama being enacted below us. Above was a thin layer of cloud, not more than fifty feet thick, through which the sun was just visible. Suddenly in front of us appeared a twin – engined aircraft, followed by eleven more, all heading towards Nieuport. I switched on the R/T: "Twelve Me110s straight ahead," I said, then opened the throttle and gave chase.

The Messerschmitts evidently saw us coming, for they went into a circle and tried to get into the clouds. For once the odds were in our favour, and four to one at that. I was still out of firing range when, to my astonishment, one of the enemy aircraft staggered and then plummeted down, down, with a strange pendulum motion as its tail came off. None of my section had fired, and since we were leading and out of range still, I could not imagine how on earth the Hun had been shot down.

By now we had closed with the enemy and turning right I got on the tail of a Messerschmitt and chased him down as he dived away, the rest of the squadron fighting to get a target! It really was pathetic. By our standards of training those pilots should never have left F.T.S., yet here they were, trying to fight four times their number and with no idea of how to do it. War is war, but I remember cursing the Hun for a cold blooded devil in sending out pilots like these to fight us. Even as I cursed I realised what a queer thought this was. We ought to be thankful for cold meat like this!

I fired several bursts at the 110 I was after and saw his port motor splutter and stop. As he tried to turn away I pulled round inside him and gave him another squirt, this time hitting his starboard engine, which was immediately enveloped in smoke. By this time we were pretty low, and as I pulled up I saw him go down into the deck.

Looking round I was in time to see the tail come off another 110, and down he went too. Since every Hun in sight had a Spitfire on his tail, I climbed up through the clouds to see if there were anything up there. As I came out on top I saw two Spitfires cruising about. As any Me110s came up through the cloud they jumped on them, sending them down again. Unfortunately for those wretched Huns the cloud was too thin to hide in – there was no escape. I came down again, and as an Me110 came towards me head on, I fired, then turned to come back after him. But another Spitfire was on his tail before I could get there. A few seconds later a dull flash appeared on the ground below, followed by a huge tongue of flame, and that was another Nazi less in the world.

After this there didn't seem to be any more Huns left so I dived down almost to the water and came home, there to find most of the aircraft already on the ground. Two more came in as I was landing, and the squadron was complete. The second squadron came in by ones and twos, and then the third squadron in formation. The latter had apparently not seen much and had been unable to find anything to fire at.

The first pilot I saw as I climbed out of my aircraft was Sgt. J...... He was grinning from ear to ear. "How many did you get, sir?" he called.

"One," I answered.

"Only one, sir! I got two."

I grinned to myself. "If people like you weren't so damned greedy, I might be able to get a few more!"

A car pulled up by the aircraft and Cras., our intelligence officer, stepped out.

"Good morning, gentlemen. Any luck?"

A chorus answered him, whereupon he was heard to mutter a few remarks about the unearthly hour at which he was forced to rise, merely on account of bloodthirsty young devils whose idea of fun was a fight before breakfast.

Having received our reports Cras. counted up the score. Seven 110s had been accounted for, and three 109s

I hadn't seen any 109s and said so, whereupon it turned out that Wilf with "B" Flight, had had a little private dogfight with some Me109s which had appeared out of nowhere. "B" Flight had apparently made the best of it! As for the 110s, Sgt. J..... had got two, and so had G....., and Grumpy, B...... and I had each got one.

Back in the mess it was still too early for breakfast, so we sat about in the anteroom swapping yarns. Tubby M....., who had been responsible for shooting down the first 110, told us a really *stirring* tale. Literally, I mean, for Tubby volunteered the information that the miracle had been achieved by use of his *stirring attack.* By stirring it was discovered he meant stirring the stick round the cockpit once his sights were on, thereby getting a hosepipe effect from his guns. This then was the secret of how to shoot down a Hun when at 1,200 yards range! However, another of his pilots had got an Me110 by means of more orthodox methods. Two more pilots were missing, apparently shot down by Flak.

But any patrol that Tubby was on invariably turned out to be an amusing one, at any rate in retrospect when he got back to the mess. He was a great humorist, and now he improved the shining hour until breakfast by giving an exhibition of his actions and reactions on a previous patrol when he had found himself short of oxygen. He had us all rocking in our seats with laughter. It was the first time I ever remember being convulsed with mirth at such an hour of the morning!

CHAPTER VII

DUNKIRK − THE LAST PATROLS

Breakfast over, we went down again on to the tarmac. The order of battle was as before. Again we circled as we left the coast to pick up the other squadron, then out over the glassy sea, down the long line of ships to Dunkirk.

The weather had not changed since dawn, and as the enemy bombers would have to come below the thin layer of cloud in order to drop their eggs, I decided to patrol just below the cloud base again.

As I turned off the harbour I glanced back over my shoulder at the mass of aircraft stretching away behind. It was an impressive sight, and I only hope it cheered up those poor devils five thousand feet below us on the shore.

Nieuport slowly appeared beneath my wings, and I turned to run back down the coast. I had just turned again at Dunkirk, and was heading back once more, when something moving on my left caught my eye. I looked round in time to see an aircraft diving down towards the shipping off the harbour. Coming hard round I dived after it, the rest of the squadron chasing after me. The aircraft flattened out over a destroyer for a moment and then turned, climbing towards the coast. As I followed there was a terrific flash below and a huge fountain of water was flung high into the air, to fall slowly back into the sea. As the disturbance subsided I saw that the destroyer had completely disappeared. So the aircraft in front of me was a Hun. A blind fury gripped me.

I was gaining on him as he strove to reach the safety of the clouds, but he was into them before I could get close enough to fire. I went up through the clouds in the hope of finding him, but he had disappeared. As I circled, waiting to see if he would appear again, some anti − aircraft fire inland attracted my attention and I caught sight of three Dorniers just above the clouds. Easing the stick forward I dropped down until I was almost in the clouds and then began to stalk the quarry. I don't think they saw me until I came round behind them and came up into position to attack. The Huns were flying in "Vic" formation and I picked out the right − hand aircraft closing in behind him. I fired a short burst from about 400 yards in the hope of killing the rear gunner, or at any rate frightening him.

41

As I closed in to shorter range, another Spitfire climbed out of the clouds to the left and turned in behind the left – hand Dornier. I grinned to myself, then concentrated on holding my aircraft steady in the slipstream from the Hun in front of me as the sights came on to his fuselage. My right thumb felt for the firing button on the stick and pressed it. A muffled "B – r – r – r – p" came from the wings and I felt the aircraft check slightly as eight streams of tracer spanned the space between us. The Spitfire bumped in the slipstream and my sights drifted off the target. I stopped firing to correct the aim and noticed tracer from the Dornier passing over my left wing. Then – "Spang!" and I looked down to see a shining furrow along the top of the wing, where a bullet had bounced off the metal taking a sliver of paint with it.

I fired again, and as the Hun seemed to rush back to meet me broke away down to one side, muscles tense, as involuntarily I tried to contract my body, half expecting to hear the sound of bullets hitting the aircraft. I made a good target for the German gunner before I got safely out of range. He had he missed me, and as I flattened out I saw the Dornier losing height very unsteadily and disappearing into the cloud. I dived down and searched frantically for him, as one more burst seemed to be all that was needed to put paid to his account. But I couldn't see a Dornier anywhere, so I made a few remarks about the parentage of the pilot and of Huns in general and turned out towards the sea.

Crossing the coast again a Heinkel passed just in front of me and I tagged on behind and gave him a couple of squirts as he climbed into the cloud. By this time my windscreen had become covered in oil, owing as I later found out to a leak in the airscrew, and it was impossible to see through the glass or use the sight. I was getting more and more annoyed, and when two more Heinkels in tight formation appeared above me I had to open the hood, pull down my goggles and peer round the edge of the windscreen in order to see what I was firing at.

A terrific blast of air hit my head as I looked out, nearly knocking my goggles off. Closing in below and to one side of the Huns I gave them the last of my ammunition, though without much hope of hitting them. But at least it had the effect of sending them up into the cloud, and as they melted like ghosts into the grey vapour above I turned and dived down to the water and headed out along the line of ships for England.

As we had run into the first lot of Huns only when it was almost time to go home, I was by now getting very short of petrol. Ten feet above the sea I raced along past the strange collection of vessels heading from hell to heaven. A mile ahead I recognised a cross – Channel steamer. I smiled to myself, remembering the long hours I had spent on her in happier days, crossing to the Continent. She would take a good two hours more to get home now, whereas I would be there in ten minutes.

Just as I came abreast of the ship the whole sea suddenly erupted immediately behind her, and only a few hundred yards away from me. I nearly jumped from the cockpit with fright! I had been rudely awakened from my dreaming by a Dornier sitting at about 2,000 feet, nearly over the top of me. As I looked, four little black objects left the belly of the bomber and came hurtling down towards the ship. I turned sharply and began to climb as hard as I could, feeling absolutely wild that the Hun had given me such a fright. He looked so insolent, sitting up there throttled right back, and letting his eggs go in that deliberate fashion. Luckily for me it hadn't helped him to aim accurately, but I felt like ramming him. I was not, however, forced to dwell further on this suicidal measure, for the Hun then turned back towards the French coast and climbed away as hard as he could, pursued by bursts of A. A. fire from a cruiser a mile or so to the north – east. Looking at the cruiser I watched the flickering stabs of flame from one of her "Chicago Pianos". Though it certainly looked a wicked and deadly performance enough, I couldn't see whether the Dornier was hit or not.

Once more I turned for home, on again up the line of ships, over the rusty wrecks on the Goodwin Sands, glistening like gold in the sun, and then the coast slipped by beneath me. I landed at M.... to refuel, then back over the peaceful English countryside to our own aerodrome.

A myriad silver dots ahead, the balloons of London, told me I was nearly home, and soon the aerodrome hove in sight. Usually I was never able to find it easily and spent the last few miles looking everywhere for a glimpse of some hangers, finally, just as I was beginning to think I had passed it, finding it as a rule hidden from view beneath the nose or a wing. But to – day I hit it straight off for once. As I sighted the hangars I put the nose down and dived across the aerodrome to pull up in a climbing turn to the left round the circuit, throttling back as I did so. My left hand went up to the hood catch, pulling the hood open far enough for me to put my elbow against it and push it right back.

The airspeed dropped to 180 m.p.h.; I pulled down the undercarriage selector, and the little white indicator pegs in the wings came slowly out until I could read "Down" in red letters on both of them. A glance at the electric indicator in the cockpit told me that the wheels were down. Then I opened the radiator wide.

The speed had now dropped to 160 m.p.h., and throttling back still more as I turned at the down wind side of the aerodrome, I waited until the clock showed 120 and then pulled down the lever to lower the flaps. I felt the aircraft slow up, the nose dropping slightly at the same time. I pulled the control to put the airscrew into fine pitch, then – stick over to the left a little and back, and the aircraft was gliding into wind towards the aerodrome. I pulled the throttle back and felt it stop. Then I remembered the mixture control was still forward in the "weak position" and was preventing the throttle from being closed. I pulled it back and then closed the throttle more as a belt of trees slid by underneath and the boundary fence came to meet me. A glance at the airspeed indicator – 95 m.p.h., O.K. – and I closed the throttle completely, easing the stick back as I passed over the fence. Back a little more still as the aircraft flattened out – hold it! – then right back, and a second later some jolting and a slight bump from the tail. We were down. Pulling the brake lever to and fro, I eased the brakes on and off to slow down without tipping up on the nose, and gradually came to a standstill. A glance behind as I put the flaps up showed me that nobody else was coming in, and I turned and taxied to the dispersal point and switched off. My fitter jumped up on the wing as I took my helmet off.

"Any luck, sir?"

I grimaced. "Look at that ruddy windscreen!"

The fitter frowned and shook his head. "Sorry, sir. It's the airscrew, I'm afraid. It's very bad on this kite."

I climbed out, lit a cigarette and wandered over to where a group of pilots stood talking to Cras. and making out their combat reports. As I approached, Cras. turned and held out a green form.

But I shook my head. "No luck, I am afraid. I pushed a Dornier into the clouds looking a bit shaky, but I couldn't find him again. He may have come down but I can't claim.

"Bad luck."

Everybody was talking and asking questions. Bit by bit I began to get an idea of what had happened to the the others. G...... had got two, a Heinkel and a Dornier, both on fire, Leonard had got a "probable" (a Heinkel), and so had Grumpy and Sgt. J..... Sgt. P..... was missing.

"Not so good," somebody remarked. "That damned cloud was just ideal for them. It was a bit thicker than it was this morning.

Still talking we wended our way up to the mess, to sit at our ease for the rest of the morning, drinking on the lawn. Robin had the best tale to tell. He had led his squadron after some Ju88s up towards Ostend, and on the way back, having finished his ammunition, he had met a Hun going home. They passed each other at a respectful distance.

A few minutes later the same thing happened again, by which time Robin was getting a bit annoyed. When, a few miles out to sea, he saw another one, he couldn't stand it any longer and charged straight at the Hun as if to ram him. They were both very low over the water, and to his absolute amazement the wretched Boche dived straight into the sea.

"Pity I hadn't got just one bullet left," he said. "I could have claimed it then."

Next day we did another patrol, but all was quiet over on the other side. The evacuation of Dunkirk appeared to be completed. When we landed at the aerodrome again we were overjoyed to find that Sgt. P...... had got back. A bullet in his oil – tank had forced him to come down in the sea, and he had been picked up by a French fishing boat, the *Jolie Mascot*. Her captain was trying to get back to Dunkirk from England but had got himself lost. P..... took over the duties of navigator and got his craft to the Belgian coast, where he took part in the rescue operations, finally coming back with some of the last of the B.E.F. A darned fine show.

Another early patrol on June 3rd, and then the next day the last show we were to do before going back to our home station. At 4 a.m. we were taxiing out, and took off flight by flight. The clouds were at 200 feet and completely covered the sky, but we managed to rendezvous above them, and after circling for a while picked up the other two squadrons. We then set course to pick up the fourth squadron from R...... and more by luck than anything else met them just as they came through the cloud. Then the wing set off on the familiar course.

The wind was south – east and the smoke from Dunkirk stretched right to London, a black ninety – mile trail! Over on the other side there was no activity to be seen. A few derelict Thames barges, a sunken destroyer, an overturned lorry on the beach, such were the only reminders of the conflict now over. Only the pall of smoke, greater than ever now that our own demolition people had been around doing their particular job.

The whole scene rather reminded me of a theatre after the audience has gone. Nothing to remind one of the show but the litter left behind. Yes, the show was over now. The enemy was within twenty miles of our coasts, but another show would be put on, many shows perhaps, and Hitler would never speak the last line.

CHAPTER VIII

NOCTURNE MILITAIRE

On June 5th we took off from the aerodrome for the last time and headed away towards our home station. It was with some regret that we left. We had had a grand time there and everybody, from the Station Commander downwards, had been kindness itself. Nothing had been too much trouble if it had helped us at all.

Our stay had been very successful too. We had succeeded in destroying 28 German aircraft and probably destroying nine others. This for the loss of the C.O. (prisoner of war), two pilots killed, "Watty" and Sgt. I..... , and one wounded, Michael. Eric and John had been slightly wounded but were fit again. Not bad arithmetic at all.

It was Eric and John who were to be the next pilots in action, but more of that later. As we headed home our thoughts were dwelling on leave. Woody, our Station Commander, had promised us forty – eight hours when we got back, and I think we all felt very carefree and happy as we came over the aerodrome, went into our own special formation, and one by one peeled off to come screaming across the aerodrome. One by one we landed and taxied up to our dispersal point, to be met by a smiling Woody and S/Ldr. P......, our new C.O. Then to the Mess for some drinks before lunch, with everybody shooting questions at us. We managed to answer most of them, I think, and cleared up the various tales which had reached the aerodrome of our doings down at H.......

A 'phone – call to my wife to tell her to pack for forty – eight hours leave and then lunch. I was drinking my coffee afterwards when I espied through the window a little grey Lancia come up the drive, a golden head showing behind the wheel. Good show – my lady hadn't wasted much time! A hurried farewell and I dashed up to my room to collect my bag and then we were away.

It was only when I got into the car and we started off that I realised that I was feeling a bit tired. It was not altogether surprising since for ten days we had been getting up at 3.15 in the morning, getting to bed usually about 11 at night. On top of that we had done quite a bit of flying and fighting. It was rather like playing a strenuous game of tennis on a hot day. You don't realise how hot you are until you stop.

All too quickly leave came to an end and we returned to the

Station to a rather inactive routine. Before long, however, the Hun began coming over at night and one flight stood by during darkness each night. On June 19th "B" Flight was on and sent up several aircraft to try to find these nocturnal raiders.

I was over in the Mess about 11 o'clock that night with S/Ldr. P......, and we strolled outside in the garden listening to the rising and falling note of the raider's engines sounding high up amongst the stars. A Hun was just passing over the aerodrome as we stood drinking a late cup of coffee just before going to bed. Suddenly, high up above us, sounded a faint whistling noise which gradually grew and grew until it sounded like an express train passing with its whistle open. "Whistling bomb," somebody remarked. Nobody seemed anxious to get under cover as they were more interested than anything else. The sound grew louder and then ended abruptly, as the bomb buried itself in the ground a mile or so south of the aerodrome − as far as we could judge.

I remember hunching myself up a little and waiting for the explosion. No sound came, however. It was a dud! Suddenly, however, from behind the Mess, came four shuddering "Crumps", and the windows rattled. Those weren't duds!

The activity died down for a while, and since I was off duty I got into my car and went home. There was great excitement when I arrived, the family standing out on the lawn watching the searchlights and regarding the whole thing as rather interesting entertainment.

Eventually we went to bed, and I had just put the light out and was drawing the blackout curtains aside, and opening the window, when I heard the unmistakable "Brrrrp" of machine − gun fire. My wife was out of bed and beside me in a flash!

I looked out into the night and there to the south three searchlights were groping against the stars, trying to find the elusive raider. As I watched, they stopped and a silver object gleamed brightly in their beams. There was another sound of machine − guns and a brief flicker of flame showed from the Hun. Then two white puffs appeared behind his tail. For a moment I thought it was smoke, then I realised they were parachutes − the crew had baled out. Another flicker of flame came from the stricken aircraft, and then it heeled over and plunged earthwards, a trail of smoke and flame behind it. The searchlights held the target still, the "blue note" from the engines echoing in the sky until the aircraft disappeared behind the trees across the road. There was silence for a split second and then a reverberating explosion and huge flash, followed by a red glare which lit up the whole heavens. Death of a raider.

It was John who had been responsible for the destruction of

this Hun. I heard the tale next morning. He had sighted his target in the searchlight beams and had attacked. In coming in close for the final burst he had himself been illuminated in one of the beams and a good burst from the German rear gunner had sent his petrol – tanks up in flames. He managed to get out, but was rather badly burnt in doing so and he was not to return to the squadron for many months.

The sequel to this was that Wilf had been chasing the same Hun and had just closed into range and was about to fire, when there was a flash just beside him and a Spitfire went up in flames. It was John – neither knew that the other was there!

Meantime, Eric had also found a Hun illuminated by the searchlight and had chased his quarry for twenty minutes before he finally caught up with it. He had fired all his ammunition but could not be certain that he had got it, only to see it disappear beneath him in a dive. The next morning brought confirmation that a Heinkel had crashed into the sea just off the coast in the position he had engaged his target. A good night's work.

The crew of John's Heinkel were brought to the Station and the officer who was the captain of the aircraft turned out to be a really nice chap – a gentleman. The same, however, could not be said for the rest of his crew! He was brought into the mess until the prisoners were taken away, and as young Leonard was away at the time, given his room to have a shave and a wash. Leonard returned at breakfast time, and walked up to his room to get the shock of his life when he found a German officer at work with his own razor! I was perhaps even more surprised after tea when my wife arrived to have a drink in the Ladies' Room with me whilst I was talking to our prisoner, for he told me he recognised her! At first I thought I had misunderstood him, but it turned out that he had seen her in Germany before the war when she had been over there motor racing,

A few nights later on, on June 26th, "A" Flight was standing by. There were quite a few Huns droning about down to the south, but it was not until just after midnight that we were called upon to go up.

I was lying on my bed in the dispersal hut listening to the snores of the luckier pilots who could sleep at any rate until I took off, when the 'phone rang beside my bed. I groped about and eventually found it.

"Take off."

"O.K."

I tumbled off the bed and out into the night. Somewhere out in the darkness an engine started up, breaking the stillness of the night. I peered in front of me trying to pick out the blue exhaust flames which would show me where my aircraft was. As I picked it out a tender came rumbling past me out on to the aerodrome – the flare – path officer going out to light up for me to take off.

As I approached my aircraft, the fitter began to run up the engine, and I stopped for a moment to listen to the music of a Merlin at full throttle. There was something very impressive, almost awe – inspiring in that thundering roar, sounding much louder in the darkness now than in daylight.

The fitter throttled back and as the engine note died to a spluttering mutter I bent down and clicked home the leg straps on my parachute, shrugging my shoulders to get comfortable in the harness as I moved to the aircraft. A heave on to the wing, and I stepped into the cockpit, settled myself in the seat and did up the straps as the fitter handed them to me.

"O.K., sir?"

"O.K.", and the man jumped down to the ground.

Turning up the cockpit lights until their orange glow lighted all the instruments, I glanced round, checking the coolant and oil temperatures and oil pressure, before running up the engine myself and taxiing out. Everything O.K., and I jerked my thumb over my shoulder, waiting until a torch flashed from behind to tell me the crew were holding down the tail and I could open the throttle.

Slowly I opened up to maximum, checked the boost pressure and revs., and then pulled the lever back, waving my hand above my head as the crew came running back to the wing – tips. Another flash from the torch and I knew that the chocks in front of the wheels had been pulled away and I could taxi out.

Out in front of me showed the faint line of lights which was the flare path. I switched off the cockpit lights to see better and then flashed on my light asking permission to take off. An answering flash came from the first light and I slowly moved forward, turning until I was pointing up the glimmering line of lamps. A glance round the cockpit to make sure all was in order, and I opened the throttle, gathering speed into the black wall of the night ahead. The last light flashed past just after I left the ground and watching the blind flying instruments, I got the undercarriage up, reset the airscrew pitch and closed the radiator slightly.

My altimeter showed 1,500 feet as I glanced out of the cockpit to pick out the horizon, a faint demarcation showing where earth met sky. The canopy of stars overhead was crystal clear, and I reckoned the visibility was a good twelve miles. It was dark, but not quite a "blackout" night. There was quite a good horizon, so I hadn't to concentrate on flying by my instruments.

I switched on the R/T and called up the Controller. His voice came crackling back to me in the earphones:

"Receiving you O.K. There are some Huns to the east of you."

I acknowledged the message and turned east, climbing towards a bank of cumulous cloud ahead. As I entered the clouds a suspicious searchlight came on and groped about, trying to pick me up. It was very eerie with the silver glow lighting up weird shapes of caves and tunnels inside the cloud. Apparently the searchlight crew below became satisfied that I was a friendly aircraft and switched off. As I came out of the top of the cloud, all was dark again save the stars overhead.

At 15,000 feet I flattened out and steered towards a group of searchlights obviously trying to pick up an elusive Hun. Cruising around just behind them I waited, peering at the beams in the hope that I might see a faint silhouette even if the E/A was not actually illuminated. For an hour and a half I followed various groups of searchlights, but without any luck; then a voice in my 'phones told me to come back and land. I turned and began to lose height, following the courses I was given until I was fairly near the aerodrome. Down to a thousand feet and I began looking round for the flare path. Over on my left a line of lights shone out. Good show, I was nearly home. Circling the aerodrome I flashed on the light for permission to land. An answering light shone out and I began my approach. Wheels down, throttle back a little, 120 m.p.h. – O.K., flaps down, and I turned at the downwind end of the flare path. A light glared out below me as the floodlight was switched on, lighting up half the aerodrome. I straightened up, losing height all the time, until my altimeter showed 100 feet. Opening the throttle a little I held the aircraft at that height until I judged I was approaching the hedge, and then throttled right back. About 50 yards short of the floodlight I opened the throttle a little and began to ease the stick back. There was a terrific bump – Blast! I had misjudged it – I was too low. I gave a burst of throttle to ease the aircraft down off the bounce, wondering if my undercart was all right. I had certainly hit the ground pretty hard! As I passed the floodlight there was a much softer bump and I was down. Running down the flare – path the left wing began to sink – so the undercart couldn't take it! I wasn't altogether surprised! Lower and lower the wing sank, until the tip touched the ground, and the aircraft slewed round, the nose dug in and we came to a shuddering standstill.

I switched off and climbed out feeling furious with myself, and walked back towards the tender coming to pick me up. As it stopped, I climbed in and sank down in the seat feeling very tired. The flare path officer came up and climbed aboard.

"Bad luck. You certainly hit the ground a wallop!"

"You're telling me! I nearly swallowed my teeth!"

I sat back as we drove back to the huts, cursing myself.

A fine example I was setting to the rest of the flight! A flight commander is supposed to be past that sort of thing.

Next morning the C.O. spoke to me. "Bad luck, that show of yours. I am not altogether surprised, though. You'd been flying all day and then on top of that a couple of hours at night — you were just too tired."

I got some comfort from that, but I still felt a "twirp"!

CHAPTER IX

"A" FLIGHT HAS SOME LUCK

July and August came and went and the autumn was beginning to draw on, but still we had no action. The Blitz had begun down south, and we were beginning to wonder if we were going to miss it.

Up to this time the squadron had been going out each day to an aerodrome near the coast to carry out convoy patrols, etc. August 16th found us at C......., basking in the sun and hoping some Hun would come in and give us something to do. Nothing much had been happening all day and as tea – time approached we tossed a coin as to which flight should go up to the Mess for tea first. I lost for "A" Flight, and we stayed there on the sunlit aerodrome until "B" Flight should return.

After about a quarter of an hour the telephone rang – the squadron was to return home. I told them "B" Flight was up at the Mess and asked whether we should go off by ourselves or wait for the others to finish their tea. "No" – "A" Flight was to go off now.

We took of and circled the aerodrome, climbing for height, then Woody's voice came through, "Climb to 15,000 feet. There might be some "trade" for you on your way back." We set course and climbed up through the sunlit haze and broken cloud.

We flew on for some minutes until I judged we must be near the coast. Then, from behind a bank of cloud sailed five Heinkels – then another five, and another, and another! A steady stream of aircraft appeared from the cloud, reminding me of a huge chorus coming out on to the stage from the wings. There must have been at least 150 of them, Heinkels and Me110 fighters and way above showed twelve thin white pencils of smoke – the top escort.

The leader of the formation must have seen us a few seconds after I sighted his formation, for the Huns turned out to sea, thin trails of black smoke from their exhausts showing that they had opened their throttles wide and were on the run.

"Keep an eye on those b......... above us," I ordered. Then, as the humour of the situation struck me, "My God, what a windy bunch!"

We were overhauling the Huns fast and the rearguard of 110s turned back to meet us, blocking our way to the bombers. Damn!

There were at least 20 of them.

The old excited feeling fluttered at the pit of my stomach. I remembered getting exactly the same feeling stepping into the boxing ring at school. Thoughts raced through my mind. How could we get to those bombers. I glanced up at the white trails far above us. They hadn't seen us or else they thought we were a decoy and wouldn't come down. Ahead the 110s were circling to meet us. I glanced back at Frankie, leading his section behind me to the left. Could one section hold off the fighters whilst the others streaked after the bombers? No — we would have to leave the Heinkels and content ourselves with a crack at the fighters.

The leading 110 was abreast of us now, turning to come in behind us. I wheeled left, Frankie taking his section in to meet him whilst I headed to cut off some of the others. A 110 turned and came straight at me from above, six streams of tracer spurting from his nose as he opened fire. Hm! Not a very experienced pilot, judging by the range at which he opened fire, and I turned my head to see his tracer going 50 yards behind me. As he flashed past, I stall – turned to come in behind him, the rest of the section breaking away, each picking out an opponent.

I dived after mine and as he turned left I pulled round inside him, got the deflection and pressed the firing button. No – dammit – I missed him and he pulled hard round and went underneath me. I turned again in time to see another Spitfire on his tail. A burst of tracer and the Hun went down in a dive – steeper and steeper and, finally, plunging vertically downwards, – disappeared into the clouds far below.

Good – that was one down – he obviously couldn't pull out of that dive – the clouds were only a couple of thousand feet up.

Turning again I climbed up towards two more Huns, getting into position behind one of them. As I got there he saw me and began twisting and turning this way and that whilst I strove to get my sights on and take a steady enough aim to fire. At last he was right in the centre of the sight, and I opened fire. One gun immediately stopped. Blast it! I wasn't out of ammunition yet – must be a stoppage.

It looked as if I was hitting the 110, but he still twisted in front of me and I broke away to get into a better position. As I did so, another Hun came round on my tail and we started circling in what the Germans so aptly term a "Kurvenkampf". The Spitfire had a much better turning circle and as I began to gain on him and come round towards his tail he broke away into the opposite turn. It was a silly manoeuvre, as it brought me on to his tail almost at once and I fired the rest of my ammunition. He broke away below me and I lost him from sight.

Feeling rather annoyed at having had no luck, I dived away towards the clouds. Glancing behind me, the fight appeared to be almost over. Away to the right a 110 was diving homewards, a Spitfire turning away from behind him and heading back towards the coast. The clouds below came rushing up to meet me and suddenly the dazzling white vapour blotted out the sun and sky. Concentrating on the instruments, I dived on down, the cloud gradually getting darker as my height decreased, until below a different shade of grey told of the sea beneath. The cloud thinned abruptly and I was out in the clear.

It was very misty down here, and for a while I couldn't pick up the horizon. The artificial horizon had been upset in the dogfight and was not working. The altimeter showed 2,000 feet, and I could tell I was still diving fast by the sound of the airstream and the noise of the engine, without looking at the air speed indicator. I eased back the stick and looked at the "turn and bank" indicator. I was in quite a steep turn. Pushing the stick over to one side I got the kite more or less straight and then a lightship appeared to my right. – It looked rather unusual as it seemed to be floating at an angle of 45°! I still wasn't straight yet, and correcting still more until the ship was in a normal position I looked ahead and saw the line of breakers on the shore, and lined up my wings on this horizon. The beach and cliffs slipped by underneath and I recognised a town to the south. 270° should be just about right to get home, and resetting the gyro compass from the magnetic compass below it, I sat back and settled down on the course, idly watching the fields and lanes disappearing slowly beneath the wings. I felt contented. We had been on the job again, and after a couple of months inactivity it was like a tonic. I was annoyed with myself for not getting anything. My eye must be a bit out. Ah well – wait till we got back and saw "B" Flight's faces! This would teach them to go and have tea first!

A town came into view beside the engine – funny I didn't recognise it, and I should be over familiar ground by now. I circled, trying to pick out some features I knew. From the look of the country I knew I was somewhere south of the aerodrome, but I wasn't quite sure whether east or west. Just then I heard the ground station at the aerodrome calling another aircraft. Waiting until they had finished, I called up and asked for a course home.

On to the new course, and the countryside began to look more familiar. Another transmission for a check bearing and I knew where I was. The aerodrome appeared in front of me and I dived down across it and came in to land. All the rest of "A" Flight was down and were talking to Cras., our Intelligence Officer, round the tail of one of the aircraft. Several of "B" Flight, including the C.O.

and Wilf, were also standing there asking questions and cursing their luck.

Wilf shook his head sadly. " Dammit, it isn't fair!"

We all laughed – at least "A" Flight did! I got hold of Cras. to ask how we had done. "Three certain and one probable," he answered.

Grumpy had one certain and a probable and Sgt. P....... had a cert. as well, and young Jock had got his first one. It was his that I had seen going down into the clouds. Sgt. P.....'s remark had the laugh when he was told his seemed a certainty all right. "Well, I knocked the port engine out of the wings, and the nose as far as the windscreen fell out as well, but he might have got home with a hell of a draught in his face!"

CHAPTER X

A QUESTION OF AMMUNITION

A week later saw the squadron in action again. On August 24th after lunch we were ordered off to the London area as a covering patrol whilst other squadrons down there were refuelling after battling with the Boche. The C.O. was away at the time and I was elevated to the leading position. It was a typical summer's day as we took off and climbed away south. The sun caught the haze below, making it difficult to see the ground.

At 17,000 feet we were over the outskirts of the Metropolis, still climbing, and watching the sun for any tell – tale glints which would tell of enemy fighters. Woody's voice came over the air to me.

"There is some "trade" to the south – east of you."

"Message received and understood." As we turned towards the Estuary one of the rear look – out section called up –

"Ack – Ack fire ahead and above."

A pause, then –

"Aircraft on the port bow, above."

Looking in the direction indicated, I saw some gleaming specks a mile or two ahead and two or three thousand feet above us. I opened the throttle wider and began climbing hard after them. Glancing down, the glint of sun on water showed the position of the Thames.

The specks grew larger and resolved themselves into Me109s, their yellow painted noses shining golden in the sunlight. Ahead and below them was a formation of Me110s and in front of them again, the bombers.

Twelve Spitfires slid in under the 109s and crept up towards the 110s in front. It was obviously out of the question to get to the bombers as they were too far ahead. The only thing to do was to wade into the 110s, of which there were about two squadrons. As we got into range I singled out a target and the rest of the formation spread out and followed in. I opened a storm of fire from almost astern and the Hun went into a steep turn. As I followed him I noticed a stream of tracer apparently going straight into him. For a moment I thought it must be from another Spitfire, but suddenly realised that it was coming just over the top of my cockpit from behind me! My heart missed a beat.

56

Pulling sharply round out of the way I found another 110 on my tail. How he got there I don't know for I certainly did not see any of the Huns break formation until I opened fire. Keeping in the turn I got away from this gentleman, and feeling rather like a replica of that famous petrol advertisement, "That's Shell, that was!" had a good look round. Nobody seemed to be a after me and I turned in after a 110 ahead, coming in from the side at him. I got a good sight on him and fired a long burst until a large portion of his port engine came right out of the wing. He lurched over on his side and fell half inverted towards the glistening water far below. Keeping a good look round, I managed to watch him on his last journey and was rewarded by the sight of a huge splash of white foam as he hit the sea just off the coast.

The fight seemed almost over now, for to the east a few aircraft were heading for the Belgian coast and a Spitfire was diving back towards home. No − there was nothing more to do but go back to the aerodrome. Then, as I turned north, a solitary 110 flew slowly past, half a mile away. Diving down a little I turned in under his tail and closed in behind him. Where he had suddenly appeared from I couldn't think, but the reason he was limping home so slowly was obvious now − his starboard engine was out of action and I could plainly see the three blades of the stationary airscrew standing mutely out from the bulge of the engine. Throttling back and somehow feeling a bit of a cad, I took very careful aim, checked the range, and pressed the firing button. Nothing happened.

I pressed it again. No − I was out of ammunition! Sitting there just behind him I swore softly to myself. The German pilot was obviously quite oblivious of my presence. What a shock he would have got if only I had had some ammunition!

Sliding out to one side I pulled up over the top of the E/A in a barrel roll, looking down through the roof of my cockpit as the aircraft became inverted. I laughed as I caught a glimpse of a pink blur in the front cockpit as the pilot looked up and saw me. He must have had the fright of his life!

Slipping down the other side of him I rolled out right way up, looking hard at the rear cockpit. The sliding cover was closed. If there was a gunner on board he must be dead.

I noticed the pilot had opened up his one good engine wide and a thin trail of black smoke was streaming back from the exhaust. I think he must have thought I was playing cat and mouse with him and I suddenly felt very sorry for him. I could visualise his feelings as he strove to get away in his crippled aircraft, expecting at any moment to hear the clatter of bullets striking the fuselage and wings and waiting to feel one plough through his body.

I climbed and turned across his nose, rocking my wings as I straightened up and flew away from him.

He would get home all right as long as he didn't over – rev. that engine. Good luck to him, anyway.

And all the way back I pondered on my feelings. Why should I have felt sorry for that German pilot? War is war and no quarter is expected or given and yet, once the heat of the moment was over, I felt almost glad that I had been forced to give him that quarter. How contrary is human nature! Tomorrow, perhaps, he would be on another raid in another machine and might shoot down one of our chaps, perhaps one of my flight, perhaps he might come upon me gliding home with a dud engine, and finish me off. I wondered if he would feel the same way I did, or whether the Nazi doctrine had killed all his decent feelings. Somehow I hoped it hadn't. Paradoxically in a fight I always hoped the other chap was a decent sort of guy. It was so clean up there in the blue – the thrill of flying and the bigger thrill of fighting.......

And yet if I had had some ammunition left I couldn't have missed him and I would have shot him down. "Cold meat!" – and I would have done it, not because I hated that German personally – I didn't know who he was but because I wanted to and got a kick out of it. But if we had not been at war could I delight in killing? No. Sanity would prevail and we should all become once more normal people. Yet that German pilot was fighting for the filthy regime which had caused the war. He probably believed in it and admired its teachings.

Damn the stupid fool for being taken in by the lies and corruption which had been poured into his ears. God! if only I had had some ammunition!

CHAPTER XI

SAD PROMOTION

August drew to a close and then on September 5th the squadron came home without the C.O. I didn't go off with the squadron that morning as I only came back from leave as they were returning. Young Leonard had got a 109, F..... had a probable Dornier, and Sgt. P....., our Czech pilot, had also got a probable 109.

Wilf rang through to the Operations Room asking for news. No news had come through yet.

"He's probably baled out," said someone.

"Hope so. Who saw him last?"

"I saw him heading into the middle of a bunch of 215s by himself. They must have got him − cross fire, probably."

The day wore on and then at tea − time came the news that the C.O.'s body had been found. He had apparently got out of his aircraft but was too low or too badly wounded to open his parachute.

A gloom descended on the Mess and there wasn't quite so much talking and laughter as usual as we sat drinking after supper that night.

Next day after lunch Russell, our Adjutant, rang me up.

"Keep this under your hat until Woody rings up, but you've got the squadron. Congratulations."

"Shut up and stop blathering," I said.

"No, really. After all, you've had the ruddy squadron once before so I suppose they think you might as well try to make a mess of it again!"

"I don't want any of your rudeness, B....," I said, coldly, using his surname. He laughed. −

"Good lord, I shall have to salute you now, I suppose!"

"you're darned right! Has Frankie got "A" Flight then?" − −

"No... F..... It's a bit tough, but after all he's had a good deal more experience."

He rang off and I went back to the tea − table. As I sat down....

"I am awfully sorry about this, Frankie, but I'm a ruddy squadron − leader and F.... goes up to flight − lieutenant and takes the Flight. I am sorry − but it's just a question of experience, you

59

see."

Frankie took it very well, although I knew he was disappointed. He had been my deputy ever since Dunkirk, and when F... came in and was told the news Frankie congratulated him as sincerely as anybody.

Drinks that night were on F.... and me. He took the promotion in his usual quiet way. He would make a darn good flight commander and he couldn't have a better deputy than Frankie.

On September 7th, the squadron went off on two patrols, the first at 11.15 bing fruitless, no E/A were seen. We were operating in a wing again of three squadrons led by S/Ldr. B...... with his Canadians. The Czech squadron followed them and we were the top covering squadron, having a better performance than the two Hurricane squadrons .

In the afternoon shortly after tea, we were off again, flying in the same formation as in the morning. Climbing south we reached 17,000 feet when a large formation of about 200 bombers and fighters was intercepted. They were flying east towards the coast and the wing turned after them and climbed into the enemy formation. We were suffering from a disadvantage in height, and it looked as if only the Hurricanes would be able to get into range as we were too far behind.

High above the squadron was the top layer of the fighter escort, Me110s and 109s. I began to climb up in an endeavour to get to them. As I did so a 110 came screaming down just in front of me, a Hurricane on its tail. As the aircraft passed the Hurricane broke away. Breaking up the squadron into sections I opened the throttle and tore after the Hun with my section. As we closed in behind him, four Hurricanes descended on him as well! Seven to one... most unfair! But the rest of the Huns were out of reach. It didn't take very long, although the German pilot fought us off magnificently, before he and his gunner baled out and their aircraft crashed in flames into a field. I watched the crew land near the burning wreck, and apparently taken prisoner by a maid from an adjoining country house, and then climbed up again in the hope that there might be some fun still about. The sky seemed to be empty, the Huns, the Hurricanes and even the rest of my section had disappeared. I heard Wilf calling up the ground station and asking where the party had gone to. I called him up and told him I was in the same boat, I had lost everybody too.

We got instructions to land and came back to the aerodrome. The rest of the squadron had had more luck than we had.

Young Jock had got a He111 in flames and damaged another. Grumpy had got two 109s and Dolly, the squadron's ever smiling Czech, had got a 110. Not so bad, after all... four down and no loss to ourselves. The bag for the wing was 20 altogether for one or two casualties. Our arithmetic was getting better and better!

Two days later the wing was in action again, a party I unfortunately missed as I was not flying that day.... and the total bag rose to 29, again for a negligible cost on our side.

F..... got a Dornier, the Admiral (Sub. – Lieut. B...) a Heinkel... and a bullet through his windscreen!.... Jock a 109, and Frankie a Heinkel. The total squadron bag was now 50 certain and 18 probables, for the cost of four killed and one prisoner of war.

September 11th, and we took off and joined up with two other Spitfire squadrons to make up the wing. Again we were to act as a covering patrol over the London area.

Thirty – six Spitfires climbed up towards the afternoon sun. I was leading the show and it felt like old times looking back at the formations behind me.

At 22,000 feet I turned east and flew along the Thames watching to the south for any trade which might be about. I had been told over the R/T that a raid was coming in towards the Capital.

As I looked a cluster of black mushrooms of smoke appeared at about 20,000 feet two or three miles away. It was the South London guns opening up. I called up the ground station and the rest of the formation as I sighted a swarm of aircraft in the middle of the Ack – Ack and turned to meet them. It was the sort of interception a pilot dreams of. We were going for them head on from slightly above. Behind the bombers I could see the fighter escort stepped up in layers above their charges; and they couldn't touch us until after we had carried out the first attack on the bombers!

I called up again on the R/T, and then we dived on the 12 leading Heinkels. I took the right hand Hun, the rest of the flight each picking out a target so as to cover the whole front of the formation. Down we went, rushing to meet them at something like 500 m.p.h., with the combined closing speed. A fleeting burst of fire and we were into them.

I think it must have shaken those Huns a lot. It must have been a rather frightening sight to see the Spitfires rushing to meet them apparently in head – on collision, forty – eight guns of the leading flight spanning the space between with white pencils of tracer.

I held on to the last minute and then ducked to one side as a huge dark green monster flashed past. I caught an impression of the whirling airscrews, a black cross outlined in white, a gun in the rear cockpit swinging after me, a pink blur of the gunner's face showing behind it. Then they were gone.

61

I turned hard round to the left to come back. To my utter astonishment almost every aircraft had disappeared. Above me the flash of the sun on wings told of a dog fight going on. No doubt the fighter escort and the rest of the Spitfires, but of what must have been over 50 bombers not one could I see! Nor could I see the rest of of the flight, much less the Squadron!

Then towards the river I saw seven Heinkels turning for home, dropping their bombs as they turned: the leading bombers which we had attacked. There didn't seem to be much to stop them going on to the centre of London if they wanted to.... only me! But no... they looked to have had enough and were going home. Well, we seemed to have got five of them down in that first attack – probably the leader had gone down and these other lads were lost and didn't know quite what to bomb. Anyway, they were on the run.

I turned after them, scanning the sky all the time for signs of fighters. Two Me110s swam into view and joined up one each side of the bombers. They made no attempt to interfere with me, one of them merely dropping back behind the Heinkels. I closed in and fired at him from dead astern. I hit him with the first burst, a shower of pieces flying off from his starboard engine as the airscrew stopped. He made no attempt to avoid my fire, he just flew straight on. Puzzled, I broke away as I overshot him and turned to come back in again. Taking a sight on the port engine I opened fire again. At the second burst a huge cloud of smoke and flame belched out and the aircraft slowly went down in a dive. Breaking away I glanced down but he was lots from view. Looking back at the other aircraft I was amazed to see the remaining Me110 diving away as hard as he could for home!

I obviously couldn't catch him and anyway the bombers were more important to knock down. The Heinkels had tightened up their formation and were steaming along as fast as they could. I picked out the rearmost aircraft and then frowned. There were only six! I counted them again. Definitely six. I looked round but there was not another aircraft to be seen in the sky. Where the other Heinkel had gone I don't know to this day. When I broke away from the 110 I temporarily lost sight of the bombers, and it must have been then that he broke away or was possibly shot down by Ack – Ack.

I closed in behind the last Hun and eased the sights on to one of the engines and fired. I stopped for a moment to steady my kite in the slipstream and then fired again. Nothing happened.

Breaking away I climbed up to one side of the formation and came down in a beam attack on the leader. Still nothing happened. No return fire came from the Huns at all. Their crews might have been dead for all the response I got to my attacks. Turning round again I closed in behind No. 6 and opened fire at his starboard engine. After a short burst a cloud of white vapour streamed out from below the engine. Ah! I'd got his radiator! I fired again but my guns stopped after a second − out of ammunition − but not before I saw flames and black smoke come licking out around the engine cowling.

I broke away above him and looking back saw there were only five Heinkels now. I could account for that − a thin streak of black smoke showed where No. 6 had gone plunging down.

Feeling rather elated on getting two down, I dived back across the Thames and headed for home and a glass of beer − it was too late for tea!

CHAPTER XII

DER TAG!

September 14th saw the wing on two patrols, but no E/A was seen. Perhaps the Hun was saving himself for the morrow. I think this was actually the case for the next day saw the record bag of 185 Huns shot down – these only the certainties, the real total therefore probably even higher.

We carried out two patrols, the first at 11.30 hours I very nearly missed as my aircraft refused to start. After about ten minutes my fitter managed to get it going and as two other aircraft had just been made serviceable I took off with a section consisting of the Admiral and Jock.

We climbed away south as hard as we could without much hope of catching up with the wing. At 20,000 feet just over the outskirts of London I sighted some Ack – Ack fire ahead. We were luckier than I had even hoped, for as we drew nearer I saw a loose formation of about 15 Dorniers with several 109s above them. They were flying west and it looked as if the wing had already been at them, as in fact they had.

Keeping an eye on the 109s, which apparently hadn't seen us, I turned in from ahead of the formation and dived at the leader, the Admiral and Jock picking a target each side of me.

We weren't quite dead ahead of the E/As and coming in at a slight angle I misjudged the deflection when I opened fire, the bullets going behind the Dornier. I flashed through the formation and pulled up in a climbing turn as a 109 came down on me. He came at me from the side and dived straight on underneath me and disappeared. Where he went to I don't know – he may have been out of ammunition and going home.

The sky was clear above, the sun shining down from the blue of the heavens on to the dazzling layer of cloud 10,000 feet below us, the Dorniers standing out starkly black against the snowy whiteness. As I came round behind the formation again I saw the Admiral's aircraft behind one of the E/A and marked the white streaks from the wings as he opened fire – then I was closing behind my own target.

I came in rather fast and fired a short burst as the aircraft bumped in the bomber's slipstream, breaking away hard down below the twin rudders as they seemed to rush almost into the cockpit. Pulling out of the half loop I began to turn again towards the enemy formation when I saw a Dornier diving past me going east. Reversing the turn I followed, firing from the quarter at the starboard engine. As I slipped in astern of the Hun a Hurricane swam up beside me firing also. I turned away to one side and saw two more Hurricanes behind him. Dammit! Who saw this Hun first?

Then I realised that the Hurricanes had probably been chasing this Dornier when I came in and attacked. Perhaps after all I was horning in on them! I looked back to see if there was anything else about. No – the sky was empty save for the Hun, the Hurricanes, and me.

Taking my place in the queue I waited my turn to fire! The German pilot seemed to be taking no evasive action at all, the Dornier just diving slightly towards the clouds. Getting impatient I pulled out to one side and began a quarter attack aiming at the starboard engine again. This time I think I hit him, but it may have been one of the Hurricane pilots who was firing at the same time, as the E/A began to dive more steeply and as it went through a hole in the clouds, two white mushrooms blossomed forth as the wretched Huns baled out. The pilot was probably dead, as only two parachutes were floating down. Throttling back I dropped one wing to get a better view of the black – crossed aircraft. Behind, rushing over trees and hedges, fields and roads to meet the stricken machine, I saw its shadow. As the two came nearer and nearer a house loomed up, apparently in the path of the raider. With a sigh of relief I watched it miss the obstacle and then shadow and master met with a huge gush of flame as the aircraft hit the ground and the petrol – tank exploded. I circled, watching the pillar of black smoke rising up towards the clear blue sky above to mark the grave of another of Goering's pride. Turning back I saw the two white shapes of the parachutes as the rest of the crew floated down. One landed in a field and then I was on top of the other. I saw the black figure at the end of the shroud lines gesticulating violently and felt tempted to give him the burst he was so obviously expecting. Anger surged up inside me as I remembered the unbroken layer of cloud over London through which these "brave" Huns had been shovelling their bombs! Looking back I saw the parachute swinging violently in my slipstream only a few feet from the top of a wood and laughed –
I hope that breaks your neck, you bloody little swine!

* * * * *

The morning's party was only a very small foretaste of what

65

was in store after lunch. The sun was only just past the zenith when we were in the air again, forming up in the usual wing formation. As we climbed away towards London, S/Ldr. B....., Woody and I exchanged wisecracks as we usually did on the way to our patrol line, in between more serious messages.

The weather was fine, the golden blaze of the sun high in the blue picking out the fleecy layer of clouds far below us. At 20,000 feet a message came crackling through in my 'phones – Woody's calm familiar voice saying, "There's some trade heading N.W. to the south of you."

"Lovely," came from B...... in reply and then ahead some black puffs of smoke showed up a myriad black specks. Huns and plenty of them!

The old feeling fluttered again at my stomach as I settled myself more comfortably in my seat, tested the reflector sight, which I knew perfectly well was working O.K., and glanced round at the rest of the squadron.

Looking back again at the rapidly growing black specks I saw above them a tangle of white condensation trails – the whole sky ahead seemed filled with aircraft. As we got closer I recognised the bombers as Dorniers, about 30 in each formation stretching away towards the coast to the south. Above the bombers weaved Me109s and 110s, the escort. Never before, or since, have I seen so many enemy aircraft in the sky at one time. There were literally hundreds of them! It was an amazing sight and one which I shall remember all my life – it made the mass fly past at the Hendon Display seem small by comparison. It must have been about the maximum effort of the Luftwaffe.

As we climbed as hard as we could towards the Huns, the leading Dorniers crossed our bows and headed away to our right with their attendant escort.

I kept glancing up at those white trails just above, a gleaming speck at the head of each showing the fighters themselves. As we headed across the stream of aircraft I heard B..... call up but I didn't catch what he said, then I saw him turn away into the nearest formation of bombers with the rest of the Hurricanes, whilst I continued up into the escort with the Spitfires to try and hold them off while the bombers were being attacked. Glancing at No.2 of my section, I noticed that he was just beginning to make a trail and looking up again as a 109 passed over the top of me I judged we were about 1,000 feet below them. I have never felt so uncomfortable in all my life; we were a perfect target and could do nothing save continue climbing into the fighters, waiting all the while to be attacked from the ideal position – above and behind. I didn't feel scared now, there was too much to occupy my attention, but my "sit – me – down" was twitching as if I was expecting someone to kick me there and all the time I was squinting up into the glare above trying to keep an eye on all those damned Huns.

Suddenly I caught sight of a flash in my mirror, and turned as a couple of 109s came down on the rear section of the squadron. We opened out and after a few seconds split up as we swam up into the middle of a whole horde of 109's and 110s.

Why they hadn't attacked before I cannot think, but probably their idea was to draw us up into them to distract our attention from the stream of unescorted bombers which I later found were following at intervals behind the leading mass if aircraft. It almost seemed as if they hadn't sufficient fighters to escort all the bombers they sent over.

Ahead of me was a squadron of Me110s and after a quick look round to see that no other Huns were immediately concentrating on me I climbed up after the rearmost 110. Unfortunately, before I could get close enough to fire they saw me and paid me the compliment of all forming a defensive circle! Remembering the pilot who managed to get inside one of these circles going round in the opposite direction and keeping the firing button pressed as the string of targets passed through his sights, I decided now was the time to do likewise. But for the fact that I was now below the Messerschmitts I think I might have succeeded, but as it was I couldn't get into the middle of them quickly enough and was forced to break away as the leader came round behind me. As I straightened out again and began to climb up, a pair of 109s descended on me, but I managed to sidestep, so to speak, and they passed harmlessly to one side and pulled up in a climb ahead of me. As I opened the throttle wide and climbed after them they did a very foolish thing. The leader turned left and No.2, instead of following him, turned way in the opposite direction, right across my nose.

He saw me as I turned after him and putting on full inside rudder as he turned, skidded underneath me. Pulling round half stalled, I tore after him and got in a short burst as I closed up on him again before he was out of my sights again. That German pilot certainly knew how to handle a 109 – I have never seen one thrown about as that one was, and I felt certain that his wings would come off at any moment. However, they stayed on, and he continued to lead me a hell of a dance as I strove to get my sights on him again. Twice I managed to get in a short burst but I don't think I hit him, then he managed to get round towards my tail. Pulling hard round I started to gain on him and began to come round towards his tail. He was obviously turning as tight as his kite could and I could see that his slots were open, showing that he was nearly stalled. His ailerons were obviously snatching too, as first one wing and then the other would dip violently. –

Giving the Spitfire best, he suddenly flung out of the turn and rolled right over on his back passing across in front of me inverted. I couldn't quite see the point of this manoeuvre unless he hoped I would roll after him, when, knowing no doubt that my engine would cut whereas his was still going owing to his petrol injection system, he would draw away from me. Either that or he blacked out and didn't realise what was happening for a moment, for he flew on inverted for several seconds, giving me the chance to get in a good burst from the quarter. Half righting himself for a moment, he slowly dived down and disappeared into the clouds still upside down, looking very much out of control.

The sweat was pouring down my face and my oxygen mask was wet and sticky about my nose and mouth. I felt quite exhausted after the effort and my right arm ached from throwing the stick around the cockpit. At speed it needs quite a bit of exertion to move the stick quickly and coarsely in violent manoeuvres.

Looking round, the sky seemed empty and I dived down to follow the 109 and see if he had crashed or whether I could find him and finish him off if not. As I reached the top of the cloud layer I noticed away to the west a formation of about 20 aircraft flying south – east.

Climbing up again as hard as I could I got up into the sun above them and waited until they approached beneath me. They were Dorniers again, with no escort. Before I came down on them I had a good look round but could see nothing else in the sky at all.

I don't think they saw me until I was on top of them and what tracer did come from the rear guns was not very close to me. I fired at the leader in a quarter attack but with the speed of the dive I couldn't get in a very long burst and had to break away quickly underneath the formation, rolling over and pulling out in the opposite direction to that in which they were flying. As I pulled out, there in front of me was another formation of about the same number of Dorniers.

I was in a fairly good position for a head – on attack and since this seemed to be about the only way I could break up a formation of this size by myself, I sailed in at them. As I fired at the leader I saw the aircraft on the right wobble a bit and wondered whether my bullets weren't going quite where I thought they were, or whether the pilot just didn't like the look of a Spitfire coming at him head on.

The Huns rushed to meet me, and I remember involuntarily

ducking my head as the leader's port wing flashed over the cockpit, then I was through the formation and turning back after them again.

Far from breaking up the formation, my efforts seemed to have had the opposite effect as the Dorniers had closed up until they were flying with their wings almost overlapping. Those Huns certainly could fly in formation and since there wasn't enough room to get through them again from the front, I pulled up to one side, got slightly ahead of the leader and then came down in a beam attack. I was certain from the sight and the tracer that my burst hit at least one other aircraft, if not the leader, but there was no visible effect, they just sailed on towards the coast.

Breaking away behind them I noticed that the last man on the starboard flank of the formation was straggling a little. A steep left hand turn and I came in behind him firing at one engine. I heard a sharp metallic bang and then my guns stopped. I broke away as obviously I was out of ammunition, and that bang I had heard was obviously a bullet from the German rear gunner. I quickly glanced over all the engine instruments but all was well – he hadn't hit the engine.

A last regretful glance after the Dorniers and I turned for home, feeling rather annoyed at not getting any of those bombers. I was sure I had been shooting straight – they must be carrying a lot of armour on them these days – Blast them!

Ah well – "Home James," and find out how the others fared.

Back on the deck once more everyone was busy over their combat reports, Cras. fussing round getting the score as he collected the completed forms, and a good score it was too. Twelve certain and five probables. Sgt. R..... had got a bullet in his engine and had forced landed, and Sgt. P..... was missing – these were our only casualties. Young Leonard had excelled himself and got three certain, two 109s and a 110, and Grumpy had got three as well, all 109s. Grumpy with some 109s always reminded me of a terrier among rats! Of the others Sgt. C.... had got a 109, F/Sgt. S.... a Dornier certain and a 109 probable, and Wilf a 110 and a Dornier, both certainties, and Jock and the Admiral each a 109.

Of the rest of the wing, S/Ldr. B..... hadn't been quite so lucky, as his squadron and the Czechs close behind had been jumped on before we could get into the escort and hold them off, but for all that they had done well, the Czechs also having a good bag. The total for the the day for the wing amounted to 52, our own casualties being covered on the fingers of one hand. That night the sun was blood red as it sank beyond the Western horizon.

CHAPTER XIII

OUT OF CONTROL

The Blitz was not yet over, but September 15th saw the climax of it. Activity continued, however, on a fairly heavy scale for several days, and the wing carried out at least one patrol almost every day. On the 18th of the month we went off three times, and the first two patrols yielding nothing, I decided I might go over to my office to get on with a bit of work.

I was there when shortly after four o'clock the wing was ordered off again. Jumping into my car, which I always had with me for these occasions, I tore round to dispersal point just in time to see 12 Spitfires taxiing away down the aerodrome. Some cad had taken my aircraft! It didn't matter from the operational point of view, as Wilf used to lead when I was away at any time, but I was furious at getting left behind. At the same time I couldn't help smiling and remembering another instance when a flight commander found his aircraft unserviceable and ordered another pilot over the R/T to give up his kite, whereat the latter developed mysterious R/T failure until he was in the air! It showed a grand spirit, and I could hardly imagine such a thing happening in a German squadron.

Alternately swearing and smiling to myself I repaired to the Operations Room, there to watch the progress of the wing. Woody, as usual had come from his office to take over and very unsympathetically roared with laughter when I told him why I was there.

As luck would have it this third patrol which I had missed was the one in which the wing got into a party, a large formation of Heinkels, Junkers 88s and Me's being sighted east of London.

I made my way back to dispersal point as the aircraft returned and waited with Cras. for the pilots to taxy in. From their faces it was quite obvious that they had had some fun. Out of the total for the wing of 28, the squadron had accounted for six plus one probable. Wilf had got a Ju88, Leonard shared a Ju88 and a probable 109, Dolly and Sgt. P....., our Czech pilots, each a He111 and Grumpy (as usual) had added to his score with a Me110. F/Sgt. S...... had also got a Heinkel and shared a Ju88 with Leonard and F....... and his section had polished off another Ju88 between them. Unfortunately F.... had had to force land at E.....

aerodrome with a bullet in his coolant tank. News came through that he was quite O.K., however, to our relief. Two days later came the news that Grumpy had got the D.F.M. We were all very pleased about it.

*   *   *   *   *   *

September 22nd was a dirty day, low rain clouds obscuring the sun. Taking advantage of this, a Dornier paid us a visit, dropping a stick of bombs along "B" Flight's dispersal point. They were only small bombs and apart from blowing one of the aircraft up on its nose and filling the cockpit with earth, no damage was done. F....... had taken off with his section just before this to try and intercept the raider and caught him over the aerodrome, getting in a burst before the Hun got back into the clouds again.

Five days later the wing was on patrol south of London and intercepted a formation of Me109s. The Hun by now had almost completely given up large scale bombing raids, contenting himself instead with sending over 109s on offensive sweeps, some of these fighters carrying bombs in order to increase their nuisance value more than anything else, I think, judging by the results they obtained.

We were flying south – east at the time and some bursts of A. A. fire ahead showed us a formation of about twenty or thirty 109s flying north in loose formation. As they saw us they turned to meet us and S/Ldr. B...... waded into them, the rest of us following. As the squadron broke up, I noticed two yellow – nosed Huns creeping round underneath us to try and attack from below and behind.

Half rolling I dived down on them, getting a short burst at each of them as they passed through my sights. I was coming down rather fast in the dive and felt the aircraft skidding slightly. My left hand felt for the rudder bias control and wound the wheel back. Still the aircraft continued to skid and trying to pull out of the dive I found that I couldn't. I was doing a fair rate of knots and the controls had stiffened up a great deal accordingly, but a backward movement of the stick did not have the customary effect! Pressing as hard as I could on the left rudder pedal had little or no effect either, as it was almost impossible to move it at this speed.

A glance at the airspeed indicator showed me that I was doing well over 400 m.p.h. and the altimeter was giving a good imitation of one of those indicators you see in lifts. To say that I was a trifle worried about all this would be a slight understatement. I had started this blasted dive at 25,000 feet and the altimeter now

71

showed 10,000. I was just beginning to think about stepping out, and then began wondering whether I could at this speed. I decided to have one last attempt at getting control.

Bracing myself against the back of the seat I put both feet on the left pedal and pressed as hard as I could, pulling back on the stick at the same time. Relieved was hardly the word, as I felt the aircraft straighten up and saw the nose rising to meet the horizon. Determined to make no mistake about pulling out of the dive completely, I kept the stick back and not unnaturally blacked out completely as the controls regained their full effect.

Easing the stick forward again I came to and was confronted with the sight of a parachute upside down and apparently ascending instead of descending. Further examination of this phenomenon drew my attention to the fact that the sun was below me! I had completed a half loop while I was blacked out without knowing it.

I rolled out right way up and circled round the white mushroom of silk, trying to recognise the pilot at the end of the shroud lines. High above me one or two aircraft were still circling round but the dog fight seemed to be over. Circling round I waited until the pilot came to rest in the top of a tree and then dived down (slowly this time!), caught a glimpse of him climbing down to the ground. He was obviously O.K. and I couldn't help laughing at his predicament. As he reached the ground he waved, and I turned for home.

Back on the aerodrome I found out that it was Gordon who had taken to the silk. His machine had been set on fire and he had had to get out in a hurry. He had left us a couple of months ago to take over a flight in the Czech squadron.

Our score for the day was good. Seven 109s down plus one probable. F........ , P......., S......., Grumpy and our Czech Sgt. P......., had each got one, the Admiral had got two and Sgt. J..... had a probable – and I had had a fright! The trouble was later traced to a "bowed" rudder, and the rudder bias out of adjustment. This had prevented me from being able to trim the aircraft straight in the dive, the ensuing skid caused the rudder to blank off one side of the elevators, thus causing the effectiveness of this control to be greatly decreased. Later I went up to test the aircraft again and all was well, the faults having been remedied.

*   *   *   *   *   *

The same day we learned that Jock and Leonard had both got the D.F.C., and we had a celebration that night in the mess to mark the occasion.

CHAPTER XIV

QUIET DAYS

It was obvious now that the Blitz was over and that at any rate for the time being the Luftwaffe had shot its bolt.

Enemy activity declined, offensive patrols by Me109s some carrying bombs to increase their nuisance value, took the place of the mass bombing raids. As a result of this there wasn't enough trade to go round! And although the wing continued patrols whenever any enemy activity occurred in the Channel, it became obvious that we should have to be very lucky to get any more action. As it happened we did have a bit of luck, but not until November 5th.

On this occasion I was unfortunate in missing the patrol, F..... leading the squadron. His R/T, however, became unserviceable shortly after taking off and F/Sgt. S..... took over the lead. Over Canterbury a considerable amount of cloud was experienced, and the squadron became separated from the rest of the wing.

Shortly afterwards a formation of 109s was sighted and attacked. The E/A dived into the clouds and disappeared, but not before F...... had fired at one from 150 yards range and seen the cockpit cover break off. He fired again, giving a five – second burst, and the 109 disappeared in a vertical dive into the clouds and apparently crashed into the sea 10 miles south of Dungeness.

Sgt. C...... claimed his first victim since joining the squadron. He climbed up after three E/A which were circling 500 feet above him and after four turns got on the tail of one, the other two breaking away and disappearing from sight. Opening fire at the remaining Hun from about 200 yards he fired six bursts closing to 50 yards before breaking away to see the 109 with smoke and flame pouring from the engine.

In the afternoon F....... again was lucky over the same area, running into another bunch of 109s and the new Heinkel 113s. This time he made certain of his opponent and had the satisfaction of seeing the E/A completely break up in the air after he had fired only about 20 rounds per gun. It was excellent shooting.

Grumpy also added another to his score, chasing a 113 across the Channel and catching it over the French coast. It was the first and only E/A of this type to be shot down by the squadron.

Unfortunately the squadron came back without H...., one of our two Czech officers, and a report was later received that a Spitfire had been seen falling in flames over the Thames at the time of the fight. His body was never found and it obviously must have been poor H..... who had been seen.

Then, on the morning of the 15th, two squadrons, S/Ldr. B.......'s and ourselves, were sent off to patrol a convoy off the Estuary.

We climbed up towards the sun and set course over the banks of rolling mist covering the tree – tops. It was a glorious morning, the sun shining down from a cloudless blue sky on to the wisps of white vapour clothing the earth below.

Out to sea the mist had cleared a little and before long B..... picked up the convoy and began running up and down the line of ships.

Owing to the limited visibility he decided to patrol fairly low at about 7,000 feet, whilst I climbed behind him to keep a look out for any higher stuff that might come in.

Away to the south over the French coast a tangled mass of smoke plumes high up in the blue showed where some Huns were having a morning trip. It was not our job to chase them, however, so I sat back idly watching the white trails weaving a fantastic pattern against the heavens.

Glancing further to the east towards Dunkirk I saw two more white plumes and watched to see which way the E/As were heading. They seemed to be coming our way.

Switching on my transmitter I called up B.... and told him I was going up higher in case the Huns should come within reach.

"O.K., pal," came back in my 'phones as I turned towards the trails. Climbing south I edged round towards the sun to try and take the Huns by surprise. There was about 10 miles separating the two aircraft, and I called up Wilf and told him to break away with "B" Flight and take the rearmost one whilst I went after the other with "A" Flight. Up and up we climbed, and after a few minutes Wilf called up and asked if I could head his chap off a bit as they weren't gaining on him very quickly.

Telling Grumpy with his section to break away and try to cut off the Hun in question, I climbed on after the other one; at about 22,000 feet he passed over the top of us heading up the Estuary and I turned in behind getting between him and the sun.

At 25,000 feet I noticed that we were making condensation trails as well and began to wonder when our quarry would see us. We were still several miles behind him and at least 5,000 feet lower but I could now pick out the aircraft at the head of its white trail of smoke. I could see that it was a twin – engined kite but we weren't near enough yet to recognise the type.

The Ack – Ack batteries were firing at the E/A and I sat watching the white puffs of the exploding shells bursting below and behind him to come floating lazily back to meet us as we climbed on and on after him.

I began to think we were never going to catch up as we didn't seem to be gaining on the Hun to any great extent and it seemed as if our climbing speed was the same as his cruising speed. Accordingly I eased the stick forward a little until we were flying level and we began to catch up. As we got nearer, I began climbing slightly again trying to get the happy medium between maximum climb and forward speed.

We were now at almost 30,000 feet and over the outskirts of London. Apparently this was as far as the Hun wanted to go, for he turned slowly round the way he had come... and then he saw us and did a very foolish thing. He dived down as hard as he could back towards the sea.

As it was I turned and dived after him, Jock and Arthur following in line astern. Down, down we went the needle of the airspeed indicator going further and further round the dial until it showed 400 m.p.h. In reality, our speed must have been nearly 500 m.p.h., as in the rarified air at these altitudes there is quite a large error of anything up to 100 m.p.h. in the instrument.

The controls were solid now with the force of the air flow over them, and it needed two hands and a lot of strength to move the stick even a little.

We were gaining on the Hun now and gaining fast, and at 10,000 feet I began to ease the sights on to the fuselage of the target. I say "ease" but perhaps heave would be a better word. I was sweating with the strain of holding my aircraft steady in the bumps as I began to get the Hun's slipstream. My head felt thick and I was almost deaf from the sudden change from the rarified atmosphere above to the increased pressure lower down.

At last I was in range and squinting through the sight I pressed the firing button.

The muffled "Br – r – r – p" of the guns came to my ears as streams of tracer leapt from the wings and flashed towards the E/A in my sight. I fired three bursts steadying my aim between each and then pulling away to the left, a stream of black smoke coming from the Hun's port engine as I did so. Straightening up I watched Jock firing and then the starboard engine spluttered and a tongue of flame licked out around the cowling. Good show! Jock. We've got him.

I watched Arthur closing behind the 110 and as he broke away the E/A pulled up in a climbing turn and I closed in from the side and gave him another squirt. He turned over on his side and

75

a parachute blossomed out behind as the burning aircraft dived through a patch of cloud and crashed in a huge fountain of white foam and steam into the blue waters of Father Thames.

We were now at 2,000 feet and watching until the German pilot had been picked up by a boat. I turned and called up the other two of the section, heading home over the carpet of mist still covering the land.

After a while I picked up a town through a gap in the mist and a few minutes later sighted a familiar landmark sticking up through the white vapour and came to the aerodrome.

Landing I found that "B" Flight had accounted for the other E/A, which had also turned out to be a Me110. The two were obviously on reconnaissance flights and it was nice to think that the Huns had lost two aircraft and a lot of photographs which they probably thought they would get without trouble.

Wilf's scheme for getting the second 110 had worked admirably and Grumpy had headed him off just as "B" Flight came up behind the quarry. Thus nine Spitfires had pounced on the wretched Hun at the same time and it was small wonder that he had not survived the encounter. He had dived headlong towards the sea in an effort to escape, the Spitfires streaming after him, and one wing had broken off before he hit the water. It was rather hard to say who had been most instrumental in getting him, as everyone except Wilf had fired.

Over a glass of beer before lunch I heard Wilf's account.

"The B......s just shouldered me out of the way," he said indignantly. "I couldn't get near enough to fire at all!" Roars of laughter greeted this remark. That the flight commander who was supposed to be leading the attack should be pushed aside, so to speak, by the rest of his flight, all determined to get in a burst, struck everybody as being extremely funny.

CHAPTER XV

THE DAY'S WORK

We settled down now for the winter and a monotonous existence again, only alleviated by the fact that the days were shorter.

Perhaps it might be well if I were to describe an average day in a fighter squadron at this juncture.

The squadron stands by from dawn until dusk. During winter this does not entail any great hardship, but during the summer months it means that the pilots are on duty perhaps seventeen hours each day.

Enemy activity to a fighter pilot is a tonic compared to long periods of enforced idleness. Once having tasted action, all other flying rather loses its meaning and tends to appear rather pointless.

Before the war I had read numerous books written by pilots about the last war, many of whom had never flown since the Armistice. It seemed extraordinary to me that anyone could give up flying once they had started, but now I begin to realise how they feel about it, and how we shall feel when the war is over and the sky will be empty of enemy aircraft. From habit we shall still keep peering into the sun looking for the tell – tale glint of a fighter above, knowing full well that no fighter will be there, and realising that the sense of futility is bound to creep in.

Flying is the supreme goal towards which all our previous flying has been directed, and now we shall have reached that goal and the game will be over. We shall still enjoy flying for its own sake but it will seem insipid. Having tasted wine, water will not satisfy.

But I am digressing. When there is no enemy activity there is training flying to be done. New pilots must be taught the applied flying which they cannot learn anywhere else but in a squadron. The experienced pilots must keep their hands in, new tactics must be evolved, night flying training carried out and so on. All this and in addition, as far as the C.O. is concerned, quite a lot of office – work.

After breakfast, then, if the Hun is quiet, the training flying commences and continues on and off all day. Good weather at dusk and some night flying probably rounds off the day's work. Except those down for flying the remainder of the pilots are free until they come on duty again at dawn on the morrow.

A pilot doesn't get very much chance for relaxation except in the winter evenings, but plenty of leave is usually forthcoming and allows him the necessary mental and physical rest he requires.

Dud weather means boredom, which is bad for morale. Given something to do, particularly with the enemy, everyone is happy. Too much action is worse than boredom, of course, and when a pilot has had a "bellyful", away he goes to a flying school as an instructor for a rest from operational flying.

Every day of the week seems the same; Sunday is just another working day. At the beginning of the war I always felt rather lost and never knew what the date was, but after a while one gets used to it and it must be Sunday of the paper boy delivers the *Sunday Pictorial* instead of the *Daily Mirror*!

Leave brings temporary and welcome freedom. No longer does the ring of the telephone – bell control your life; but the Adjutant has got your address, and you might receive a telegram, "Return Unit Immediately," should circumstances demand it. As a matter of fact, during the Blitz I found it very hard to get chaps to go on leave – they were all afraid of missing a chance of getting at the Hun!

Now, however, leave was eagerly looked forward to. The wing still carried out patrols in the hope of catching some 109s and on November 28th a small formation was seen over Ramsgate and F...... had a crack at them. The net result was three down, and no loss to the squadron, Leonard having got one certain, F/Sgt. S...... another, and Grumpy and Sgt. F....... sharing another. This was the last action the squadron was to have up to the time of writing, and brought the squadron score up to 91 certain and 30 probable, for our own casualties of under double figures. Although this score did not compare with those of other squadrons nearer the scenes of activity, at the same time we felt justly pleased with ourselves at arriving at that score with the loss of so few of our own chaps.

The old faces were, however, fast disappearing through postings to other units. G...... and Eric had left us some time before to take over flights in other squadrons. Frankie soon followed them and then Wilf left to take command of a new squadron which was forming. Grumpy and F/Sgt. S..... had also been posted from the squadron to become instructors. Wilf, G..... and F/Sgt. S.... had all been awarded "Gongs" (medals to you!) after Dunkirk and Grumpy during the Blitz, to which was added a bar before he left us. F...... and Jock were soon afterwards given the D.F.C. and then two old faces were welcomed back to the squadron in John and Michael. John took over "B" Flight after Wilf's departure, but although he showed himself to be an excellent flight commander it soon became obvious that he hadn't fully recovered from his experience that night in June. He resolutely refused to admit it and was furious when eventually he was posted away as an instructor to give him a rest from the cares and worries of a squadron and to give him a chance to get really on his feet again.

New pilots kept arriving to fill the vacancies left, some to be posted again to new squadrons just forming after we had trained them up. And so it went on. Sometimes a section would be sent off to try and intercept a solitary Hun snooping about in the cover of the clouds on days of bad weather, but it was like looking for a needle in haystack.

And then one day we got a job after our own hearts again. A sweep was being carried out over Northern France by some bombers escorted by fighters, and the wing was to provide a covering patrol for the main formation.

We flew down to H....... where the squadron had been stationed during Dunkirk, there to refuel before going over to the other side. Memories came flooding back as I led the squadron down and came in to land on the familiar aerodrome. It looked just the same as it did seven months before. A few filled – in bomb – craters showed up from the air and the faces we saw were new.

The pilots gathered in the Watch Office talking and smoking while last – minute instructions were given and the aircraft refuelled. Then we went out on to the tarmac again to the spluttering and rumbling of engines being started up.

I climbed in and ran up the engine with more care than usual, then waved away the chocks and taxied away down the field, the other Spitfires following one by one behind me, to turn into wind and wait whilst the leading Hurricanes had taken off.

Raising one thumb I waited for the answering signal from the other section – leaders and then we were away, thundering across the green turf to rise slowly over the far hedge and climb up after the other squadrons circling the aerodrome and waiting for us.

As I got into position I called up L..... leading the Hurricanes and the wing turned south and climbed away towards the French coast.

We had instructions to patrol between Calais and Boulogne and at 25,000 feet we turned over Cap Gris Nez and flew down the coast. Almost at once the Flak opened up at us from the Calais area, and I turned to watch the black woolly puffs of smoke blossoming lazily out just behind us, and listening for the sound of the shell exploding which would tell me that the bursts were getting too close for safety. The German batteries were putting in some quite good shooting and some of the shells seemed to be exploding very close to us although the familiar "Bop!" was inaudible.

After a few minutes the Flak stopped and we ran on down the

coast only to be fired at again as we reached Boulogne. The Huns didn't seem very keen on wasting ammunition and after a few rounds ceased fire and all was quiet once more. It looked very peaceful and lovely down there in the typical French countryside with the sun shining down on the carpet of snow on the ground. They seemed to have had more of it over there than we had the other side of the Channel.

Suddenly down behind us something moving caught my eye. Looking round I saw an aircraft diving inland ten thousand feet below us. It looked like a 109, but I couldn't be sure at that distance. I wondered if he had seen us and wished I had seen him sooner – we might have been bale to have got to him, but it was too late now. We shouldn't catch him this side of Paris.

As I turned over Cap Gris Nez I heard Woody's voice calling me, telling me to come home. Disappointedly I turned and flew back over the blue waters of the Channel glistening in the afternoon sun. Blast those Huns! Where had they all got to and why wouldn't they come out and play?

Then the white cliffs of Albion slid slowly beneath the wings and we dived away northwards towards the aerodrome.

CHAPTER XVI

IN THE PALE MOONLIGHT

Daylight activity was almost negligible now except for the odd E/A coming in under cloud cover on days of bad weather.

Goering was concentrating all his efforts on night attacks and to help combat this day squadrons began operating during the periods of moonlight. In consequence of this increased activity by fighters, at night, the enemy's losses began to reach encouraging totals.

On March 14th, six pilots were standing by for night operations and as the sun sank in the west the thunder of engines being run up in readiness for the coming flights, reverberated across the darkening 'drome. One by one the stars came out and as the last light of the sun faded, the eastern horizon began to gleam as the moon rose slowly into the night sky.

Half an hour slowly passed and then the telephone – bell rang in the Mess Hut as we sat smoking and talking.

"First two aircraft off!"

I jumped to my feet, grabbing overalls from a nearby chair, and made for the door, Arthur at my heels. As I opened the door I called over my shoulder:

"Ring the flights and tell them to start up, somebody."

Into my car and down the road to stop outside "B" Flight hut. As I got out of the car I glanced round to see where my aircraft was. The faint silhouettes of six Spitfires showed against the sky on my left and I caught sight of the little flickering stabs of flame from the exhausts of one as the fitter sat warming up the engine. That was mine.

I nipped into the flight hut to sign up for the flight, giving a hasty "Good evening," to the flight sergeant and then out again to run to my aircraft. The fitter got out of the cockpit as I approached and stood on the wing bending down waiting to help me into the cockpit as I did up my helmet.

"O.K., sir?"

"O.K., thanks," and he jumped down. Checking everything in the cockpit I waved my hand over my head and waited until the dim figures of the fitter and rigger waved an O.K. from each wing – tip, and opened the throttle. Another wave and the crew saluted and I taxied out towards the dim line of lights of the flare path to the right.

A green light came speeding down the aerodrome slowly over the far boundary; the starboard navigation light of Arthur's aircraft as he took off. Glancing towards the light showing the position of the floodlight, I signalled on the identification lights for permission to take off, and as an answer flashed out, I adjusted the elevator and rudder trimmers and turned down the cockpit lights.

Peering out over the side of the cockpit, the cold blast of air from the prop brought tears to my eyes, until I had turned into position to take off, and settled back again behind the windscreen.

As I opened the throttle and eased the stick forward, the green light of the undercarriage indicator shone out dazzlingly in the dark cockpit as the throttle lever operated the automatic switch. Six seconds later the bumps of the undercarriage ceased and we were airborne. My right hand dropped to the control lever and after a moment the green light on the instrument panel changed to red as the wheels thudded up into the wings. Adjusting the airscrew pitch, throttling back and closing the radiator and the cockpit hood, switching off the navigation light, I switched on the R/T and called up the ground station.

The controller answered me and I turned on to the course he gave me and began to climb up. It was a wonderful night, The midnight blue of the sky paling round the dazzling silver orb of the moon. Below the ground showed up startlingly clear, roads and fields, hedges and rivers standing out plainly visible in the moonlight. What a night for bombing!

At 15,000 feet I got instructions to circle and await further instructions. Peering down I made out the outlines of houses and streets below. A few minutes later, Woody's voice came to me over the air.

"There are several raiders in your vicinity now at your present height. Keep circling, they will pass very close to you."

"O.K., O.K."

Minutes passed, and then below me to the right I suddenly picked out the glint of something moving. As I looked, I picked out the faint form of a twin – engined aircraft flying north. Calling up the R/T told Woody and received his acknowledgement.

Diving down I followed the aircraft and as it turned left over the city I got a perfect plan view.... then, as it straightened up the glint of the moon on the wings faded and it disappeared. Frantically I turned this was and that, in an endeavour to pick up the aircraft again, but it was no good.

Suddenly brilliant flashes of flame sprang from the ground, followed a few seconds later by a cluster of flashes just below and in front of me. The guns were having a crack at the raider. Although the explosions of the shells gave me a good indication of where the E/A was, I couldn't pick him up again, and after a while fresh instructions were passed to me.

I had been up about an hour now and since there was a good head wind waiting for me on the way back, Woody decided it was time to come back. Twenty minutes later I was over the aerodrome again at 1,000 feet, awaiting permission to come in to land. There were some Huns overhead and I would have to wait until they had gone, before I could have the floodlight switched on on the ground. It was hardly necessary in view of the brightness of the moonlight but my landing would give away the position of the aerodrome to the E/A overhead, and they might give us a present of a stick of bombs.

I was still circling when the controller's voice called me asking how much petrol I had left. Pressing the button beside the gauge on the instrument panel showed me that I still had about thirty gallons left. I passed this information to the controller, and received a course to steer after one of the Huns.

Climbing up, I set course and saw above me against the dark blue of the sky the silver trail of a condensation plume. Good show! This was the answer to a night fighter's prayer. Up and up I went until I was just below the trail and then flattening out I tore along until abruptly I came to the end of it − Nothing was there! The Hun had either dived down or left this particular condensation area. I judged that he was some miles ahead of me as the end of the plume looked some minutes old by the way it had thickened out. I called up the controller again and he confirmed my suspicions. The Hun was too far ahead now for me to catch him. Regretfully I turned back and dived down. A few minutes later I was circling the aerodrome again.

I flashed for permission to land and the light came back from the field. I lowered the undercart and flaps and turned in to land. As I approached the down wind hedge the floodlight came on. The moon was so bright that the light on the ground in front of me seemed almost dim, although actually it was of some thousands of candlepower and it was only as I felt the wheels bump on the ground as I flashed into the beam that I realised again how bright it really was.

Taxiing in I switched off and climbed out of the cockpit. As I jumped down to the ground and pushed my helmet off my ears, the fitter's voice echoed in my ear:

"Aircraft all right, sir?"

"Yes, thank you."

"Did you see anything, sir?"

"Yes, I saw one but lost him."

"Bad luck, sir," and the man jumped up on the wing and began unscrewing the filler cap on the top tank ready for refuelling.

From the roar of the engine and slipstream I now found myself revelling in the peaceful silence of the night. The only sounds which came to my ears were the chugging of the tractor bringing the petrol tanker out to my aircraft and the faint hum high overhead of a Spitfire climbing up into the moonlit heavens to try to find the dark invaders of the night.

Lighting a cigarette I made my way to where I had parked my car and throwing my helmet and gloves into the back seat, pressed the starter and motored slowly back to the Mess hut.

The electric light had been turned out by now and in the light of two hurricane lamps I made out the dim forms of figures sprawled out in the armchairs snatching some sleep ere they were called to take off. A can of cocoa was simmering on the coal stove in the middle of the room and finding a cup I dipped into the steaming liquid and settled myself in a chair to enjoy it. The quiet voice of Cras. in the chair next to me broke the silence.

"Did you see anything?"

"No, it's all right, you can go to sleep again."

I heard a soft chuckle and the Intelligence Officer closed his eyes.

All was peace again save for the noise of a Hun droning slowly overhead and the sound of breathing from the still forms around me.

CHAPTER XVII

MORE MOONLIGHT

The next night the Hun was active again and so were we.

Two aircraft were despatched at a time and my turn came at eleven o'clock. It was another glorious night and as I took off I couldn't help marvelling at the beauty nature was providing and the evil use man was making of it. There is nothing in the world quite like night flying and I don't think one can fully appreciate the beauty of a moonlight night save in the air. You seem so much nearer nature herself and when the clouds cut off the silver light from the earth beneath, to climb up through the white vapour and see it shining like a white carpet below brings you into a new world, the loveliness and loneliness of which makes you catch your breath in awe. The sound of the engine and the rush of air past the cockpit fade into silence as the spell takes hold.

I was rudely awakened from my thoughts by the insistent voice of the controller asking if I was receiving him. I came back to earth as it were and switched on my transmitter. "Receiving you loud and clear, are you receiving me? over."

An affirmative came back to me and instructions for course and height, and I turned on to the given course and began to climb. Fresh instructions kept crackling in my 'phones as the controller directed me after a raider. Although I got very close to him I saw no sign of another aircraft, and after a while I was given a new course which took me out to the north – east of the aerodrome. At 15,000 feet I cruised around following the courses given to me and the circled as the controller got me in the path of an incoming raider.

"One E/A approaching you from the east at 15,000 feet."

"O.K."

Still turning I strained my eyes towards the east hoping all the while for a glimpse of a shadowy shape coming towards me, but nothing materialised. Then....

"Keep a good look out. Plots show he is right on top of you."

My heart began to beat a little faster and I found myself praying for a glimpse of the Hun. Still I saw nothing and then came the anticlimax.

"He has passed you."

I chased the invisible quarry for several minutes and then the controller called me again.

"E/A has turned away to the north. I don't think it's worth chasing him any more. Come back and then circle."

"O.K."

As I turned east again a line of intensely white flickering light suddenly appeared miles away towards the coast.... incendiaries. I watched the lights slowly turn to a steady red glow and knew that they had found a mark and had set something on fire.

The four minutes being up I circled again yawning a little as I awaited more instructions. To the north another stick of incendiaries suddenly lit up on the dark earth beneath. One by one they flickered out and the lights died. Good.... those must have been on open ground.

A few seconds later a parachute flare lit up in the sky to the north – east and then another and another.

I called up on the R/T and asked if I could go and investigate, and received an O.K.

As I headed out towards the flares there came a flash and one of them disappeared. A gun had opened up from the ground and hit one, putting it out. A few seconds later came another flash and another flare went out.

In answer the Hun dropped three more and then another three. He seemed to have an unlimited quantity of the darned things!

I still did not appear to be much nearer the scene of activity and at that moment the controller called me up and told me to circle at my present position. There was another Hun coming in very close to me, and I started getting all excited again!

I think I had circled for about a minute when a stick of incendiaries appeared in the ground almost underneath me. I turned quickly and came round on a course parallel to the line of bombs. I now had a very good idea of where the Hun was, as a bomb hits the ground only a few hundred yards behind the aircraft which drops it. In addition to that I could tell what the raider's course was from the direction of the line of incendiaries.

Alas, in spite of all this I could see nothing. Then behind me to the north appeared another stick of incendiaries. Blast the fellow! He had turned right round and I yanked the kite round in a steep turn after him. It was rather like a game of blind man's buff and then to add insult to injury a stream of big white sparks whizzed past my starboard wing – tip. Tracer! The b..... was firing at me! Swearing and cursing to myself I rammed the nose down out of the way so that I could see ahead, but he wasn't there. He must have caught sight of me silhouetted against the moon.

Just then the controller's voice told that the Hun was now a mile or two to the west of me. He must have turned round underneath me after he fired. Still feeling furious I turned west and tore after him. But no.... my luck was out and when he turned away to the north, the controller called up and told me to come back and land.

A glance at the petrol – gauge confirmed his suggestion as a wise one and I turned on to the homing course he gave me and began to lose height. Corrections of the bearing were passed to me every few minutes and after a while I caught sight of the gleam of water below me and recognised the landmark. Another ten miles and as I came lower I picked up the flare – path and the aerodrome.

At a thousand feet I circled the aerodrome waiting until another Spitfire had landed. I have told earlier of an unfortunate night landing. Even in good moonlight and when conditions are favourable all the sense need to be on the alert. On this occasion, unlocking the hood I pushed it back with my elbow until it locked home in the open position. A rush of cold air filled the cockpit and I leant forward a little to get the utmost protection from the windscreen. My eyes felt tired and the night air made them water and I had to keep brushing the tears aside with my glove.

Pushing the undercarriage lever out of the top "gate" I pulled it down until it locked at the end of its travel, the red "UP" of the cockpit indicator going out to be replaced a few seconds later by a green "DOWN" as the wheels locked home in the downward position.

I throttled back as I came down the left – hand side of the flare – path and as I reached the end, checked the speed on the luminous airspeed indicator and pulled down the flap lever. The aircraft slowed and the nose dropped as the flaps came down and feeling for the rheostat control of the cockpit lights I turned it until a faint orange glow from the hooded lamp lit up the airspeed indicator and altimeter so that I could read them more easily.

110 m.p.h. I put on left bank and turned half a mile from the downwind hedge until the nose came round in line with the flare – path. The altimeter was showing 300 feet, the needle slowly moving round the dial as I lost height. I could see the hedge of the aerodrome boundary quite easily in the brilliant moonlight. The floodlight shone out in front of me and as the hedge disappeared under the leading edge of the wing I throttled right back and let the speed fall of to 95 m.p.h. The red light fifty yards inside the aerodrome boundary flashed past and then the airscrew lit up in a shining disk as I passed the floodlight and the beam illuminated the aircraft. A bump.... pause.... and the another, followed by a continuous jolting, and we were down.

One after another the lamps of the flare – path slipped by as I eased on the brakes, and as the aircraft slowed right down, turned off towards the dispersal point and taxied to where a dim figure was flashing a guiding torch to show me where to park the kite.

As I neared him he came running to meet me and grabbing the wing – tip guided me in towards the chocks and pile of cockpit and engine covers marking my parking place. braking, I gave a burst of throttle and turned the aircraft into wind and switched off, the engine spluttering until with a final kick the airscrew stopped, and all was quiet save for the whirring of the gyros behind the instrument panel.

I climbed out and answered the crew's usual enquiry about the aircraft.

"Yes – everything O.K., thanks."

Back to the flight hut to sign up after the flight that everything was in order, then a talk on the 'phone to the controller about the trip, and then back to the mess – hut for a cigarette and some cocoa, to flop down in chair and take my ease until, perhaps, the telephone would ring and it would be my turn to go off again.

CHAPTER XVIII

ALMOST LIKE OLD TIMES

The moonlight period was over and thirty – five Huns had been knocked down in seven nights by fighters and guns. March had gone out and April had come in with a promise of spring weather. The month was eight days old and the aerodrome was basking in the noonday sun when the telephone rang in the mess – hut. This was not an unusual occurrence and I answered it without interest. Then I woke up as I heard an excited voice from the Operations Room saying that there was a "thirty plus" raid in the Channel and all aircraft were to come to "readiness." I hadn't heard those once familiar words for months now and as I passed the information over my shoulder to the rest of the pilots, their faces lit up as they leaped into activity, grabbing their flying kit and making for the door and the aircraft.

A couple of minutes later we were all ready and waiting when the order to take off came through. Three minutes afterwards 11 Spitfires were thundering across the aerodrome leaving me still wrestling with an engine which refused to start. After what seemed an age it fired, coughed, and then picked up again.

In a matter of seconds the crew had the chocks away and I opened the throttle wide and took off from where I was, racing cross wind over the green expanse of the aerodrome to rise over the far hedge and climb up towards the squadrons now wheeling high above me.

The rest of "B" Flight formed up on me after a few minutes and we climbed away towards the midday sun after "A" Flight and the Czech squadron which was leading. They were climbing hard and I found I could make little headway on them.

It was a perfect spring morning with a visibility of at least a hundred miles. The whole of S.E. England was laid out like a map beneath us and beyond the shining ribbon of the Channel the French coast stood out clear and distinct. A broken layer of white fleecy clouds at 3,000 feet speckled the sunlit earth and blue waters of the North Sea with endless shadows. It was the sort of day when one thanks God to be alive and yet here were we, going as fast as we could in the hope of getting a chance of killing some Germans. And yet we would be cleansing the earth in doing so, that we and many millions of others might enjoy the cleanness of

Nature on just such a day as this. Yes.... I feel sure God had amended His commandment in our case, and I fell to thinking of the cowardly hypocrites who clung to that same commandment. "Thou shalt not kill!" – boloney! I am not of a religious nature but I have a bit of conscience, and I certainly had no regrets in killing as many Huns as possible. Maybe it was rather a drastic way of teaching them their sorely needed lesson, but it was the only way open to us now. And with that I came back to the job in hand. We were now at 18,000 feet, almost over the Estuary with the others still about a mile ahead and a couple of thousand feet high. As I watched the leading squadron white plumes began to form behind each aircraft to spread out into a one thick woolly trail half a mile astern.

I heard F..... call up L..... , the English C.O. of the squadron, and draw his attention to the trail, and the Hurricanes lost height until they were clear of the condensation layer. Such blatant advertisement of our numbers and position was not conducive to a surprise attack should we meet the enemy. At last I came up just behind "A" Flight as they turned north – east off the coast to follow the other squadron of which I had now lost sight.

At that moment the controller's voice came over the R/T saying that there were some E/A to the south of us and at the same time F.... called up saying he had sighted some aircraft diving away below us and requesting permission to investigate. I answered with an "O.K." and flew up and down watching one or two smoke trails which were weaving about high up further out to sea. I wondered whether they were a decoy sent to try and draw us away from the shipping we were guarding in the Thames. At length the plumes turned and headed towards the land. I climbed up a little and watched until I could see the little gleaming specks of the aircraft at the head of their white tails, and as they passed over head the sun glinted on the undersides of their wings as they banked and I saw the red, white and blue roundels at each wing tip. O.K. They were Hurricanes.

Up and down we flew, tacking on the down sun run so that the sun was never at our tails. Minutes passed and still no formation was seen coming from the direction of the French shore.

At last the controller called up again saying that the enemy activity had dispersed and all was quite quiet again, but that we were to stay on patrol in case anything further should come in.

Every now and then another squadron of Spitfires passed us on the same patrol line and somewhere near at hand was the Czech squadron, although I couldn't see them. Twenty minutes passed and then I heard F..... calling up the ground station. His transmission was rather faint and I wondered where he had got to and whether he had managed to find any E/A. The controller answered him and then I heard him say he had chased some aircraft which had turned out to be Spitfires.

As I turned at one end of the patrol line I saw far away to the south – west six little white plumes standing out sharply against the deep blue of the sky. Ours or theirs I wondered. As I watched the smoke curved round and streamed out towards the French coast. Might be ours after something but it looked rather like a small bunch of Huns going home.

I kept an eye on them out of interest more than anything else as they were much too far away to interest us, and finally saw the plumes stop as the aircraft dived down and left the condensation layer.

And all the while I was squinting into the sun and scanning the sky for a glimpse of something suspicious but nothing caught my eye. Then I heard the ground station calling L.... , telling him to come back and land. As L.... acknowledged the message it was passed on to F.... and me, and I turned towards the land and began to lose height.

Down we went, although at that height only the position of the nose and the feel of the controls told that we were diving, except for the needle of the rate of climb and descent dial which was showing 2,000 feet per minute down. My ears began to sing and the noise of the engine and the rush of air past the cockpit seemed less as I began to go a little deaf with the increased pressure of the lower air.

I pushed a finger and thumb into the top of my oxygen mask and pinched my nose and blew until both ears cracked and the rush of noise came back to me. Every few thousand feet I went through the same procedure, relieving the pressure on my eardrums and restoring the normal hearing.

At four thousand feet the steady dive gradually became bumpy as we approached the top of the clouds and came into the disturbed air currents. The white masses of vapour rushed up to meet us, enveloped us, and then darkened below us as the ground came into view.

The bumps had increased now as we were in the rougher air just below the clouds and the aircraft tossed about in the eddies. Automatically I corrected with the stick as first one wing and then the other dropped. The other sections of the flight closed up on me in tight formation and I began looking round for a familiar landmark. Ah yes, that stream with the railway beside it – we were on our course, and I began peering ahead for a glimpse of the bunch of trees just south of the aerodrome. After a minute I picked it out and turned slightly until the nose of my kite was

91

pointing at it. At the same time half a mile to the right 12 Hurricanes emerged from the cloud above, diving towards the aerodrome now visible ahead.

At a thousand feet we roared across the green expanse and turned left round the circuit. Switching on the R/T I called the ground station and told him I was now over base and then told the other section leaders to break away and land individually with their own sections. Then I came in and landed, to be followed in quick succession by the rest of the flight and finally by "A" Flight who had by now almost reached the aerodrome.

I taxied in, waved away the other aircraft in my section each to his individual dispersal point. I switched off, climbed out and walked to the flight hut to sign up for the flight, and to light a cigarette whilst the others came in.

Then back to the mess for a welcome drink before lunch. There might be better luck for us this afternoon.

CONCLUSION

And now as I sit penning the last of this book, the sun is streaming through the window, lighting a vivid pattern on the paper before me. Glancing back through the chapters I realise what fun it had been writing them and reliving those fights over the sunlit coast of Belgium and the lovely countryside of Kent. I have tried to take you up high into the blue with me to meet the Luftwaffe and to give you an idea of what it's like up there. I hope I have succeeded.

I am no "ace" and I know of many who could tell you a far far better tale than I, besides whose experiences mine are nothing. It isn't too easy writing a book in these times. Time is the great enemy, and I have had to write in spare moments between flights and after the squadron has been released in the evenings.

Mine is only one side of a the picture, the easiest side, I think. Compare it with that of the bomber boys.... perhaps one day their story will be recorded by one of them, and that will be a book worth reading.

But before I put my pen down for the last time I want you to think of the lads who are, so to speak, behind the scenes, the fitters and riggers, the engineer officers, the flight sergeants (the backbone of the Service), the Controllers in the Operations Room, and all the other ground personnel who make it possible for the pilots to do their job. Working in the background, no glamour, no "gongs", just getting on with it. So to them I say, "Thank you."

The spring of another year of war has come. Hitler has walked into Jugoslavia — well, some of the way, anyway — and his forces have reached the Egyptian border. Perhaps he thinks he's winning — well, perhaps he does, they say he's mad, anyway! But the day of reckoning will come, come what may, and then will follow the task of making Germany fit to exist in a civilised world. Some task, but we will do it and — Just a moment, the telephone has rung.... "Hello... Operations?... Yes... Yes, speaking... Thirty plus over the Channel? Good show... Do you want us off right away? ... O.K., cheerio."

"O.K., boys, we're off. Somebody tell the flight."

Sorry — I must go now — I can't write more.

Where the hell's my "Mae West?" — Ah, I've got it — I wonder if this is the beginning of another Blitz — invasion, maybe — well, let 'em all come — the more the merrier — so long!

Part Two

SPITFIRE SQUADRON

The story of Squadron Leader Brian James Edward Lane DFC
and Number 19 (Fighter) Squadron 1939-1941

by

Dilip Sarkar

Above. Squadron Leader Brian Lane DFC.

Below. Eileen Ellison, later to become Mrs. Lane, pictured with her pre-war race winning Bugatti. (Mrs. Margaret James.)

Squadron Leader and Mrs. Lane snapped on the occasion of Frank Brinsden's wedding, February 1941. (Flt. Lt. W. Cunningham.)

The elementary cockpit of the Avro Cadet. In centre of picture note the Gosport speaking tube for instructor/ pupil communication. (Mr. J. B. Wray.)

An Avro Cadet training aircraft, possibly flown by Brian Lane whilst a pupil at Air service Training, Hamble. The photograph was taken by John Wray who was on the same course. (Mr. J. B. Wray.)

"Ace" Pace, a buff on the Great War 'aces', the epitome of the prewar fighter pilot, photographed at Duxford, winter 1939. Note the black flying overalls, and No. 19 Squadron badge above left breast pocket. (Air Cmdre. J. Coward.)

Left–Right: Sergeant Potter, Flying Officer Matheson, and Pilot Officer Watson. During the squadron's first engagement with the enemy on May 26th, 1940, Peter Watson was shot down and killed. (Wg. Cdr. P. I. Howard-Williams.)

No. 19 Squadron during the 'Phoney War'. Left–Right, front row: Flying Officer Pace, Pilot Officer Brinsden, Flight Lieutenant John Banham, Flight Lieutenant Wilf Clouston, unidentified, Middle row: Flying Officer Petre, Flight Lieutenant Withall, Pilot Officer Llewellyn, Pilot Officer Eric Ball. Rear row: unidentified, Pilot Officer Watson, Squadron Leader Cozens (CO), Pilot Officer Gordon, Flying Officer Sinclair, Flying Officer Coward, Flight Sergeant Steere, unidentified, Flight Sergeant Unwin, Sergeant Potter, unidentified. (Wg. Cdr. F. N. Brinsden.)

Following Squadron Leader Stephenson being shot down and made prisoner, No. 19 Squadron's next Commanding Officer was Squadron Leader Phillip Pinkham AFC (Centre). This photograph is taken from his Pilot's Flying Log book. (Mr. J. M. Pinkham.)

Operations room caravan, Fowlmere Farm. formerly a Great War airfield, on July 24th, 1940, No. 19 Squadron set up permanent home at Fowlmere. (Wg. Cdr. P. I. Howard-Williams.)

Below. 'Before the Blitz', a photograph taken at Fowlmere, Duxford's satellite airfield, and so captioned in the Flying Log Book of Pilot Officer Arthur Vokes. Left–Right: Squadron Leader Brian Lane, Sergeant Jack Potter, Sergeant 'Jimmy' Jennings, Pilot Officer Ray Aeberhardt, Flight Sergeant George 'Grumpy' Unwin, Flight Sergeant Harry Steere, Flying Officer Frank 'Fanny' Brinsden, Flying Officer Walter 'Farmer' Lawson, Flying Officer Leonard Haines, Pilot Officer Arthur Vokes, Flight Lieutenant Wilf Clouston (note that he is wearing a German life jacket) and Flying Officer Thomas. (Author's collection, The Malvern Spitfire Team.)

Sergeant Jack Potter at Duxford. On September 15th, 1940, Potter chased a German aircraft far out over the Channel but was shot down himself, ditched his Spitfire off the French coast and was taken prisoner of war. He died in 1977. (Wg. Cdr. P. I. Howard-Williams.)

Pilot Officer Arthur Frank Vokes. Vokes, of Erdington, Birmingham, was a member of the Vokes air filters family. Having joined No. 19 Squadron in June 1940, he assumed command of the squadron on August 28th, 1941, following the death in action that day of Squadron Leader 'Farmer' Lawson, and Flight Lieutenant 'Jock' Cunningham being shot down and taken prisoner. Tragically, one week later Vokes was killed in a flying accident and was buried at Bircham Newton. (Author's collection, the Malvern Spitfire Team.)

Flight Sergeant George 'Grumpy' Unwin DFM at Fowlmere during the Battle of Britain with his Alsatian, 'Flash'. At the end of the battle Unwin had destroyed 14½ German aircraft and had received a bar to his DFM. (Wg. Cdr. G. C. Unwin.)

'QV-I' receiving an armourer's attentions, Sergeant Jennings in the 'office'.

After the battle. The photograph which helped inspire the writing of 'Spitfire Squadron'. After an engagement over London during September 1940, the strain of combat clearly shows on the faces of Squadron Leader Lane, Flight Lieutenant Lawson, and Sergeant Lloyd, who discuss the sortie with No. 19 Squadron's Intelligence Officer.

Briefing, Fowlmere style. Left–Right: Flying Officer Frank Brinsden, Sergeant Charnock, Flying Officer Leonard Haines, Squadron Leader Brian Lane, Pilot Officer 'Uncle Sam' Leckrone (an American volunteer serving with 616 Squadron), Sergeant David Cox, Flight Sergeant George Unwin, unidentified, Sergeant Jennings, others unidentified.

Left–Right: Sergeant Lloyd, Flight Sergeant Unwin, unidentified, Pilot Officer Hugh 'Cocky' Dundas (616 Squadron), Flight Sergeant Harry Steere, Squadron Leader Brian Lane.

No. 19 Squadron Spitfire Mk 1a being rapidly 'turned around' at Fowlmere between sorties, September 1940.

Sergeant Jennings taking off in 'QV-I' X4474, to commence a 'beat up' of Fowlmere for the benefit of official photographers.

'Admiral' Blake in the cockpit of a No. 19 Squadron Spitfire. Blake was shot down and killed in a surpise attack by 109s over south London on October 29th, 1940. Note the Spitfire's unusual fared in rear view mirror.

'Jock' Cunningham, 'Admiral' Blake, Frantizek Dolezal and Frank Brinsden relaxing at Fowlmere. The front page of Flying Officer Brinsden's newspaper reports on the sinking of the liner Lustiana, carrying evacuee children to America, by a German U-Boat. (Author's collection, the Malvern Spitfire Team.)

Flying Officer Frantizek Dolezal, a Czech pilot serving with No. 19 Squadron during the Battle of Britain. 'Dolly' later led the Czech Wing and his final score of aerial victories was 5½.

Walking in after a successful combat, September 1940, Flight Sergeant Unwin (left) and Flight Lieutenant Lawson (centre), both clutching combat report forms, with Sergeant Lloyd.

The 'Scramble' photograph (below) is often used to illustrate pilots dashing to their Spitfires. The top photograph, however, shows that the scramble was not so urgent! Left–Right: Pilot Officer Vokes, Sergeant Cox, Flight Sergeant Unwin, unknown, Sergeant Jennings, others believed to be of No. 616 Squadron. (Author's collection, the Malvern Spitfire Team)

Left–Right: Flying Officer Leonard Haines describes a successful combat to Frank Brinsden (left) and the American 'Uncle Sam' Leckrone (right), the latter of No. 616 Squadron.

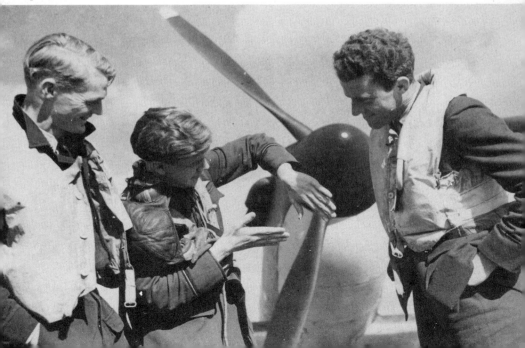

Fowlmere crew room, October 1940. Squadron Leader Lane sits in the left corner. To his left, smoking pipe, is Flight Lieutenant Colin MacFie, and, feet on table, Squadron Leader Billy Burton, both of No. 616 Squadron who also operated from Fowlmere as part of the 'Duxford Wing'. Sitting in front of the door is Flying Officer Hugh 'Cocky' Dundas, also of 616, reading the casualty list in 'Flight'. (Mr. J. M. Pinkham.)

Wing Leader, Squadron Leader Douglas Bader pictured with his No. 242 Squadron Hurricane at the time he commanded Duxford's controversial 'Big Wing'. (Imperial War Museum)

The wreckage of Unteroffizier Hotzelmann's
Bf109 at Hardy Street, Maidstone on
September 5th, 1940.

Top: The crew of Von Arnim of 4/KG4.

Below: The wreckage of Von Arnim's
He111 at Six Mile Bottom, June 19th,
1940.

The enemy, Oberleutnant Gerhard Schoepfel, an Experte of III/JG26. On November
5th, 1940, Flight Sergeant George Unwin's Spitfire was seriously damaged in combat
with 109s; in the same action Schoepfel claimed two Spitfires destroyed, one of which
may have been Unwin's. (Via Dr Alfred Price.)

Pilot Officer Scott took this photograph from his own Spitfire. The pilots were: Leading-Squadron Leader Lane and clockwise – Flight Lieutenant Lawson, Pilot Officer Vokes, Pilot Officer Stevens and Flight Lieutenant Cunningham. (Wg. Cdr. D. G. S. R. Cox.)

No. 19 Squadron at Fowlmere, October 1940. Left–Right, back row: Sergeant Charnock, Flying Officer Brinsden, Pilot Officer Hradil, Sergeant Fulford, Sergeant Lloyd, Sergeant Boswell. Front row: Flying Officer Parrott, Pilot Officer Dolezal, Flight Lieutenant Lawson, Flight Sergeant Unwin and Sergeant MacGregor. (Flt. Lt. A. N. MacGregor.)

Sergeant David Cox sat in Arthur Vokes's Spitfire, Fowlmere, 1941. In 1942 he joined No. 72 Squadron, and later flew in North Africa. Cox later commanded both Nos. 222 and 1 Squadrons, his final score being 8⅓. (Wg. Cdr. D. G. S. R. Cox.)

Sergeant Ken Wilkinson, posted to No. 19 Squadron as a replacement pilot towards the end of the Battle of Britain, poses with his Spitfire, Duxford, October, 1940. (Flt. Lt. K. Wilkinson.)

By the time Brian Lane returned to the UK, a new German fighter had appeared which out classed the Spitfire Mk V. On June 22nd, 1942, as the result of a navigational error, Oberleutnant Arnim Faber of III/JG2 landed by mistake at RAF Pembrey in South Wales, thus delivering to the RAF an intact Focke Wulf 190A-3 fighter. (Drinkwater Family.)

Arnim Faber awaits an escort to take him into capitivity. (Drinkwater Family.)

Squadron Leader Lane photographed at Fowlmere by David Cox in May 1941, one month before he left the squadron for staff appointments at home and abroad. The Spitfire is P7849 'Armagh', one of a number of aircraft presented by the Belfast Telegraph Spitfire Fund. (Wg. Cdr. D.G.S.R. Cox.)

A still from the cine gun camera of Oberleutant Schoepfel showing a Spitfire being shot down on June 27th, 1941. On December 13th, 1942, whilst serving as supernumery with No. 167 'Gold Coast' Squadron, Squadron Leader Lane led a sweep over the Dutch coast from which he was not to return. His section were attacked by Focke Wulf 190s, and Lane was shot down over the North Sea by Oberleutnant Walter Leonhardt of II/JG1. (Schoepfel via Dr. Alfred Price.)

Sadly, Eileen Lane died prematurely of cancer in 1967, and, as Squadron Leader Lane's parents are believed dead, no other members of his family could be found. However, a friend of the late Mrs. Lane, Mr. Owen Fargus, has in his possession a silver cigarette case once owned by Brian Lane. His initials can be seen engraved on the lid, and the underneath is badly dented with a hand scratched inscription: '11.11.38 Magister L8136', which presumably refers to a flying accident suffered by the owner and in which the case was damaged. (Andrew Long, the Malvern Spitfire Team.)

CHAPTER ONE

Brian James Edward Lane was born on June 18th, 1917, at
Harrogate in Yorkshire, and joined the Royal Air Force on a
Short Service Commission in 1936. He reported for duty at Air
Service Training, Hamble, on March 22nd, 1936, successfully
completing that course prior to being posted to No.11 Flying
Training School at Wittering on June 3rd. John Wray joined the
Royal Air Force with Brian, and recalls their training days:

"In those days officers and non commissioned officer (NCO) pilots on
limited service engagements spent three months at an Elementary Flying
Training School where they completed fifty hours dual and solo flying, and
engaged in associated ground school subjects. They then proceeded to the
Depot at Uxbridge for general introduction into the Service including the issue
of, or, in the case of officers, the purchase of uniform. This lasted about one
month. Then on to the Service Flying Training School for one year or ten
months conversion onto service type aircraft and instruction in its use as a
military weapon. Ground associated subjects were also studied and the whole
training experience was now in a service environment with we officers learning
to be such and the NCOs learning to be NCOs. My course at 11 Flying
Training School, Wittering was drawn from two Elementary Flying Training
Schools, one from Hamble and one from Ansty near Coventry. I had been at
Hamble with Brian Lane and we both went to Wittering together. At Hamble
we had flown the Avro Cadet bi – plane, the smaller brother of the Tutor, and
Avro's answer to De Havilland's Tiger Moth.

"Brian was rather languid and slow in those days and was not what one
imagined a fighter pilot to be. He was always known as "Dopey" Lane. He had
deep set eyes with black rings underneath, nothing, I am sure, to do with his
lifestyle, just natural characteristics! During those now far off days of training,
only the very good pilots on the Flying Training School course went to fighter
squadrons, which meant, of course, the minority. For example, I was posted to
an Army Co – operation squadron because, so I was told by the Chief Ground
Instructor, "In Army Co – Operation squadrons they need gentlemen because
you may have to take port with the General".

"'Dopey' Lane was posted to a fighter squadron upon conclusion of our
course at Wittering. I saw him afterwards on a number of occasions when he
was with 19 Sqn at Duxford, and ran into him on other stations when his
squadron was refuelling at forward bases such as Manston. In conclusion, I
would like to make one point abundantly clear: "Dopey" Lane was no dope
when it came to the question of being the leader of a fighter squadron."

Also on Brian Lane's course were several young airmen destined
for greater things. One was R.A.B. Learoyd, later a Flight
Lieutenant with No.49 Squadron who led a formation of nine

97

Hampdens to bomb the Dortmund Ems Canal on August 12th, 1940, and whose aircraft took the brunt of the ground defence fire. Learoyd brought his badly damaged aircraft back to Scampton after destroying the target. For his actions he was awarded the Victoria Cross. Another was "Sammy" Hoare, an Old Harrovian, later to become a successful night intruder "ace" with a total score of twenty – one and a half victories. Another future fighter "ace" was Peter Burnell Phillips, better known as "B.P.", who survived spinning in at Wittering but was later called upon to resign for low flying. Upon the outbreak of war he re – joined the RAF and became a Sergeant Pilot, flying Hurricanes with No.607 Squadron during the Battle of Britain. After receiving a DFM and a commission in November 1940, he was killed in a flying accident the following year with his score standing at five victories. An amusing character seems to have been Simon Maude who, John Wray remembers, forgot to have his "wings" sewn onto his uniform for the course dining in night. In desperation he stuck them on with paste, only to have the coveted brevet fall off into his soup!

John describes his own first year of war as "somewhat bizarre", and indeed it was. After his posting to an Army Co – Operation squadron, he went to France in September 1939 and took part in the early operations over Germany. His first wartime injury was as a result of being laid out in a football match, after which he spent a few days in hospital and then on sick leave prior to ferrying a replacement Blenheim from Odiham to Glisy. Rather unfortunately, John was shot down by the French near the site of the Battle of Crécy, and then followed a second period in hospital. Recovered once more he was posted to 1 Flying Training School as an instructor, but in July 1940, during the Battle of Britain, he was shot down by a Messerschmitt Bf110 near Southampton whilst giving flying instruction to a pupil in a Fairey Battle. His injuries sent him back to hospital for the rest of July and August, whereafter he again served with 1 Flying Training School until 1941 when he transferred into Fighter Command, remaining flying Whirlwinds, Typhoons and Tempests until 1944 when he became leader of 125 Wing, 2nd Tactical Air Force, flying Spitfire XIVs. He continued as an officer in the post war Royal Air Force and eventually retired after thirty years service.

Upon conclusion of the training course at 11 Flying Training School, Wittering, on January 8th, 1937, Pilot Officer Lane reported for flying duties with No.66 (Fighter) Squadron at RAF Duxford. No.66 Squadron had been formed from a flight of No.19 Squadron, also based at Duxford, and at the time Brian Lane arrived the squadron was flying the Gloster Gauntlet bi – plane fighter. He was to remain with No.66 Squadron for only a short time, being posted on June 30th, 1937, to fly Gauntlets with the recently formed No.213 (Fighter) Squadron at Northolt. Brian remained with the unit as it passed through such stations as Church Fenton and Wittering, during which time the squadron re – equipped, in 1939, with the new eight gun mono – plane fighter, Sydney Camm's Hawker Hurricane.

Throughout Brian Lane's early days in the peacetime air force the clouds of war gathered across Europe. Following defeat in the Great War of 1914 – 1918, and in the wake of the economic, military and territorial conditions imposed upon the country at the subsequent peace settlement at Versailles, Germany had been gripped in economic depression and suffered dangerous political instability. The conditions were perfect for the growth of fascism and the German people eventually looked to one man, Adolf Hitler, and his followers, the National Socialist Workers Party, or Nazis, to lead Germany into a more optimistic future. The Nazis crooned anti – semitism and blamed Germany's defeat on the Jews and Communists who had "stabbed the country in the back". Hitler told the broken German people that they were the "Master Race", of Aryan descent, and that they needed "living space", so must therefore increase their territories, and conquer "inferior" peoples to become their slaves. After Hitler became Führer, or leader, in 1933, Germany prospered. At Versailles Germany's armed forces had been severely restricted. Hitler set about rectifying this situation and secretly re – built his illegal air force with modern military mono – plane aircraft, his army with modern tanks, which were prohibited under the terms of the peace settlement, and his navy with new submarines, also prohibited by Versailles. In Britain and the rest of Western Europe disarmament was the major policy, and little money was spent by governments on the advancement of military power and machinery. Hitler soon set about regaining the territory Germany had lost at Versailles. His troops marched into the de – militarised zone of the Rhineland, on the German – French border, and later into the Sudetenland area of Czechoslovakia, the greater percentage of the population of these countries being German speaking. The forbidden union of Austria and Germany also took place; Versailles was ridiculed. Britain and France took no action and their governments pursued a policy of appeasement, of giving in to the dictator's demands. In fairness to Neville Chamberlain and his fellow ministers they had little choice but to adopt this policy as Britain was in no position to meet Germany on the battlefield. At the time of the Munich agreement in 1938, when Chamberlain and Hitler signed the "white paper", guaranteeing peace between their respective countries and that no further territorial demands would be made by Germany, the first Spitfires had only just started to reach Fighter Command's squadrons.

On Friday, September 1st, 1939, Hitler's forces invaded Poland. Until that time it could have weakly been argued that Hitler's territorial ambitions had been purely to rectify what was seen through Germany's eyes as the injustice of the Versaiiles Peace Treaty. Clearly the invasion of Poland heralded territorial ambitions far more sinister. On Sunday, September 3rd, 1939, Britain and France declared war on Germany, Hitler having taken no heed of their instructions to remove his forces from Poland, or suffer the consequences. Chamberlain having broken the traumatic news to the British people that summer's morn, Britain remained as peaceful as ever whilst a bitter struggle for freedom took place on the other side of Europe. Chamberlain broadcast to the German people the following day:

> "He gave his word that he would respect the Locarno Treaty; he broke it. He gave his word that he neither wished nor intended to annex Austria; he broke it. He declared that he would not incorporate the Czechs in the Reich; he did so. He gave his word after Munich that he had no further territorial demands in Europe; he broke it. He gave his word that he wanted no Polish provinces; he broke it. He has sworn to you for years that he was the mortal enemy of Bolshevism; he is now its ally. Can you wonder his word is, for us, not worth the paper it is written on?"

At last the storm had broken. The British Expeditionary Force and Advanced Air Striking Force were swiftly despatched to France and the nation mobilised for war. Amongst the first to be affected were many territorial reservists, amongst them my late grandfather who had served with the 3rd Battalion of the Grenadier Guards between 1928 and 1931, thereafter being committed to nine years on the reserve list. Subsequently market gardener Herbert Henry Smith once more found himself Guardsman 2611042 and exchanged his agricultural tools for a uniform and weapons of war. He left his Worcestershire home and family on September 1st, bound for a war on the shores of France where his father had lost his life fighting against the same enemy in the Great War. With the optimism of the nation epitimised by popular slogans such as "Home by Christmas" and "We're gonna hang out the washing on the Siegfried Line", Guardsman Smith could not suspect that it would be nearly six long years before his return, his whole life disrupted, having been a prisoner of war deprived of his family and the Worcestershire countryside he cherished so much.

One week after the outbreak of the Second World War, Brian Lane was promoted and posted to No.19 (Fighter) Squadron at Duxford as a flight commander. No.19 Squadron held the distinction of having been Fighter Command's first unit to receive the new Supermarine Spitfire when on August 4th, 1938, test pilot Jeffrey

Quill delivered Mk I, K9789. By the outbreak of war the squadron were efficient in their handling of R.J. Mitchell's creation, which was soon to prove a deadly adversary for its German counterpart, the Messerschmitt Bf109. The squadron diary recorded the following entry on September 3rd, 1939:

"Due to partial mobilisation completed during the preceeding few days, declaration of war against Germany found the squadron almost on a war footing and ready for any eventuality. Flying personnel: S/L H.I. Cozens AFC (CO), P/O F.N. Brinsden (Adj), F/L L.C. Withall (OC "A" Flight), F/L A.J. Banham, (OC "B" Flight), F/O Clouston, T.G. Pace, J.B. Coward, A.I. Robinson, G.C. Matheson, P/O G.L. Sinclair, G.E. Ball, A.J.A. Llewellyn, G.W. Petre, L. Marples, M.D. Lyne, L.A. Haines, J.H. Bowring, F/Sgts H. Steere, G.C. Unwin, Sgts J.A. Coleman, J.H. Potter, P.S. Gunning, T. Boyd, A. Bruce (RAFVR). The majority of the flying personnel are quite conversant with the characteristics of the Spitfire Mk Ia, with which the squadron has been fully equipped for almost a year".

Flight Lieutenant Lane's arrival at Duxford on September 10th was not altogether welcomed by many No.19 Squadron pilots, as Frank Brinsden, a New Zealander who was later to enjoy a long career in the Royal Air Force, explained:

"He was received politely but coolly as "Sandy" Lane when he arrived from Wittering to command "A" Flight of No.19 Squadron. Coolly because the residents of No.19 Squadron thought that a number of them could have filled the bill without calling in an outsider who, despite the small number of officer pilots in Fighter Command at that time, was unknown to us. However, within a week or two Brian's calm diginity and professional skill showed through and the sobriquet "Sandy" was never used again; within the squadron he became "Brian". The somewhat derogatory tag of "Sandy" was quite incongruous. His dignity was not a pose and he enjoyed squadron sorties to the local as much as we all did, and we were all equal to him. However, I recall a formal dressing down I received from Brian Lane after which my respect for him was enhanced; in later years, as a Commanding Officer myself, I used the same technique with comparable result."

Following the flurry of activity as the nation mobilised for war, and as wives and sweethearts bade their loved ones farewell on railway platforms crowded with troops bound for France, the events following the declaration of war became an anti – climax. The expected air raids did not materialise and after Hitler had conquered Poland he sat pondering his next move on the chess board of Europe. The winter of 1939 was a cold one, and, due to the enemy's inactivity, the war became known as the "Phoney War". In France the soldiers of the British Expeditionary Force spent the winter dug in in trench systems, waiting for the enemy to make his move. At home the nation waited too, hardly daring to hope that Hitler's fury was not, after all, to be turned westwards. It seemed that the dictator's blitzkrieg had now become the "sitzkrieg".

Two hundred and sixty one Hawker Hurricane fighters were despatched to France, but no Spitfire equipped fighter squadrons left these shores. The Commander in Chief of Fighter Command, Air Chief Marshal Sir Hugh Dowding, recognised the great threat to this country with regard to a German seaborne invasion in the event of the collapse of France and refused to release any of his precious few Spitfire squadrons for anything but home defence. For Flight Lieutenant Lane and his fellow pilots of No.19 Squadron, the remainder of 1939 and up to the spring of 1940 was somewhat monotonous and not far removed from peace time days of training flights, albeit with a degree of uncertainty as to the future.

On October 1st, 1939, a pilot with No.19 Squadron, Wilf Clouston, was promoted to Acting Flight Lieutenant and took over command of "B" Flight. Clouston was a New Zealander, born in Auckland in 1916 and had also joined the Royal Air Force in 1936. Just five days after taking over the flight Clouston was involved in a flying accident when his Spitfire, K9854, collided with K9821 flown by Pilot Officer G.E. Ball. The collision had occured whilst the two aircraft were flying from Watton to Duxford. Fortunately Clouston, who had much of the tail of his aircraft chopped off by Ball's airscrew, managed to force land on Newmarket racecourse. Neither pilot was hurt. Accidents during training were common. A particular incident worthy of note had occurred the previous year when, on March 9th, 1939, Sergeant George Unwin found himself in trouble when his Spitfire, K9797, suffered an engine failure:

"I forced landed at Sudbury in Essex. A coolant pipe had broken causing the engine to partially seize up. I decided to land on a large playing field and was doing fine with undercarriage down until the school children who were playing on the various pitches saw me descending (I was apparently on fire and trailing smoke). They ran towards me and on to the path I had selected for a landing. I was then at less than 100' and decided to stuff the Spitfire into the thick hawthorn hedge just in front of me. The impact broke my straps and I gashed my right eyebrow on the windscreen but was otherwise unhurt. For this I received an Air Officer Commanding's commendation."

On October 20th, 1939, the squadron moved to Catterick to offer some protection to northern bound convoys and to act as security against incursions by enemy aircraft in that part of the country. The squadron was stationed there for just one week, returning to Duxford on October 27th. However, on one of the few days spent at Catterick a section of Wilf Clouston's "B" Flight, namely himself, Pilot Officer John Petre and Sergeant Harry Steere, caught sight of an enemy bomber over the sea south of Flamborough Head. When the Spitfires sighted the enemy aircraft it was just about to attack a convoy. The Royal Navy opened up with anti – aircraft fire which drove away the raider but also forced the fighters to break off their attack. An opportunity unfortunately missed through no fault of the pilots. As winter set in it was to be some time before No.19 Squadron had another chance. Being stationed at the inland station of Duxford in 12 Group the unit was not favourably positioned to take part in the meagre fighting which was taking place, usually over convoys.

Michael Lyne, a Pilot Officer at the time, described for me his experiences with No.19 Squadron during those early days:

"I arrived at the squadron fresh from Cranwell in August 1939. Brian Lane was my second flight commander and I found him to be a charming and encouraging superior. Our aircraft were Spitfire Mk I with fixed pitch two bladed wooden airscrews. Duxford had a grass runway of 800 yards, and, with the poor take off and on landing the poor braking effect of a coarse pitch propeller, we needed every yard of it. I was astounded at the boldness of Squadron Leader Cozens in conducting formation landings at night in this aircraft, especially as the lighting consisted of the World War One style paraffin flares.

"In spite of the war most of September 1939 was given over to practice flying, formation, high altitude and night flying. The blacking out of all towns and villages made this harder than we expected. In February 1940 one of our most experienced pilots, a New Zealander, Pilot Officer Trenchard, was killed in a night flying accident.

"By October we were operational, going forward to spend the days at the bomber airfield at Watton, in tents and forbidden the Officers Mess because the CO did not like the way we fighter pilots looked in our flying boots and heavy sweaters ready for unheated and unpressurised flight at high altitude; in some ways it was still very much a peacetime air force.

"On October 20th we made a sudden move to Catterick, with groundcrews and equipment being carried in four engined Ensign transports. This was in response to the German attack on the Firth of Forth, each squadron moving north one stage. We did a few convoy protection patrols near Flamborough Head and returned to Duxford a week later.

"In November we started to patrol from the new Norwich airfield of Horsham St Faith. The mess was not ready and we all lived in a house called "Redroofs". There was no night flying so our social life was active. When we were at Horsham on a Sunday we gave an unofficial flying display at low level for the local population. This system of forward basing and coastal patrols continued throughout December and into January 1940.

"The flying conditions over this period were often very frightening, there being no proper homing or landing aids and a very poor and out of date cockpit radio. After a spell above cloud you let down gently and hoped that you were over the sea or Fens. Sometimes the ground did not show up until you got to 300', when the problem became one of trying to recognise somewhere in the rain and mist. A lovelorn section leader, Flying Officer

Matheson, nearly did for me in these conditions when he took us back from Horsham in terrible weather so as to keep a date in Cambridge!"

Having been the first Spitfire equipped squadron in Fighter Command, it was logical that No.19 Squadron should continue to receive new versions of the aircraft, fitted with various improvements, to evaluate under operational conditions. On November 1st, 1939, a Spitfire was collected by Squadron Leader Cozens which was fitted with the new De Havilland constant speed (CS) airscrew. This was a great advantage over the fixed pitch two bladed propellers fitted to the original Mk I Spitfires which had given Michael Lyne cause for concern. The pitch of an airscrew relates to the angle at which the aircraft's propeller bites into the air. Altering the angle of the bite has an effect similar to changing gear in a motor car. With the old fixed pitch airscrews it was impossible to alter the angle, but the new CS design gave the pilot fluent control of his propeller's pitch throughout a whole range of settings from coarse to fine, the term "constant", therefore, being somewhat misleading. Squadron Leader Cozens immediately commenced intensive flying and reliability trials with this aircraft, discovering that the new propeller much improved acceleration and handling, particularly at low speeds, two factors crucial to survival and success in combat. Fortunately, thanks to Squadron Leader Cozen's evaluation work, and that of the Supermarine test pilots, all operational Spitfires were fitted with the CS airscrew in good time for the critical Battle of Britain of summer 1940.

As the golden hues of autumn 1939 faded into drab winter greys the monotony of training flights and ground defence co – operation sorties, to test the reactions of nearby airfields, began in earnest. Very few patrols were ordered and this situation continued into December, only one offensive sortie being flown that month. This was an interception of what was later discovered to be a friendly aircraft. In January 1940 Squadron Leader Cozens, who had done a great deal to establish the Spitfire in squadron service, was promoted to Wing Commander and left No.19 Squadron for a staff appointment. His replacement was Squadron Leader Geoffrey Stephenson, a former Chief Flying Instructor. On February 7th the squadron received a new pilot fresh from the Central Flying School at Upavon. He was Flying Officer Douglas Bader, already famous in Fighter Command for having flown aerobatics with the Royal Air Force to the highest possible standard before the war, and for the flying accident in which he lost both of his legs. Invalided out of the service, he mastered his artificial limbs, and the indomitable Bader argued his way not only back into the RAF, but into the cockpit of a Spitfire. Michael Lyne clearly remembers Bader's short time with No.19 Squadron:

"By March the weather was better, but we now had Flying Officer Douglas Bader to cope with. He was very brave and determined but was having a hard time coming to grips with the Spitfire, especially in cloud. More than once my friend Watson and I, lent to him as a formation by the CO, emerged from cloud faithfully following Bader only to find ourselves in a steep diving turn."

In early March, Bader damaged a Spitfire in somewhat embarrassing circumstances. At this time No.19 Squadron was deploying three aircraft on a daily basis to the airfield of Horsham St Faith, near Norwich, which was still in the process of construction. On this occasion Bader led his section to take off out of dispersal on a short run of the airfield and slightly down wind. This would have been advantageous in saving precious time, at only minimal risk, if he had not forgotten to engage "low gear" for take off by putting his propeller into fine pitch. Half way through take off the other two pilots realised what had happened and opened their throttles wide, just in time to avoid the boundary hedge. Bader's Spitfire cartwheeled across a ploughed field, throwing clods of earth skywards. The aircraft was written off, as were the pilot's artificial limbs which were damaged beyond repair.

In "Spitfire!" Brian Lane describes how George Unwin became known as "Grumpy" after being left off the squadron battle order for its first patrol over the Dunkirk beaches. George pointed out to me that this was not in fact the case as his nickname was given to him by Douglas Bader as an indirect result of the legless pilot's accident at Horsham St Faith:

"Sometime after Bader's accident we were at Horsham and Bader persisted in filing his new pair of tin legs, to get them in perfect working order, and I remonstrated with him for scratching and scraping whilst I was trying to sleep. The film "Snow White and the Seven Dwarfs" was very popular at that time and Bader replied "Oh Shut up Grumpy". From then on that was my nickname."

Other squadron nicknames included "Ace" for Flying Officer Pace who was a buff on the Great War fighter "aces" and an avid reader of flying comics, fictional of course, all glorifying the stupendous exploits of mythical fighter pilots. Wilf Clouston dubbed Frank Brinsden "Fanny", although Frank never knew whether the word was meant as either the British or American interpretation!

Douglas Bader was soon promoted to Flight Lieutenant following the accident, and left No.19 Squadron to fly Spitfires with Squadron Leader "Tubby" Mermagen's No.222 "Natal" Squadron which he joined as a flight Commander. Just eight weeks after leaving No.19 Squadron he was given his own squadron of Hurricanes, No.242 (Canadian) Squadron, with which No.19 would shortly become closely associated.

After an uneventful April, the squadron was able to chalk up its first victory on May 11th, 1940, when Flight Lieutenant Clouston, Flying Officer Petre and Flight Sergeant Steere destroyed a Junkers Ju88, the crew of which were all picked alive up from the sea. Justice indeed that Clouston, Petre and Steere should strike the first blow for the squadron having been cheated of their prey by the Royal Navy the previous October.

The "Phoney War" had now ended. The day before the Junkers slid into the glowing graticules of Blue Section's gun sights, Hitler's field grey tide had swept into Belgium, Holland, Luxembourg and France. On May 13th General Guderian's XIX Panzer Corps crashed across the River Meuse at Sedan. By May 21st both Rotterdam and Antwerp had fallen. The Germans crossed the river Somme in the advance towards the Channel ports and the British Expeditionary Force found itself in a full scale retreat, along roads choked not only with the retreating military but also with thousands of refugees fleeing the invader. With the modern, hard hitting and fast tactics of the new type of warfare unleashed by Hitler, a new word was added to the military vocabulary: "Blitzkrieg", or "Lightning War", against which the outdated tactics and equipment of the British Expeditionary Force were virtually powerless. The retreat ended at the port of Dunkirk, from where the British flotilla of "Little Ships", comprising military and civilian craft of all shapes and sizes, commenced evacuating a total of some 338,226 British and Allied troops during "Operation Dynamo".

Needless to say such an operation required air support to prevent the Luftwaffe from pounding the defenceless troops on the beaches below to a pulp. The troops did suffer terribly and the RAF's prestige sank to its lowest ebb in the eyes of the army. The soldiers had been bombed and strafed for weeks without, they believed, protection from their own fighters. In reality Fighter Command's squadrons were operating continously between their airfields and Dunkirk, attempting to prevent German air attacks actually reaching the beaches. The distance was such that the RAF fighters were operating at extreme range across the English Channel and each squadron had only fifteen minutes fuel endurance at combat speeds before having to return home. Most air battles had been fought unseen by those on the ground, taking place at high altitude, above cloud cover, or behind German lines. Fighter Command squadrons flew 4,822 operational hours during the evacuation, destroyed 258 enemy aircraft and damaged 119, compared to their own loss of 87 aircraft.

On May 18th, No.19 Squadron was visited by 12 Group's commander, Air Vice Marshal Trafford Leigh – Mallory, and it was decided that the squadron was, after all, to move temporarily to France. However, the rapidity of Hitler's push west towards the

Channel ports put a stop to the plan. One week later No.19 Squadron moved south to Hornchurch, in Essex, and next day met the enemy for the first time en masse. The squadron flew two sorties on that day, and of the first the squadron diary has this to say:

"Squadron led by Squadron Leader Stephenson went on patrol in the morning, Dunkirk – Calais. Met twenty one Stukas escorted by thirty Me 109s. Approximately ten enemy aircraft shot down. Squadron Leader Stephenson and Pilot Officer Watson failed to return, Flying Officer Ball wounded in head and arm".

Brian Lane flew Spitfire N3040 on his first sortie over Dunkirk and recorded the following in his log book:

"Yellow section comprising F/O Brinsden and Sgt Potter, squadron patrol Dunkirk to Calais. Took off 0740, over Calais 0750. Sighted twenty – one Ju 87s over Calais after half an hour. Blue, Red and Yellow sections attacked, Green watching for escort. Got in a couple of attacks before Ball yelled "Fighters!" and thirty Me 109s descended on us. General dog fight ensued. Saw Watson hit by cannon from an Me 109, later a parachute in the water off Calais. Potter saw him bail out. Had a smack at various Me 109s and then got chased by three of them. Got a good burst in at one doing a beam attack and he disappeared. Got away from the other two and headed for Hornchurch and a drink. Probable bag one Ju 87 and one Me 109. CO and Watson missing."

Flight Lieutenant Lane's personal combat report relates the action in more detail:

"On 26.5.40 I was on patrol leading Yellow Section of No.19 Squadron. We were at approximately 10,000' over Calais when we sighted 21 Ju 87s proceeding out to sea. I was astern of Red Section, who attacked the starboard rear section of the E/A, Blue Section attacking a section on the port side of the formation. I attacked as soon as I could, selecting an E/A to starboard of the formation, as it turned left.

"I fired one burst at approx. 400 yards from below and astern. Tracers appeared to enter E/A which climbed and stalled. I fired again from about 200 yards and E/A went into a dive. The escorting Me 109s were by this time attacking and I was forced to break away, but sighted the Ju 87 diving towards the sea. No fire was experienced from the rear gunner and the E/A appeared out of control.

"I looked round and observed an Me 109 attacking a Spitfire which was almost immediately hit forward of the cockpit by a shell from an E/A. The Spitfire went into a steep dive and I subsequently observed a parachute in the sea about half a mile off Calais.

"A dog fight now ensued and I fired bursts at several E/A, mostly deflection shots. Three E/A attached themselves to my tail, two doing astern attacks whilst the third attacked from the beam. I managed to turn towards this E/A and fired a good burst in a front quarter deflection attack. The E/A then disappeared and was probably shot down. By this time I was down to sea level and made for the English coast, taking violent evasive action. I gradually drew away from the E/A's using 12 lb boost which gave an air speed of 300 mph."

Michael Lyne remembers the morning combat:

"On May 25th we were sent to Hornchurch to take the place of squadrons shot to pieces in the early stages of the battle of Dunkirk. To us the mess had a new atmosphere, people clearing the rooms of kit belonging to casualties and the Station Commander insisting on closing the bar and sending us to bed to be ready for the battles that awaited us. On May 26th we were called to patrol over the beaches. I will always remember heading off to the east and seeing the columns of black smoke from the Dunkirk oil storage tanks. We patrolled for some time without seeing any aircraft and received no information from the British radar, then called RDF (Radio Direction Finders). We had received excellent VHF (Very High Frequency) radios shortly before, but they were only of use between ourselves on that patrol. Suddenly we saw ahead, going towards Calais where the Rifle Brigade was holding out, about forty German aircraft; we were twelve. Geoffrey Stephenson aligned us for attack in sections of three on the formation of Ju 87s. As a former CFS A1 instructor he was a precise flier and obedient to the book, which stipulated an overtaking speed of 30 mph. What the book never foresaw was that we would attack Ju 87s doing just about 130 mph. The CO led his section (Watson No.2 and me No.3) straight up behind the Ju's which looked very relaxed, they thought we were their fighter escort, but the leader of these had been very clever and had pulled his formation away towards England, so that when they turned in towards Calais he would protect their rear. Alas for him we were coming, by sheer chance, from Dunkirk rather than from Ramsgate.

"Meanwhile, Stephenson realised that we were closing far too fast. I remember his call "No.19 Squadron! Pepare to attack", then to us "Red Section, throttling back, throttling back, throttling back."

"We were virtually formating on the last section of Ju's, at an incredibly dangerous speed in the presence of enemy fighters – and behind us the rest of the squadron were staggering along at similar speed. Of course the Ju's could not imagine that we were a threat. Then Stephenson told us to take a target each and fire. As far as I know we got the last three, we could hardly have done otherwise, then we broke away and saw nothing of the work of the rest of the squadron, but it must have been dodgy for the last section as the Me 109s started to come round. As I was looking round for friends after the break I came under fire from the rear for the first time – and did not at first know it. The first signs were mysterious little corkscrews of smoke passing my starboard wing. Then I heard a slow thump, thump, and realised that I was being attacked by an Me 109 firing machine guns with tracer and cannons banging away. I broke away sharpish and lost him.

"I made a wide sweep and came back to the Calais area to find about five Ju's going round in a tight defensive circle. The German fighters had disappeared, so I flew to take the circle at the head on position and gave it a long squirt. It must have been at this stage that I was hit by return fire, for when I got back to Hornchurch I found bullet holes in the wing, which had punctured a tyre.

"Alas my friend Watson was never seen again, and Stephenson made a forced landing in France and was taken prisoner. He survived the war but was killed in America as the result of a flying accident."

In the spring of 1986, two Spitfire wrecks surfaced above the shifting sands of the English Channel near Calais. The machine at Coquelles, the remains of which were not substantial but included a relatively intact Merlin engine, was later identified as N3200, the aircraft in which Squadron Leader Stephenson had been shot down on May 26th. The remains were last reported in the British aviation press in May 1987 as having been recovered for display at the Calais World War Two Museum.

As the pilots of No.19 Squadron landed at Hornchurch after their first sortie, minus Watson and Stephenson who were now categorised simply as "Missing", they had been blooded at last, like many other pilots of Fighter Command, in the skies off the French coast. Flying Officer Eric Ball, who had destroyed a Messerschmitt Bf109 during the combat, had also been wounded. Peter Howard – Williams, a Pilot Officer at the time, recalls:

"I went to Hornchurch with No.19 Squadron as a very junior pilot. I remember going back to Duxford to collect the first Spitfire fitted with hydraulic automatic undercarriage. I flew over Hornchurch raising and lowering the undercarriage in quick time. Previously we had to pump up the undercarriage by hand, a real problem if you were the outside man of a squadron formation take off across the grass at Duxford.

"I also remember Eric Ball landing at Hornchurch and stopping in the centre of the airfield. A bullet had gone through his helmet and hair – parting it for him and leaving a small wound."

However, the fighting that day was not yet over as the squadron were to fly a second sortie into the battle zone. With the Commanding Officer now a prisoner of war, it fell to Flight Lieutenant Lane to lead the squadron until a replacement was found for Stephenson. Lane described the sortie in his log book:

"Leading squadron on patrol of Dunkirk and Calais. Green Section reported eight Me 109's just above us off Calais. Observed Me 109 chasing Sinclair into cloud. Hun pulled up and gave me a sitting target from below. Gave him a good burst which he ran straight into, lurched and went straight down. I followed him but he hadn't pulled out at 3,000' and must have gone straight in. Blacked out completely but pulled out in time. Landed at Manston and stayed for tea. Lovely near the coast in this weather."

Shortly after landing at Manston he made out this combat report on the action:

"At 1600 hrs I was leading three sections of the squadron on a patrol over

109

Dunkirk area at 8,000' when the rear section reported eight Me 109s 1,000' above. The E/A dived in ragged formation to the attack and the squadron broke formation to escape. I saw an E/A diving to attack F/O Sinclair who escaped into cloud. The E/A pulled out of the dive just above the cloud and headed for France. I chased it and delivered a climbing attack from astern firing a burst of 4 – 5 seconds at about 300 – 200 yards range. The E/A lurched onto its side and fell in a vertical dive. I followed it down and pulled out at 2,500', when the E/A was well below me."

It was off Gordon Sinclair's tail that Brian Lane had shot down the Messerschmitt Bf109.

Following the combat over Dunkirk, Flying Officers Petre and Sinclair had also claimed an Me109 destroyed. Having landed at Manston with Flying Officer Brinsden and Sergeant Jennings, Lane returned to Hornchurch to find that Sergeant Irwin was "missing" and Pilot Officer Lyne had been shot up but managed to force land on Walmer beach. Michael Lyne recalled for me that rather traumatic experience:

"In the afternoon Brian Lane led us on our second patrol over the evacuation beaches. The German fighters must have been smarting after their trouble with us in the morning. Suddenly we were attacked by a squadron of Me 109s. As before we were flying in the inflexible and outdated formation of "Vics of three". Later the basic unit became the pair, or two pairs in what was known as a "Finger Four". Such a formation, as the Germans were already using, could turn very quickly, with each aircraft turning on its own, but the formation automatically reformed in full contact at the end of the manouevre.

"Because of our formation we quickly lost contact with each other after the Me 109's attacked. I found myself alone, with a pair of Me's circling above me left handed whilst I was going right handed. The leader dropped his nose as I pulled up mine and fired. He hit me in the engine, knee, radio and rear fuselage. I was in a spin and streaming glycol. He must have thought I was gone for good, so did I. But for a short time the engine kept going as I straightened out and dived into cloud, setting compass course shortly before the cockpit filled with white smoke which blotted out everything. In a few seconds the engine seized and I became an efficient glider. On breaking cloud I saw Deal some way off, but remembered the advice to hold an efficient speed, so with 200' to spare crossed the surf and landed on the beach. That adventure ended my flying until February 19th, 1941."

Over Dunkirk Fighter Command had tried to put into practice the months of training in text book attacks which, with their tight, smart formations, were impractical for modern air fighting, as previously described by Michael Lyne. Due to the tight formations required by the Fighter Command area attacks, of either vics of three aircraft or sections in line astern, each aircraft in close proximity to its neighbour, the Royal Air Force pilots were unable to search the sky for the enemy without fear of collision. Thus in the early days many Fighter Command pilots went to their deaths totally unaware of the presence of their assailant. A prime example occurred during the Battle of Britain when on Sunday 18th August, 1940, Oberleutnant Gerhard Schoepfel of Jagdgeschwader 26, from his position high in the sky with the sun behind him, pounced on the Hurricanes of No.501 "County of Gloucester" Squadron who were flying over Canterbury. Within a matter of seconds he sent four Hurricanes plunging earthward, three pilots being wounded and one killed. The remainder of the squadron flew on oblivious to the destruction behind them. When battle was joined the tight formations were split up and pilots fought alone. The Luftwaffe, however, utilising combat experience gained in both the Spanish Civil War and the Polish campaign, used the "Schwarm" formation developed by the great "ace", Werner "Vatti" Molders. The "Schwarm" consisted of four aircraft flying loosely in line abreast, like the four fingers of an oustretched hand, each pilot able to concentrate on looking for the enemy without fear of collision. When battle was joined the "Schwarm" broke into the "Rotte" or fighting pair of two formations of pairs, each aircraft protecting its partner. Later this tactic, which has ever since remained the basic formation of fighter combat, would be used by Fighter Command and known as the "Finger Four". Pre – war tactical thinking in Britain hinged largely on the mistaken theory that "the bomber would always get through". The Fighter Command 'book' foresaw orderly queues of fighters in line astern peeling off one by one to attack lone enemy bombers flying straight and level. What they did not predict was fighter versus fighter combat, particularly that in which many aircraft were involved, all moving at in excess of 350 mph, clearly a situation where such tactics and tight formations were totally impractical. In the Second World War the advantages of height and sun were as important as in the First, and the dogfights of large numbers of fighters, albeit faster, were not dissimilar. The old adage "Look for the Hun in the sun" became well voiced and again took on a deadly serious meaning. George Unwin elaborated for me on the thinking of the time:

"The tacticians who wrote the book really believed that in the event of war it would be fighter versus bomber only. What they could not foresee was Hitler's modern ground tactics that would take his armies to the Channel ports in an unprecedented period of time, thus providing bases for his fighters in the Pas de Calais and putting England within their limited range. Our tight formations were all very well for the Hendon Air Pageant but useless in combat. Geoffrey Stephenson was a prime example; without modern combat experience he flew exactly by the book – and was in effect shot down by it."

Over the coming months the pilots of Fighter Command would become much more tactically aware with experience, and the "book" would eventually be altered accordingly. For the time being, however, the killing ground of Dunkirk provided the Spitfire squadrons with their first true lessons in modern air fighting.

Following the combats of May 26th, the pattern of the next few days remained the same, the pilots of No.19 Squadron usually up before first light and flying two sorties a day. All of the squadron's Spitfires returned safely from the first sortie on May 27th; Brian Lane's log book describes events:

"Took off at 1100 hrs, squadron patrol of Calais and Dunkirk. Section with Flt Sgt Unwin, Sgts Potter and Jennings. Sighted an He 111 and attacked over Gravelines. Heavy AA fire nearly wrote the squadron off. Chased Heinkel in and out of cumulus, came in and put all I had into him. No visible effect! Fire from top gun stopped after first burst so I think that must be one less Hun in the world. Unwin got separated from me and was set upon by three Me 110s."

From the second sortie all of No.19 Squadron's aircraft returned, but all were hit. Sergeant Jennings attacked a Dornier Do215, as did Flying Officer Petre and Flight Lieutenant Clouston, who also definitely destroyed another. Flight Lieutenant Lane, Flying Officer Brinsden and Flight Sergeant Unwin chased a Henschel Hs126 reconnaissance aircraft inland as far as Ypres where Unwin made his first "kill". Again Brian Lane's log book relates events:

"Evening patrol, leading squadron, Dunkirk. F/O Brinsden and Flt Sgt Unwin observed Archie inland of Dunkirk and went to investigate. Found one Hs 126 and chased him. Twisted and turned like hell, and after a couple of bursts I lost him. Brinsden had a crack at him but Unwin got him and pushed him into the deck after Brinsden and I had reformed. Returned from Ypres to Dunkirk right down on the deck. I have never seen anything so peaceful – no sign of war at all except the big smoke pall over Dunkirk."

On the morning of May 28th, No.19 Squadron operated as part of a wing formation for the first time, in conjunction with Nos.54 and 65 Squadrons. Although no action was seen on that sortie the same wing met fifty Me109s later that morning. The squadron diary recorded the combat as follows:

"Near Dunkirk met four Me 109s, F/S Steere and F/S Unwin got one each. All of our aircraft returned but F/O Petre had altimeter shot away by HE bullets and small pieces of metal entered one of his legs."

Flight Lieutenant Lane's log book, the notes recorded in which he used to write "Spitfire!", gives a more detailed account:

"Same "Balbo" ran into fifty Me 109s. Got into the usual dogfight and got a nice shot at one E/A. Fired about twenty rounds when guns stopped. Another E/A was just getting on my tail so I didn't wait but half stalled out of the party. Discovered that I had no air pressure so came home. 65 Squadron bagged three Do 215's, Unwin an Me 109."

On the same day Squadron Leader "Tubby" Mermagen's No.222 Squadron and Squadron Leader Robin Hood's No.41 Squadron arrived at Hornchurch. Over the next few days No.19 Squadron would lead a wing consisting of these squadrons and No.616 "South Yorkshire" Squadron, an Auxiliary Air Force unit. The end of May proved uneventful combat wise, but on May 31st, No.19 Squadron received its new Commanding Officer, Squadron Leader Phillip Pinkham AFC, like Geoffrey Stephenson also formerly a Chief Flying Instructor without combat experience. It therefore fell to Flight Lieutenant Lane to continue to lead the squadron into action over Dunkirk.

On June 1st, Brian Lane led Nos.19, 222, 41 and 616 Squadrons into action on the first of two sorties flown that day. The wing encountered twelve Me110s, in Lane's words "straight from FTS I should think. Terrific sport." He definitely destroyed one of the enemy machines:

"At approximately 0540 hrs I was leading No.19 Squadron two miles NE of Dunkirk at 4,000' when I sighted twelve Me. "Jaguars" ahead. I immediately attacked in line astern and the E/A turned towards coast. A dog fight ensued just over the beach. I continued to attack E/A and observed one engine stop and the starboard one emmitted large quantities of vapour, presumably coolant. E/A dived towards the ground and had not pulled out at 50'. I turned and attacked another E/A head–on. E/A passed below me to avoid collision, and I lost sight of him. Burst appeared to enter nose of E/A. During the combat I observed one E/A dive straight into the sea and another crashed on the shore and burst into flames."

The second patrol of the day was the last during the squadron's detachment to Hornchurch, and Brian Lane's log book notes are of some interest:

"Dunkirk beaches. Most amazing sight this evacuation. Thames barges, sailing boats, anything that will float, and the Navy. God help them down there!

"They need more than we can give them. Ran into a bunch of Do 215's and He 111's. This layer of 10/10ths cloud at 4,000' made things a bit difficult as the sods kept darting into cloud after dropping their bombs. Had a good bang at a Do 215 which disappeared in cloud. Tore round firing at odd Heinkels as they appeared below cloud, but couldn't do much as windscreen was completely iced up. Headed for home at sea level along the line of ships. Passed a cross Channel steamer and saw the sea erupt just behind him. Nearly jumped out of the cockpit as I was bloody close to the wretched ship. Looked up and saw a 215 cruising along at 2,000' right on top of me it seemed. Felt an awful twirp as I had no ammo or petrol so could not do anything about it. Sqn. Ldr. Hood, (41) reported the same thing but he met his Hun at sea level. He made a stall as if to attack and the wretched Boche fell into the sea without a shot being fired. Was his face red!"

From the German point of view the Luftwaffe pilots, in attempting to prevent the evacuation of the British Expeditionary

Force from the Dunkirk beaches, were clearly employed in performing a role which would have been best conducted by ground forces. At 10.30 am on May 24th, Hitler visited the headquarters of his Army Group "A" at Charleville. Guderian's panzers had crossed the Aa Canal that morning but had outstripped their infantry support and supplies. Many of the tanks were also worn out as a result of two weeks continuous advance. Before they could be used in the swing to Paris a regroup was necessary. Hitler, seeing his prize as Paris and not the pitiful remnants of the defeated allied armies, whose weapons and equipment were strewn all over France and Belgium, made the decision to halt Guderian's forces and withdraw the panzers from the Aa. It was two days later before Guderian persuaded Hitler to continue the advance, but by then it was too late. The defences around the Dunkirk perimeter had become established and the evacuation had begun in earnest. The Luftwaffe aircrews were also taxed to near exhaustion by the intense fighting endured during the campaign. The fighter pilots, tasked with providing protection for the bombers, met in combat for the first time, the Supermarine Spitfire, a fighter which could best their Messerschmitt Bf109 "Emils". Previously the Jagdflieger had met in battle the obsolete Polish and French fighters, and the Hawker Hurricane, none of which could fight the Emil on equal terms. Now, for the first time, went up the cry "Achtung, Schpitfeuer!"

June 2nd, 3rd and 4th saw the wing of Nos.19, 222, 41 and 616 Squadrons on patrol again, but with nothing to report. With "Operation Dynamo" having been completed on Monday June 3rd, and allied forces still in the Dunkirk perimeter surrendering on June 4th, No.19 Squadron returned to Duxford the following day. Flight Lieutenant Lane returned home in Spitfire N3040 which he had flown on all but two of his Dunkirk sorties. He wrote in his log book:

> "Squadron returned to Duxford. Visibility so good that I couldn't see Duxford anywhere! Did a 19 peel off and then peeled off on 48 hours leave. Pretty good."

Not all of No.19 Squadron's pilots, however, had participated in the fighting. On May 13th a Volunteer Reserve pilot, Sergeant David Cox, joined the squadron at Duxford straight from Operational Training Unit. Due to the very limited amount of flying time on Spitfires that he had been able to record in his log book, Cox was not allowed to operate with the squadron over Dunkirk. Instead he found himself left behind to ferry replacement aircraft to Hornchurch, and conduct test flights on repaired Spitfires, both extremely necessary chores which enabled the pilot to gain more flying experience on the potent fighter. When the squadron returned to Duxford following its detachment to Hornchurch and involvement in the evacuation's air battles, young Sergeant Cox was to hear from Flight Sergeant Harry Steere that the air war was certainly not a glamourous game. Steere told the intently listening youngster how he had set an Me109 on fire and had subsequently flown up alongside his stricken victim to see the German pilot trapped due to a jammed canopy. The sight of his opponent unable to escape and enveloped in flame made the Spitfire pilot physically sick.

During "Operation Dynamo" 224,686 British and 141,445 French and Belgians were snatched to safety. The price was heavy, 226 Naval and civilian craft had been sunk in the process. As the fighting continued in France, Winston Churchill, who had replaced Neville Chamberlain as Prime Minister on September 10th, 1939, told the House of Commons:

"We shall fight on the beaches, in the fields, in the streets and in the hills. We shall never surrender."

On Saturday 22nd June, 1940, French representatives signed the armistice in the same railway carriage at Compiègne as had Imperial Germany in 1918. On Monday 24th the French signed a second armistice with the fascist dictator Mussolini. Britain was now alone and braced herself to take the full onslaught of the enemy. David Scott – Malden was a young Pilot Officer at the time undertaking his training on Spitfires at Aston Down in Gloucestershire prior to joining an operational squadron. On June 17th he recorded in his diary:

"The French give up hostilities. Cannot yet conceive the enormity of it. I suppose it will not be long before we start defending England in earnest."

Churchill stirred the nation's spirit with yet more startling rhetoric:

"The Battle of France is over. I expect that the Battle of Britain is about to begin...The whole fury and might of the enemy must very soon be turned on us. Hitler knows that he will have to break us in this island or lose the war. If we can stand up to him, all Europe may be free and the life of the world may move forward into broad, sunlit uplands. But if we fail, then the whole world, including the United States, including all that we have known and cared for, will sink into the abyss of a new Dark Age made more sinister, and perhaps more protracted, by the lights of perverted science. Let us therefore brace ourselves to our duties, and so bear ourselves that if the British Empire and its Commonwealth last for a thousand years, men will still say "This was their finest hour"."

The young pilots of No.19 Squadron had flown over Dunkirk untested in combat. Within sight of the port's blazing oil tanks they had met the enemy successfully, despite the handicaps of no previous experience in modern fighter combat and being hampered by impractical tactics. Although the squadron had suffered losses, the pilots were satisfied with the number of casualties inflicted upon

115

the enemy. They were now confident in their ability, and that of their Spitfires, to take on and beat the Luftwaffe. As Britain stood alone, the last bastion of freedom and defiance in Western Europe, it was with optimism and eager anticipation that No.19 Squadron, and other units of Fighter Command, now awaited the enemy's onslaught.

CHAPTER TWO

Following their involvement in the air battles covering the Dunkirk evacuation, the pilots of No.19 Squadron returned to Duxford in Cambridgeshire and there awaited the enemy's next move. Meanwhile Hitler enjoyed a sight – seeing tour of Paris and his troops performed a victory march along the Champs Elysee. Although the air war had entered a lull, German bombers made nuisance raids at night on various targets in the British Isles, no doubt to probe the British defences and gather information.

The squadron found itself pressed into the night fighter role in an attempt to combat the nocturnal intruders. The Spitfire was not a good aircraft for night fighting. Two long banks of exhaust fore of the pilot glowed brightly, ruining his night vision, and the narrow track undercarriage posed problems in night landings. The squadron's pilots performed twenty night patrols during the month of June 1940. During one of these, on the night of June 18th – 19th, Flying Officer "Johnnie" Petre, flying L1032, destroyed a raider. This is believed to be the first nocturnal victory scored by a Spitfire. On the same night Flying Officer Eric Ball also shot down a German bomber. The squadron diary takes up the story:

"On the night of June 18th – 19th Flt. Sgt. Steere made a patrol without seeing anything. Flg. Off. Petre, Flt. Lt. Clouston, Flg. Off. Ball and Plt. Off. Lawson, "B" Flight pilots, were ordered to investigate a raid near Mildenhall. Flg. Off. Petre sighted an enemy aircraft first near Newmarket and shadowed it in the direction of Bury St Edmunds. When he was about to open fire a Blenheim was in the way, so he sheered off to one side and made a quarter attack, allowing for deflection. He saw his tracer hit one engine which poured out volumes of black smoke. At this moment he was caught in searchlights and an explosive bullet from the rear gunner hit his petrol tank and forced him to jump from the blazing Spitfire. Petre landed safely but was badly burned about the face and hands. The Heinkel crashed in flames near the New Market (sic) to Royston Road near Six Mile Bottom. Three prisoners were taken, one crew member being dead as he had failed to use his parachute. Flg. Off. Ball was instructed to investigate a raid over Newmarket and found an enemy aircraft illuminated by searchlights and recognised it as a Heinkel 111. Over Colchester he attacked from dead astern, closing from 200 – 50 yards, broke away and repeated, by which time the enemy aircraft was enveloped in clouds of smoke and losing height. Enemy aircraft crashed at Margate and the crew were all killed."

Ball had actually brought down the He111 of Leutnant Hans – Jurgen Bachaus from 4/KG4. The Heinkel fell into the sea at 02.15 hours of Sackett's Gap near Margate, but contrary to the squadron's records only one of the four crew was killed, the other three being taken prisoners.

Petre's Heinkel was a "P" variant of 4/KG4, coded "5J + AM". Oberleutnant Von Arnim, Feldwebel Maier and Feldwebel Hanck were captured, the unfortunate member of the crew being Unteroffizier Gersch. The Blenheim was a machine of No.23 Squadron flown by Squadron Leader O'Brien who was also shot down and took to his parachute. Pilot Officer King–Clark was killed in his attempt to abandon the doomed night fighter, and Corporal Little was killed in the subsequent crash.

Petre was very badly burnt and admitted to the General Hospital at Bury St. Edmunds. Later that morning the wounded pilot received a visit from Group Captain Woodhall, Duxford's station commander, who completed a combat report on Petre's behalf, forwarding same to HQ Fighter Command in lieu of the usual personal combat report. Woodhall described Petre as being on the "dangerously ill list", and that "it would be unwise for him to have too many visitors for some days". Frank Brinsden remembers that Petre's Spitfire "literally blew up in his face" and that the young pilot "suffered terribly disfiguring burns which I am happy to say have been less obvious with the passage of time."

From the destruction, death and injuries arising from Petre's combat with the bomber, two amusing stories have nevertheless come to light:

Flying Officer Gordon Sinclair had introduced Brian Lane to a Cambridge girl, Eileen Ellison, whom the quiet young fighter pilot later "went off and married without fuss." Eileen was a very successful racing driver during pre–war days who had done extremely well at the Brooklands race track where, in 1932, she had won the coveted Duchess of York's race for women drivers in her famous Bugatti. She had also earned respect and admiration for her performance on the long and difficult hill–climbs on the continent. Frank Brinsden recalls that on the morning of Petre's night victory Eileen Lane visited the Officers Mess at Duxford looking for her husband, who was unavailable, and was unwittingly shown into the Ladies Room by the Duty Officer; unwittingly because within one of the Heinkel crew members was being held captive. On Mrs. Lane's entry the German airman rose to his feet and greeted her, as they had known each other on the continental motor racing circuits!

The second tale was related by James Coward, who had left No.19 Squadron temporarily and to whom news filtered through of Petre's success:

"A Scottish soldier recently returned from Boulogne, where the Germans had allegedly shot all Scottish prisoners, saw the Heinkel's pilot descending in the searchlight beam and was waiting for him with bayonet fixed. Apparently, the very arrogant German, who spoke excellent English, said, "There is no point you taking me prisoner, the Führer will be over here next week and it is you who will all be prisoners," to which the Scot is said to have replied "Who's takin' prisoners?" and, prodding with his bayonet, forthwith escorted his captive to the Guard Room."

Peter Howard – Williams also recalls Petre's victory:

"I started night flying in Spitfire N3199 in the middle of June, 1940, on circuits and landings. On the night of June 18th, I was flying R6623 on a local night recce, when I was recalled and experienced pilots were scrambled. Petre subsequently destroyed a Heinkel 111, and one of the crew was killed. The rest were captured and one was locked up in one of the guardroom cells as he proved to be rather fierce and belligerent. Von Arnim came to the mess, spoke good English and was well entertained. He was the navigator and captain of the aircraft, which seemed odd to us as in the R.A.F. the captain was always the pilot. I remember that I gave him a pair of R.A.F. wings. Von Arnim did say that his father or grandfather was commanding the German armies in North Africa. After a pleasant evening, during which there was no hostility, he was given a room for the night in the mess. I do recall that there was a stink the next day as the intelligence people who came to question Von Arnim did not think that he should have received such good treatment. All Von Arnim said about the war was that Germany would win simply because Hitler had said so. Apart from that we all had a few beers and thoroughly enjoyed the experience."

Petre's combat record previous to the Heinkel He111 kill consisted of one damaged Me109 and a Ju88, a third of a share in the destruction of a Do215, and an Me109 destroyed.

The nocturnal patrols continued and Flight Lieutenant Lane flew virtually every night. Perhaps fatigue began to tell, as on June 26th he recorded in his log book, "Landed at 0200 hrs rather too heavily for undercart, tut, tut!'.

July 1st, 1940, saw Sub – Lieutenant Giles Arthur Blake of the Fleet Air Arm report to the squadron from No.7 Operational Training Unit at Hawarden near Chester. As a result of the serious calls made on Fighter Command earlier in the summer, and in expectancy of the coming air battles, a number of pilots were received by Fighter Command on loan from other branches of the service and the Royal Navy. Blake, who was to prove his worth as a fighter pilot in the summer that was to eventually claim his life, became a popular member of the squadron and was known, perhaps inevitably, as either "Sailor" or "The Admiral" by his air force colleagues.

On the same day Brian Lane's log book was examined by his Commanding Officer. He had flown a total of 189.30 hours since June 1st, 1939, 14.05 of which were at night, giving him a grand total of 732.25 hours. On an Air Ministry form gummed into his log book recording the totals, Squadron Leader Pinkham also gave Lane the rating of an "exceptional" fighter pilot, and as being "above the average" as an aerial marksman.

Squadron Leader Phillip Campbell Pinkham AFC, more commonly known to his friends as "Tommy", hailed from Wembley, North London, and was a great nephew of Sir Charles Pinkham, formerly Deputy – Lieutenant of the County of Middlesex and one time chairman of Middlesex County Council. He had been educated at Kilburn Grammar School, after leaving which he had joined the London Yeomanry and became the prize recruit of his year. In 1935 he joined the Royal Air Force, after eighteen months in insurance, and was trained at No.6 Flying Training School, Netheravon, before a posting to fly Gauntlet bi – plane fighters with No.17 (F) Squadron at Kenley in February 1936. The following August he was posted to the Meteorological Flight at Mildenhall where his duties became the recording of data for the weather men. After a distinguished service at Mildenhall he was posted to instruct at No.11 (Fighter) Group Pool, Andover, on January 17th, 1938. At the Air Fighting School, Flight Lieutenant Pinkham flew Demons, Battles and Gladiators, until March 21st, 1939, when he flew a Hawker Hurricane, L1870, for the first time, on a ten minute flight from Filton to base. From then on the Hurricane became the most common type in his log book. However, on June 5th he took off in Fairey Battle N2061 on a training exercise with Pilot Officer Rochfort and the aircraft's engine cut on take off, believed to have been caused by a petrol vapour lock in the fuel system. An immediate forced landing was made. Pinkham attempted to land in a field but although the Battle crashed into trees on the airfield's boundary, both instructor and pupil escaped unhurt.

After war was declared on Germany the training units were faced with preparing the service for war by providing enough pilots. From this time onwards an increasing number of names appear in Squadron Leader Pinkham's log book who were later to fly Hurricanes in the Battle of Britain, amongst them Beamont, Pilkington and Dewar. In March 1940, 11 Group Pool, recorded in Pinkham's log book as "Ye schoole of ye air fightinge" became No.6 Operational Training Unit at Sutton Bridge and was commanded by himself. Poles and Finnish pilots also began to pass through the training units at this time and, on March 27th, Pinkham received a message of appreciation from the commander of 12 Group for his work in training Finnish pilots. Obviously an officer with a skill for teaching, he received the Air Force Cross in the King's birthday honours that year for his work with both 11 Group Pool and No.6 Operational Training Unit. In July the honour was confirmed and he received a personal message of congratulations from Sir Archibald Sinclair, Secretary of State for Air. Throughout his log book

Pinkham's flying ability, whether as a fighter pilot, a meteorological pilot or an instructor is consistantly recorded as "above average". A young officer no doubt destined for high office in the service, his request for a combat command coincided with Stephenson's loss over Dunkirk. Fate had played a hand. Squadron Leader Pinkham officially took over No.19 Squadron on June 3rd, 1940.

The Supermarine Spitfire Mk I had met its German adversary, the Augsburg built Messerschmitt Bf109E, for the first time over Dunkirk. During those combats it was discovered that the "Emil" packed a very powerful punch in the shape of two 7.92 mm Rheinmetal Borsig machine guns mounted on top of the engine, and two 20 mm Oerlikon MG FF cannons, one in each wing. Much to the Royal Air Force's discomfort the Oerlikon 20 mm weapon was found to be particularly devastating, especially when compared to the effect of the eight .303 Browning machine guns with which Spitfires and Hurricanes were armed. It was therefore natural that work should be conducted in Britain to include 20 mm armament in the wings of Camm's and Mitchell's fighters. The first cannon armed Spitfire to reach squadron service was R6261, which went to No.19 Squadron for trials in June, and was followed soon after by R6770 and R6776. Frank Brinsden recalls how "chuffed" the squadron's pilots were to learn that they were to re – equip with cannon armed machines, but, as the squadron diary records on July 1st, Squadron Leader Pinkham left his men in no doubt that there was much work to be done to introduce the Hispano Suiza cannon into service:

"Sqn. Ldr. Pinkham gave a lecture on the merits and de – merits of cannon equipped Spitfires. It was evident that new attacks would have to be developed to cope with the type's disadvantages and to make full use of the advantages of the new armament. No. 19 Sqn is soon to be fully re – equipped with cannon Spitfires, although so far we have but three."

DISADVANTAGES (At the moment)
1. Stoppages too frequent. Stoppage of one cannon makes it very difficult to keep a steady sight with the other.
2. Fire period restricted to six seconds making defence against other fighter aircraft very difficult.
3. Lack of spread.

ADVANTAGES
1. Terrific destructive power.
2. High muzzle velocity decreasing amount of deflection necessary in deflection shooting.
3. Increased range and accuracy.

Squadron Leader Pinkham busied himself with testing the new aircraft and devising new tactical formations so as to use the weapon to its best advantage. On July 4th, the squadron flew training flights to practice such a tactic. "A" Flight's sections dived in echelon from 2,000 feet above and to the side of three target aircraft to dead astern. They closed rapidly and gained very steady sight for the two cannon at high speed. Break away was carried out downward and to one side. The attack was then renewed from above and to the side. The one big disadvantage to this tactic was that German bombers tended to fly just below cloud base, enabling them to rapidly disappear, which thus prevented a high speed diving attack from above. However, Pinkham had confidence in his new method and the formation was pasted up at dispersal in diagrammatic form. Basically it relied upon two sections of two aircraft in line astern and was highly manoeuvrable, not unlike, in fact, the German "Schwarm" or "Finger Four".

Tactics may have been progressing but the cannon itself was proving to be extremely unreliable, and jamming during practice firing at Sutton Bridge became all too frequent. Shell case stoppages caused during their ejection from the weapon were partially overcome by the fitting of a rubber pad to the downward cartridge deflection plate which prevented the used round rebounding and being trapped by forward movement of the breech block. During practice firing on July 4th, only one shell hit the target cone. A few days later Pilot Officer Sutherland flew a cannon armed Spitfire to the Air Fighting Development Unit at Northolt, only to return with the news that No.19 Squadron's armourers and pilots knew more about the new machine than the experts did!

Another technical improvement was that the new De Havilland constant speed airscrews (as discussed in chapter one) began to replace the existing, two setting only, variable pitch propellers currently fitted to the squadron's Spitfires. The new airscrew shortened the take off run, improved flying control at lower air speeds and reduced petrol consumption. On July 4th, Flight Lieutenant Lane carried out an air test in R6770 and wrote in his log book "Air test in aircraft with CS airscrew and automatic undercart. Very nice and labour saving".

Whilst the squadron's armourers continued in their attempts to solve the jamming of the cannon, and the pilots continued practising new formations and test firing of the weapon, operational commitments continued. The Battle of Britain "officially" started on July 10th, and its first phase was German attacks on Channel bound convoys bringing much needed food and supplies to the beleagured island. No.19 Squadron, therefore, regularly found itself engaged on providing protection for such convoys and experienced pilots continued attempting to pass on their knowledge to new men in training flights. On July 13th, Flight Sergeant Steere was engaged in dogfight practice with Sergeant Birch, who was on the verge of becoming operational. Inexplicably Birch dived into the ground off a steep turn from 2,000 feet and was killed. He was a gifted contributor to "Punch" magazine and an obituary notice later appeared in that publication.

The convoy patrols were a somewhat monotonous, albeit very necessary, task for the pilots. On July 22nd, a new policy of sending "A" Flight to Coltishall on daily detachment commenced. Firstly this gave the cannon armed Spitfire pilots an opportunity to operate from the coast, and therefore have more chance of contacting the enemy, and secondly to relieve No.66 Squadron whose pilots had completed a seemingly endless number of such patrols. No.222 Squadron, in which Douglas Bader was a flight commander, was also at Coltishall at this time. Wallace "Jock" Cunningham, a Pilot Officer in No.19 Squadron, recalls:

> "We were lying in the sun at Coltishall along with Douglas Bader and other 222 Sqn. pilots. It was just before our involvement in the Battle of Britain proper and Brian Lane had recently received his "gong" for his good leadership of the squadron and general activities at Dunkirk. Douglas was kidding him and asked Brian "What's that?" in his usual cocky fashion, pointing to Brian's DFC ribbon. "I must get one of those" said Bader, and, as we all know, he did."

Despite flying many patrols the enemy were not met. The nearest the Spitfires came to catching a raider was not until July 24th, when Pilot Officer Aeberhardt sighted a Dornier Do215 three hundred yards, away which promptly vanished into cloud.

On the same day "A" Flight moved from Duxford to its satellite airfield at nearby Fowlmere, an old Great War aerodrome, and set up permanant home. During the squadron's previous stay at Fowlmere, coded "G1", only two Nissen huts existed, but on this occasion there were six. The Spitfire pilots moved into the billets recently vacated by the Defiant pilots of No.264 Squadron. "Admiral" Blake became Messing Officer and the squadron diary recorded: "The irrepressible Plt. Off. Howard – Williams re – started his excellent bar".

The weather now turned for the worst with days and nights of torrential rain and thunder. The grass airfield at Fowlmere quickly became a swamp, inches deep in mud, and duckboards were sent for. On the night of July 26th six aircraft of "A" Flight, returning from Coltishall, had to execute night landings at Duxford where the beacon was illuminated. R/T reception had been poor and Flight Lieutenant Lane had not received the order to return to Coltishall.

The appalling weather persisted until July 28th, when fine skies provided a complete contrast to previous days. Red Section, led by Flight Lieutenant Lane and consisting of Sub – Lieutenant Blake and Pilot Officer Cunningham, was up for an hour, and despite experiencing severe icing problems Blake sighted a Ju88 flying in the opposite direction. The section gave chase, lost the bomber in cloud, and found it again, at which time the enemy pilot executed violent turns, putting his nose down and escaping into cloud at full boost. On returning to Fowlmere, Yellow 3, Sergeant Roden, crashed on landing in Spitfire R6627 but was fortunately uninjured.

The following day the squadron diary records how the whole of "B" Flight was

> "sent off in a big alarm from Coltishall when all available squadrons left the ground. "B" Flight was ordered to attack approaching enemy bombers. No enemy aircraft were sighted but 66 Sqn. got two He 111s. "B" Flight returned after a vain search of one hour and five minutes".

The Battle of Britain was building up over southern England but the 12 Group pilots remained frustrated and relatively idle whilst their 11 Group counterparts engaged the enemy, in numbers, on a daily basis. For No.19 Squadron the frustration was worse as they were still experiencing problems with the Hispano Suiza cannon. The Commander – in – Chief of Fighter Command, Air Chief Marshal Sir Hugh Dowding, monitored closely the progress and problems with the squadron's Spitfires. On July 24th he wrote to Sir Archibald Sinclair, explaining some of the thinking behind the weapon and outlining its defects:

> "If and when the German bombers armour the backs of their engines, the eight gun fighter will be quite useless for the attack of bombers except when employing deflection shooting which is very difficult to apply accurately against high speed targets. We may, therefore, be driven to adopt the cannon fighter as the standard type. I cannot say that we shall have to do so because the initiative rests with the enemy. The ideal arrangement is to prepare alternative wings so that the armament can be quickly modified if the change becomes necessary.
>
> The defects of the original cannon armed Spitfire fighter are that:
>
> a) It only has two guns.
> b) These guns were designed to operate on their bellies but have been mounted on their sides. This has led to technical difficulties.
> c) Each gun carries a drum containing 60 rounds, and it is impossible to re – load in the air. The ammunition is expended in 5 seconds."

On August 2nd, Blue Section, led by Flight Lieutenant Clouston, patrolled a convoy off the Norfolk coast and intercepted an He111. Each member of the section fired at the enemy aircraft and had a good burst at it. Clouston, flying a machine gun equipped Spitfire, disabled the bomber's starboard engine and possibly killed the rear gunner. The Heinkel pilot resorted to evasive tactics and escaped eastwards having made full use of 9/10ths stratus cloud at 15,000 feet.

Over the following days considerable test firing went on with the cannon Spitfires. Yet more stoppages were experienced, most still due to the spent cartridge case ejection being from the weapon's side instead of from the bottom as intended by the manufacturers. The weapon had been mounted on its side due to the thin cross section of the Spitfire's wing. The squadron armourers had carried out considerable work in the fitting of deflector plates, but the problem was still not entirely solved. It was extremely frustrating for all involved as there was no doubt of the cannon's effectiveness given careful sighting and firing at correct range.

August 11th saw a new Spitfire delivered to No.19 Squadron. This was X4231, which was armed with two 20 mm cannon and four Browning machine guns. Although it was initially feared that the fighter would be slightly underpowered, Squadron Leader Pinkham flew the aircraft on a test of one hour and ten minutes, writing in his log book "Quite normal and obviously the right combination". The squadron diary states "General opinion is that the new Spitfire is a step in the right direction". However, the diary's next sentence provides us with the squadron's first vote of no confidence in the cannon Spitfires: "Possibly another step in the same direction would be re – equipping with the old eight gun machines".

Dowding still monitored the trials carefully, and on August 12th received the following letter from Lord Beaverbrook, the Minister for Aircraft Production:

"Dear Sir Hugh,

"Will you keep the Spitfire with cannon guns as long as you like, and do with it what you will. I have arranged this with Air Commodore Laing of No.41 Group.

I am only too gratified to be able to do anything which might be of assistance to you in the magnificent fight you are putting up."

Across the other side of the English Channel German troops congregated in the sea port towns and prepared for "Operation

Sealion", Hitler's proposed invasion of Great Britain. Barges of all shapes and sizes were being converted in the Channel ports to carry a seaborne invasion fleet. Bomber Command harrassed these activities by night, and on August 12th "B" Flight of No.19 Squadron, led by Squadron Leader Pinkham, flew to Eastchurch Airfield from where they were briefed to strafe German motor torpedo boats or "E" – Boats. As recorded in Pinkham's flying log they were to "escort the Battle boys on a beat up of the other side". For some reason the sortie was not carried out. However, Squadron Leader Pinkham's log book records an amusing incident on the journey to the coastal airfield:

> "Chasing Clouston who was chasing a Bombay carrying "B" Flight's ground crew into a big air battle over the Thames Estuary. Bombay forced down at North Weald – Thank Heaven!"

The Luftwaffe having attacked convoys and radar stations, the latter representing Britain's first and crucial line of defence, had by now turned their attentions to the airfields of Fighter Command. The Battle of Britain was now in its third, and most critical phase. Tuesday, August 13th, was scheduled by Luftwaffe chiefs as being "Adler Tag", or "Eagle Day", in which the German bomber fleets were to destroy Fighter Command on the ground. Weather conditions on the long awaited day, however, were not perfect early on, and the Dornier Do17s of KG2 which set out to bomb Sheerness and the airfield at Eastchurch, failed to receive the recall signal postponing the attack until the afternoon. The No.19 Squadron diary states that "B" Flight's personnel, still at Eastchurch, were "most thoroughly bombed". Approximately 250 bombs were dropped on the airfield and low flying raiders machine gunned those taking shelter on the ground. Fortunately no injury was sustained by "B" Flight and no Spitfires were damaged. Sergeant David Cox was unfortunate enough to be on the ground during the raid:

> "I was awakened by the bombing at about 7.30 am. I rushed out of my room, which was in a wooden hut, into a corridor where I met Flight Sergeant Tofts, who was in charge of the servicing of "B" Flight's aircraft. He grabbed me by the arm and we ran into the only brick shelter available, a urinal, and Tofts pushed me onto the floor saying "This is no time to be squeamish, lad!" Thirty odd people were killed in that raid, although fortunately none were from 19 Squadron."

KG2, however, was badly mauled by the Spitfires and Hurricanes of Air Vice – Marshal Keith Park's 11 Group. Later in the morning the Germans attacked the airfields at Odiham and Farnborough in Hampshire, which together with a raid on Portland met stiff opposition from Fighter Command. With better weather during mid – afternoon, "Adlerangriffe", the "Attack of the Eagles", was launched with simultaneous mass raids against Portland, Southampton and the Thames Estuary. The airfields of Detling and Andover were also bombed. The fighters of 11 Group were stretched to the limit in dealing with these large scale attacks across such a wide front, but nevertheless accounted for the destruction of forty – four enemy aircraft; a further thirty – six are reported as having returned to their bases damaged, some carrying wounded or dead crew members.

One type of German aircraft to suffer on "Eagle Day" at the hands of 11 Group was the Ju87 "Stuka" dive bomber. Much vaunted following its success as flying artillery in support of ground forces in previous offensives, the Stuka had a pyschological advantage. As it dived onto the target its banshee like siren struck fear into the hearts of its enemies. However, the Stuka was no match for the fast Spitfires and Hurricanes and was eventually withdrawn from the Battle of Britain. On "Eagle Day" thirteen Spitfires of No.609 "West Riding" Squadron left Warmwell to engage the enemy over Lyme Bay. The enemy formation, consisting of forty Stukas and a fighter escort of a similar number of Me110s and Me109s, was heading northwards from the Channel when the Spitfires made a surprise attack from down sun. Twelve of the No.609 Squadron pilots made claims following the subsequent combat, and the squadron diary records that it was a particularly bad day for the "species Ju 87". A total of ten Stukas and two Me109s were claimed as destroyed, three Stukas probably destroyed, and three Stukas, two Me109s and one Me110 damaged.

By dusk on August 13th the Luftwaffe had failed to achieve its objective, but there was to be no respite for the front line squadrons of 11 Group as intensive attacks continued. Meanwhile the squadrons of 12 Group, particularly those of the Duxford sector who were within striking distance of the battle zone, were anxious to be called upon to get at the enemy. News of the bitter fighting filtered through to No.19 Squadron. On "Eagle Day" Pilot Officer Arthur Vokes wrote in his log book "Big air battle above clouds over Thames Estuary", and Squadron Leader Pinkham wrote "Terrific air fight in afternoon which we rather missed".

Friction between the controllers of 11 and 12 Groups was becoming constant. Understandably 11 Group commited its own squadrons to battle in the first instance, and in the second called on 12 Group to reinforce. The problem with this method was that, due to the distance the 12 Group squadrons were away from the battle zone, they often found themselves called upon ·too late by 11 Group. An example occured on August 15th, as David Cox remembers:

"The squadron was scrambled to intercept a raid on Martlesham Heath airfield. The attack was carried out by some twenty five Messerschmitt 110 fighter bombers of Erprobungsgruppe 210, led by their brilliant commander

Rubensdörffer. The enemy were completely undetected until only a few minutes from Martlesham. Only three Hurricanes of 17 Squadron managed to get airborne from Martlesham before the 110s arrived over the airfield. Our chances of intercepting the raid were impossible, taking into consideration that Fowlmere to Martlesham was sixty air miles. Taking an optimistic speed for 19 Squadron's Spitfires of 300 m.p.h., it would take twelve minutes from take off to reach Martlesham. I doubt that at 2,000' the Spitfire Ib was capable of 300 m.p.h. as its maximum speed was not reached until 19,000'. I would suggest that 280 m.p.h. was the maximum possible for that height, but even at 300 m.p.h. the squadron could not achieve the impossible."

On August 16th the German bombers again pounded Park's airfields, despite having continued to suffer serious losses since the ill fated "Eagle Day". During the early evening of the 16th, "A" Flight, led by Flight Lieutenant Lane and consisting of Flight Sergeant Unwin, Sergeant Roden, Flying Officer Brinsden, Pilot Officer Cunningham, and Sergeants Potter and Jennings, met the enemy en masse for the first time since the fighting of "Operation Dynamo". The squadron diary relates events:

"Thirty miles due east of Harwich, 1730 hrs. On returning to Coltishall, "A" Flight were asked to investigate. The investigation proved to be approximately 150 enemy aircraft consisting of bombers and fighter escort. Enemy aircraft were moving approximately southwards, bombers in front, escort of 40 – 50 Me 110s stepped up behind, and further escort of Me 109s at 1,000' to 1,500' above and to starboard of main formation. "A" Flight attacked in two sections of three and four aircraft respectively. Three definitely shot down and one probable, all Me 110s. Sgt Roden's aircraft had several bullet holes but no other damage. The Me 110s, on being attacked, commenced milling in an attempt, which was successful, to keep us from the bombers. Generally speaking the enemy showed little enterprise. As far as could be observed the Me 110s had no rear gunners. Six of the seven Spitfires involved in the engagement had cannon stoppages. Results would have been at least doubled had we been equipped with either cannon and machine guns or just eight machine guns. During the engagement the Me 109s did not attack".

Brian Lane, leading the flight in Spitfire R6919, recorded events in his log:

"Returning from Coltishall investigated 'X' Raid above cloud with seven aircraft of "A" Flight. Turned out to be about 150 Huns!! Waded into escort of Me 110s but ruddy cannons stopped on me".

It is most unusual that the Me110s should fly without a rear gunner; Sergeant Bernard "Jimmy" Jennings flew R6924 as Yellow Two and noted the fact in his log book, adding that he suspected the formation to be practising. Unfortunately Jennings did not add to his score during the engagement as his cannons jammed virtually immediately.

Amongst the successful No.19 Squadron pilots was Sergeant Jack Potter:

"I fired at several Me 110s but could not definitely claim to have scored. I then pursued an Me 110 and fired at very short range from above and saw almost the whole of his starboard engine disappear. He flicked over to port and as he did so a large piece of the front section broke away. My ammunition exhausted I returned home".

Also successful was Pilot Officer Cunningham, who destroyed an Me110. He filed the following combat report:

"I attacked as number four of Yellow Section and fired, no hits. I broke away and fired at another Me 110, out of range I think. On a burst at another Me 110 he broke away to the right and I had a large expanse of underside offered to me at which I fired a long burst. He dived down through cloud, probably out of control. Stoppage in starboard gun after 30 rounds".

Flight Lieutenant Lane added confirmation of Cunningham's victory at the bottom of the Glaswegian's report:

"I saw this enemy aircraft roll over and dive vertically through cloud. I consider this a definite casualty as the enemy aircraft made no attempt to evade action".

Wallace Cunningham recalled:

"`A' Flight was returning to Duxford and was directed out from Clacton, catching up with a large German formation. I remember mainly Jennings on the R/T bemoaning his jammed 20 mm cannon, full of indignation at the unfairness of life in general."

Flight Sergeant George Unwin flew as Red 3 in Flight Lieutenant Lane's Red Section. He remembers that combat:

"We left Coltishall at 1715 hrs and were ordered to 15,000', which was altered to 12,000'. After 20 minutes a large formation of enemy aircraft were spotted, escorted by Me 110s at the rear and Me 109s above. As we "went in to attack the bombers, the Me 110s saw us and attacked. I attacked one of the Me 110s and gave him a short burst. He half rolled and went down almost vertically. I could not see what happened to him as I was attacked by another. I out turned him and found myself with a perfect target at close range. My starboard cannon had a stoppage, but I fired the remainder of my port cannon's ammunition into the 110. Bits fell off the enemy aircraft and he went into a steep dive, during which the tail came off. I followed him down and when I came out of cloud I saw the end of a splash into the sea which I assume was him."

It must have been extremely frustrating for the Spitfire pilots to meet the enemy in such circumstances only to have their cannons jam, especially after playing a lesser role in 12 Group whilst Park's fighters engaged the enemy on a daily basis. No doubt had this not been the case, as the diary records, results on August 16th would have been even better with possibly both Lane and Jennings increasing their score.

On August 19th, Squadron Leader Pinkham reported concerning the Spitfire armed with both cannon and machine guns:

"Owing to recent operational commitments it has not been possible to carry out an exhaustive trial of the aircraft and the following is merely a report on trials undertaken to date. As far as flying qualities are concerned the difference between this aircraft and the normal Spitfire is not noticable. Its take off, climb, landing speed and run are quite normal. It appears to stall at the same speed as the normal Spitfire. It is quite as manoeuvrable as the ordinary Spitfire up to 30,000'. A test to determine the service ceiling has not yet been carried out, but it has already been climbed to 32,000'. The guns have been fired independently and together and have functioned satisfactorily".

On the same day, Green Section, flying cannon only armed Spitfires and led by Flying Officer Leonard Haines, intercepted and shot down an Me110. Haines's cannons suffered stoppages during the combat and this action was referred to in a further report by Squadron Leader Pinkham on August 24th:

"The ejection stoppages experienced were similar in each case; the empty case was not thrown clear of the gun or had bounced back into it, the next round being fed in jamming the empty case with the breech block partly forward. The mark of the breech block was clearly visible on the live round, though rather lower than normal. When firing in action on 19.8.40, F/O Haines had similar stoppages on both guns in aircraft No. 6882, the port gun firing 5 rounds and the starboard gun 22.

"It would appear that the stoppage is caused by the installation and is due to the effect of the gun being mounted on its side, combined with the small width of the ejection shute. It is not clear how this can be cured until the gun is mounted the right way up and a belt feed introduced. Further the magazine is supported on its neck by a magazine positioning stop which is only effective for positive "G". If any skidding or slipping or negative "G" is applied the magazine is entirely supported by the neck. This is thought to have been the cause of the failure at the neck of the starboard magazine in aircraft No. 6776 after firing 9 rounds in action."

Regarding Flying Officer Haines's claim for the Me110 on August 19th, David Cox has some interesting recollections:

"Green Section comprised Haines, Steere and myself. We were given a vector of about ninety degrees, which was in the direction of the east coast. We flew at about 2,000' under 10/10th cloud. As we approached the coast near Aldeburgh, the cloud started to break up and I, who was flying on the left and looking out to sea, saw a twin engined aircraft. As was the rule, being the pilot who had the enemy in sight, I took over the lead. At about 300 yards I opened fire with my cannons in a quick burst of about three seconds. I then broke away allowing Haines and Steere to attack. On making my second attack I saw the port engine catch fire, which rapidly enveloped the whole aircraft. Three of the crew baled out. Haines said it was a Messerschmitt 110 bomber. I had my doubts as I thought they only had two crew members, but as

Leonard Haines was a senior Flying Officer I entered it in my log book as a Messerschmitt 110. However, German records show no losses of any 110s on that day, but there is a Dornier 17Z* reported as shot down at 6.30 pm, the exact time of our combat."

* This was Do17 U5+DR of 7/KG2

On Saturday, August 24th, six large raids occurred, the fourth of which, at 3 pm, penetrated to the eastern outskirts of London. On this occasion 12 Group was called upon by the 11 Group controllers to reinforce Park's fighters. No.19 Squadron was scrambled at 3.45 pm, led by Flight Lieutenant Lane, to intercept an approaching formation of around fifty enemy aircraft. The Spitfires caught the enemy formation moving eastwards at 1500 feet over the Thames Estuary. The six Spitfires of "A" Flight, consisting of Flight Lieutenant Lane, Red 1, Sub–Lieutenant Blake, Red 2, Sergeant Roden, Red 3, Flying Officer Brinsden, Yellow 1, Pilot Officer Cunningham, Yellow 2, and Sergeant Jennings as Yellow 3, attacked the Me110s from behind. In the resulting mêlée Flight Lieutenant Lane destroyed one Me110. In his log book he wrote:

"Squadron took off at 1545, self leading. Ran into a bunch of Huns over Estuary. Had a bang at an Me 110 but had to break away as tracer was coming over my head from another behind me. He appeared to be hitting his fellow countryman in front of me but I didn't wait to see if he shot him down. Had a crack at another and shot his engine right out of the wing – lovely! Crashed near North Foreland. Last trip in "BLITZEN III"!"

Lane's combat report provides greater detail, and recounts the incident in which he found a straggling Me110 but was unable to attack as his ammunition was expended:

"At approximately 1600 hrs over North Weald A.A. fire was sighted to the east and I turned towards it, at the same time sighting a number of enemy aircraft above at about 15,000'. I climbed up and at approximately 1610 hrs got astern of a ragged formation of about 40 Me 110s and Do 215s with an escort of approximately 10 Me 109s above and to the rear. The Me 110s were at the rear of the Do 215s. I approached from below and from the sunward side, and almost got within range when Me 110s sighted us and turned towards us. A dogfight ensued and I opened fire from below and astern of the nearest Me 110 but was forced to break away as tracer appeared over my head from an enemy aircraft astern of me. This tracer appeared to be hitting the enemy aircraft that I was firing at, but I observed no result. I got below another Me 110 and fired with slight deflection at the port engine and observed a large part of the engine or mainplane fly off. Enemy aircraft dived down and I observed it crash in the sea. No rear fire was experienced from the Me 110s. The Me 109s appeared to be painted yellow on upper surfaces and pale blue below with yellow roundels around all the markings, including those on under side of mainplane. Me 110s had normal camouflage. After the fight I observed a lone Me 110 flying east with its port engine out of action. I attacked but had no ammunition left. I flew alongside the enemy aircraft which immediately opened up flat out. There appeared to be no gunner in the rear cockpit."

Sergeant Jennings was more fortunate in this combat than during that of August 16th. In the dogfight with the Me110s he claimed destruction of one, and a second as probably destroyed. His log book reads:

"R6917. Intercepted 30 Do 215s, 10 Me 109s, 10 Me 110s. Shot starboard engine also rudder and tail unit off starboard side of one Me 110, also rudder and tail unit off starboard side of another Me 110. Port cannon stopped after 37 rounds, other fired 60 rounds."

Sergeant Jennings had actually attacked four Me110s, from slightly above, which were flying in a fairly wide formation. As the nearest enemy aircraft slid into his reflector gunsight, he squeezed the brass gun button. Cannon shells ripped through the air and smashed into the enemy machine, knocking off the top of its starboard engine and propeller, sending the aircraft plunging earthwards in a vicious engine turn. Jennings dived under the remaining enemy machines, turning first to starboard, then to port, before climbing and attacking a lone Me110. A long burst of cannon fire smashed through the enemy's tail section, knocking off part of the tail unit, including starboard rudder. The enemy yawed, pursued by Jennings who was suddenly presented with a target of two Me110s in front of him. With his starboard gun the Spitfire pilot fired a long burst. His port cannon jammed, but an Me109 passed between his sights and the target, having dived on Jennings from above and overshot. He rapidly searched the sky for other enemy fighters. Seeing none he attacked another Me110 but did not hit this machine before the starboard cannon also jammed. Yellow 3 sensibly broke off for home.

Above Red and Yellow sections who were engaging the Me110s, Green Section, consisting of Pilot Officer Aeberhardt, Pilot Officer Burgoyne and Pilot Officer Parrott, engaged the Me109s in a running fight and attempted to prevent the enemy fighters reaching "A" Flight. Green Section scored no victories but succeeded in their objective.

Once again the squadron had been faced with overwhelming odds, just nine Spitfires against at least fifty enemy machines. They had claimed the destruction of two Me110s, and probably that of a third, for no loss to themselves. However, once again the cannon had let the gallant pilots down, only two of them being able to fire their entire ammunition without mishap.

As Red, Yellow and Green Sections fought above the Thames Estuary, No.19 Squadron received four Czech pilots on attachment from No.310 Squadron, a Czech Hurricane unit also based at Duxford and to which Gordon Sinclair had been posted as a flight commander. Pilot Officer Dolezal, Pilot Officer Hradil, and Sergeants Plzak and Marek are reported in the squadron diary as being "very keen to have a crack". Like the Poles, the Czechs earned a reputation for their aggressiveness in the air. This is not surprising when the anxieties for their families, still in their occupied homelands, are considered.

On Monday, August 26th, No.19 Squadron was ordered to patrol Debden at 10,000 feet. The following incident did nothing to improve relations between 11 and 12 Groups, as David Cox remembers:

> "The actual raid came in at 1,000'. As 19 Squadron were at 10,000' and above 10/10th cloud, we saw nothing of what was going on. It appears that the Observer Corps had reported a raid coming in at 1,000', but the 11 Group controllers thought this must be a mistake and consequently asked 19 Squadron to patrol at 10,000'. The subsequent intelligence report stated that the "Spitfires from Fowlmere were slow in getting off the ground", which was certainly not the case."

By the last day in August, Saturday 31st, Göring had maintained his attacks on Fighter Command's airfields. Despite serious damage, particularly at Biggin Hill in Kent and Kenley in Surrey, none had ceased to remain operational. The Luftwaffe intelligence chief, Hans Jeschonnek passed to German aircrews information to the contrary. August 31st saw the indescriminate bombing of East Anglia by 250 aircraft in 5 waves, and later raids on the East End of London and Kent by waves of firstly 100 plus and secondly 200 plus bombers. The day was also to see Fighter Command suffer its highest losses throughout the entire summer's fighting.

On August 31st, Flight Lieutenant Lane and "A" Flight were off duty. At 8.30 am "B" Flight patrolled over Duxford and Debden at 20,000 feet in readiness for a German attack on those airfields. Sergeant Jennings, in R6917, discovered that his oxygen system was not functioning correctly as he reached 17,000 feet so returned to Fowlmere, which he found to have been bombed. Flight Sergeant Unwin had spent the raid in a slit trench, being unable to get airborne as his aircraft was undergoing a routine inspection. The rest of the squadron, led by Flight Lieutenant Wilf Clouston, was vectored south and intercepted a formation of 60 – 100 enemy aircraft consisting of Do17s, Me109s and Me110s. Clouston, leading Blue Section, and Flying Officer James Coward, leading Green Section, attacked. Coward had been posted from No.19 Squadron to No.266 on November 5th, 1939, but had returned on August 30th, 1940. The sortie on August 31st was to prove somewhat traumatic for Coward, who was flying X4231. This was the cannon and machine gun armed Spitfire usually flown by Squadron Leader Pinkham:

133

"We were scrambled from our satellite airfield, Fowlmere, and intercepted 15 Do 17s escorted by 80 Me 109s, just south of Duxford. Flt. Lt. Clouston led us into a copybook Fighter Command No 1 Attack from dead ahead, turning in three sections line astern, to come up in sections echeloned port behind the enemy who were in sections of three in vic line astern. The fourth section, led by Flg. Off. Frank Brinsden, was detailed to climb up and intercept the fighters. I got a cannon shell through the cockpit which shattered my left leg below the knee, also severing the elevator controls, and I had to bale out. I put a tournequet round my thigh, using my helmet radio lead, and landed by parachute about four miles north of Duxford on the Royston to Newmarket Road. I was admitted to Addenbrooke's Hospital in Cambridge and was out of the battle from then on."

Flying Officer Brinsden, mixing it with Me109s, was shot down in R6958, but baled out unhurt:

"At about 1500' plus, whilst still climbing and with the controls therefore sluggish, I was attacked head on from up sun by a 110 which I then noticed was part of a large formation. There then followed an almighty bang, loss of control and me over the side pretty sharpish. I landed by parachute at Starling Green, near Saffron Walden, and R6958 crashed at Brent, Pelham. I was very lucky not to have caught fire because I reeked of petrol and was violently ill during the descent, possibly caused by the parachute's motion."

Flight Lieutenant Clouston and Pilot Officer Burgoyne shared in the destruction of an Me110. Sergeant David Cox accounted for the destruction of a second machine; he recalls the combat:

"We were caught on the hop! Most of us were still in bed as the squadron was in a state of "stood down". We got a panic message to scramble at once. I put on my flying boots and flying jacket over my pyjamas. We took off at about 8 o'clock and climbed south to about 17,000'. It was jolly cold up there as the flying jacket only came down as far as my waist!

"We soon came in sight of the enemy, about 30 Dorniers with a large number of Me 110s above and behind. I was No 3 in Blue Section which was led by Flg. Off. Coward. We were above and behind the bombers but below the Me 110s. We were put into echelon starboard and dived onto a section of the Dorniers. Before I could open fire I was attacked by the Me 110s so I took evasive action, a very, very sharp left hand climbing turn, after which I found myself alone and no longer in contact with the squadron.

"I then climbed up to about 20,000' and flew south east. Over Clacton I saw about 20 – 30 Me 110s milling around in a left hand circle and about 2,000' below me. I dived down onto the circle and fired at one Me 110 that had got detached from the formation. My cannons operated perfectly as I was keeping a straight line with no turning. The Me 110 turned slightly to port and then dived away steeply with his port engine belching black smoke. I was then attacked by four other Me 110s, and, being out of ammunition, got the hell out of it!

"Apparently the Me 110 I destroyed was "3U + HS" of II/ZG76. The

134

crew, Oblt. von Bergen and Uffz. Becker were rescued from the sea by some fishermen and brought ashore to be taken prisoner."

Nineteen year old Pilot Officer Ray Aeberhardt had been involved in the action, during which his aircraft, R6912, was damaged by enemy fire. Whilst attempting to land without flaps at Fowlmere, R6912 crashed and turned over, the pilot being killed in the resulting fire. Raymond Andre Charles Aeberhardt, who had joined the squadron from No.5 Operational Training Unit in early summer 1940, lies buried at Whittlesford churchyard in Cambridgeshire. David Cox recalls:

"When I got back to Fowlmere I landed over the smoking remains of Plt. Off. Aeberhardt's Spitfire. I visited his grave several times after the war and at first it was on its own with a large headstone and was always looked after. After about twenty years it became overgrown and obviously uncared for. I tried to tidy it up myself and put some flowers on it. The last time I visited the grave it had been moved to be with the other RAF graves, and, like them, was now carefully tended. I always remember young Aeberhardt as a very nice young officer who would always have a few words with us NCO pilots."

After the fight on August 31st, the squadron diary again recorded that "the score would most definitely have been higher given eight machine guns". The problems with the cannon were still no where near resolved and Flight Lieutenant Lane made representation to the Commanding Officer on behalf of the pilots. On September 1st, Squadron Leader Pinkham reported as follows to Group Captain Woodhall:

"In all of the engagements so far occurring it is considered that had the unit been equipped with eight gun fighters it would have inflicted far more severe losses on the enemy. Furthermore, Captain Adams from the Ministry of Aircraft Production, who recently visited the unit to report on the guns, has stated that the guns at present installed in the cannon Spitfire would never function satisfactorily until they are mounted up – right, or possibly with a modification to the existing wing. It would take some months before this modification could be completed and it is considered most unfair that pilots should be expected to attack enemy formations of the size encountered at present with unreliable armament. It is most strongly urged that until the stoppages at present experienced have been eliminated this squadron should re – equip with Browning gun Spitfires. It is suggested that a way of doing this would be to allot the present cannon armed Spitfires to an OTU, and withdraw Browning gun Spitfires from there for use in this squadron."

Group Captain Woodhall took heed of his subordinate's recommendation and reported further to HQ 12 Group:

"It is very strongly recommended that until the teething troubles of the cannon armed Spitfires have been overcome 19 Sqn should be equipped with eight gun Spitfires. At the present time, after five engagements with the enemy using these aircraft, the pilots have no confidence in their weapons for the following reasons:

a) Frequency of stoppages.

b) The fact that no tracer ammunition is used with cannon up to the present and pilots have no indication as to where their rounds are going as they do with eight gun Spitfires.

c) I can confirm that Captain Adams made the statement, and in addition he stated that he was reporting to the Ministry of Aircraft Production that until a modification to the existing wing was made it would be useless to carry on with the present mounting of cannons in Spitfires".

The following day, September 2nd, Flight Lieutenant Clouston led one standing patrol over Debden airfield and Squadron Leader Pinkham three. The enemy were not met on any of the sorties. However, an atmosphere of gloom had descended over the squadron as news had been received that due to the problems with the cannon, the squadron was to be withdrawn to Digby in Lincolnshire, right out of the battle area. The pilots felt that through no fault of their own, due to the problems between 11 and 12 Groups in co – ordinating efforts, and because of their unreliable armament, they had not had an opportunity to meet the enemy on the same terms as other squadrons.

On September 3rd, Squadron Leader Pinkham led all of No.19 Squadron's available aircraft, eight Spitfires of "B" Flight, on a standing patrol over Duxford and Debden. He received information from the controlling ground station that enemy aircraft were attacking North Weald aerodrome. The Luftwaffe had now switched from bombing fighter airfields in Kent, England's front line, to those in Essex. Hornchurch, Debden and North Weald airfields were now being attacked in a sensible attempt to push Fighter Command to use airfields further north, and thus be a greater distance away from the proposed invasion beaches in the south. As Squadron Leader Pinkham headed towards North Weald for his first combat with the enemy the raiders unloaded their bombs and caused severe damage to the airfield, which remained operational, to the great credit of its personnel. The Spitfires arrived as the enemy had finshed bombing and, flying in pairs line astern, the squadron attacked the enemy formation from above and in front. The formation consisted of 60 bombers and 150 fighters. Squadron Leader Pinkham was unsuccessful in the action as he too suffered the frustration of jammed cannon. Flying Officer Haines claimed the destruction of an

Me110, and both Sub – Lieutenant Blake and Flight Sergeant Unwin the probable destruction of two more. The machine attacked by Unwin is believed to have been a Bf110C – 4, W.Nr. 3120, of Stab I/ZG2, which was also attacked by Pilot Officer Carpenter of No.222 Squadron, and possibly Sergeant Furst of No.310. The enemy aircraft was abandoned by the crew, Oberleutnant Messner, the Gruppe Technical Officer, and Unteroffizier Santoni, who were both captured unhurt. Their aircraft, "3M + CB", crashed at Edwins Hall, Stowmaries, Essex.

On the same day news was received from 12 Group's Commander – in – Chief, Air Vice – Marshal Trafford Leigh – Mallory, that No.19 Squadron was not to be withdrawn to Digby but would remain in the Duxford sector, exchanging its cannon armed machines for Mk Ia's equipped with eight Browning machine guns. Flight Sergeant Unwin flew the cannon armed R6776 from Fowlmere and collected the Browning armed P9546 from Duxford. "QV – H" was to be Unwin's regular mount for the next few days of fighting.

On Thursday, September 5th, a formation of around seventy German aircraft crossed the English coast at Dungeness and headed inland to attack Fighter Command airfields in 11 Group. Leigh – Mallory's 12 Group were called upon, and at 9.47 am Squadron Leader Pinkham led No.19 Squadron on a scramble out of Fowlmere. The five Spitfires of "A" Flight and six of "B" Flight were ordered to patrol Hornchurch at 15,000 feet. Over the patrol line Sergeant Jennings sighted an ememy formation of forty Do17s approaching from the west and heading down the Thames Estuary. Above the bombers was the ever present escort of some forty Me109s. Jennings informed the squadron of the enemy presence and led his comrades towards the German formation. Having sighted the enemy himself, Squadron Leader Pinkham ordered "A" Flight to attack the fighters and "B" Flight the bombers. "B" Flight climbed to make their attack in pairs from the rear. Blue 2, Flying Officer "Farmer" Lawson, lost sight of Blue 1, Squadron Leader Pinkham, in the sun and attacked the rearmost vic of three Dorniers. As he did so the Me109s dived on "B" Flight. Blue 2 saw parts fall off one of his targets, but he was forced to break away when his aircraft was hit by cannon fire from behind, an assailant he never even saw. Serious damage was suffered by Spitfire N3286, but Lawson managed to return safely to Fowlmere. Contemporary squadron records do not detail Pilot Officer Vokes as having taken part in this action, but his log book records that he flew in Squadron Leader Pinkham's section as Blue 3. He later chased an Me110 out to sea, but was unable to catch up with the "Zerstörer".

Black 1 and Black 2 then attacked the same formation from

astern. Black 2's second burst knocked a Dornier's starboard engine out and Black 2 then attacked a second bomber. The section was then attacked by the German fighter escort. Black 1 saw an Me109 in front and below him which he attacked from astern. Although the Me109 wobbled and turned, obviously having been hit, the pilot did not subsequently make any claim regarding this machine. Black 2 attacked another German fighter without result, but was then pursued by a further four Me109s. Green 1 and Green 2 approached the bombers but were intercepted by the escort diving from above. Green 1, Flying Officer Haines, turned sharply and the enemy fighters overtook him, enabling him to get onto the tail of the second Messerschmitt. Green 1 pursued his victim across Kent at hedge top height. Over Ashford, Green 1's bullets found their mark. The Me109E – 4 of 1/JG54, climbed to 800 feet where the pilot, Unteroffizier F. Hotzelmann, baled out. Hotzelmann broke his legs in a heavy landing in the grounds of Melbourne House, John Street. His aircraft, "White 9", crashed into the rear of No.6 Hardy Street, Maidstone, burying itself deep into the lawn and exploding. Fortunately the occupants of the house were sheltering in a cellar and had a lucky escape. Green 2, the Czech Sergeant Plzak, singled out an enemy aircraft which was diving to escape the attention of another squadron. After two bursts from the Czech's machine guns the Messerschmitt Bf109 poured black smoke, but he was forced to break following an attack by two more of the fighter escort which he fortunately lost by diving and performing an Immelmann turn.

"A" Flight, led by Flight Lieutenant Lane, had climbed in line astern to reach the Me109s, which were 5,000 feet higher and already diving to attack "B" Flight. As the Spitfires climbed towards the blinding sun they lost sight of their quarry and despite searching for them over east Kent for fifteen minutes were forced to return to Fowlmere. Pilot Officer Eric Burgoyne of "B" Flight returned with P9391 damaged but repairable. Of Squadron Leader Pinkham nothing had been seen since Blue Section commenced their attack on the rearmost vic of Dorniers; the wait for him to return was to be in vain. As Pinkham steered his Spitfire, P9422, towards the bombers he is believed to have been caught in the combined cross fire of the three enemy aircraft. Quite possibly he may also have been hit by an Me109. Later a Spitfire was discovered to have crashed in remote countryside near the village of Birling, in Kent, and shortly afterwards No.19 Squadron were informed that their squadron commander had been killed. Apparently Squadron Leader Pinkham had attempted to bale out of his stricken fighter, but probably due to wounds to his chin, chest and hip, he only managed to do so when perilously low, too low in fact for his life saving silk parachute to open.

Air Vice – Marshal Leigh – Mallory wrote a letter of condolence to Squadron Leader Pinkham's parents in which he commented: "In him I feel that the service has lost an exceptionally promising young officer". The pilot's body was handed over to his family for burial and the service took place the following Tuesday at St Andrew's, Kingsbury, London. As the coffin, covered in the Royal Air Force ensign, entered the church the sirens wailed their piercing announcement of an approaching air raid. In accordance with the Bishop's instructions, the Reverend Bridgewater announced that the church was not an air raid shelter and invited those who wished to leave and take cover in a more appropriate premises to do so. No one left the congregation. As the funeral service drew to a close the sirens sounded the "all clear". Squadron Leader Phillip Campbell Pinkham AFC RAF, aged just 25 years old, was buried in St Andrew's churchyard. His flying log book was stamped simply "Killed in action". Appropriately, in memory of his sacrifice, the people of the area commenced collecting to purchase a Spitfire to be known as the *Borough of Willesden*, in honour of "Tommy" Pinkham.

On the day of Squadron Leader Pinkham's death in battle, Flight Lieutenant Brian Lane DFC was promoted to Squadron Leader. Flying Officer Lawson was promoted to Flight Lieutenant and made commander of "A" Flight. The vacancy could also have been filled by Flying Officer Frank Brinsden, a section leader with comparable experience who had been Brian Lane's deputy flight commander.

So it was that Brian Lane, at the tender age of 23, came to command No.19 Squadron, an appropriate move as it had fallen to him to lead the squadron into battle during "Operation Dynamo", and on the majority of occasions in which the squadron had been engaged with the enemy. It would be over the next few months that this fine young man's abilities as both a fighter tactician and a leader of men would be given the opportunity to rise to the fore.

CHAPTER THREE.

Fighter Command's system of defending the United Kingdom included the division of the country into four separate groups. Each group had its own head – quarters and commander, but was answerable to the Commander – in – Chief of Fighter Command, Air Chief Marshal Sir Hugh Dowding, at the command's head – quarters at Bentley Priory. London and the south east of England became 11 Group, commanded by Air Vice – Marshal Keith Park. The south west of England was protected by Air Vice – Marshal Sir Christopher Quintin Brand's 10 Group and the Midlands by Air Vice – Marshal Trafford Leigh – Mallory's 12 Group. The north of England and Northern Ireland came under the auspices of Air Vice – Marshal Richard Saul's 13 Group.

The New Zealander Keith Park was the son of a professor and came to England to serve as a gunner in the Great War. In 1917 he transferred to the Royal Flying Corps, later receiving a permanent commission in the Royal Air Force. Having received his first squadron command in 1920, he passed through the Staff College and served as air attaché at Buenos Aires. By 1938 he had become Dowding's right hand man as Fighter Command's senior Staff Officer, and was shortly afterwards made commander of 11 Group. With the benefit of hindsight Park has been described as possibly the Royal Air Force's greatest expert on all aspects of fighter direction. During the air battles of Dunkirk he logged one hundred hours in his personal Hurricane watching his young pilots in action. This patient observation was to pay off as Park proved himself a brilliant tactician during the Battle of Britain.

Air Vice – Marshal Trafford Leigh – Mallory was born at Mobberley in Cheshire on November 7th, 1892, and joined a Territorial battalion of the King's (Liverpool) Regiment on the outbreak of the Great War. Shortly afterwards he received a commission in the Lancashire Fusiliers and was seconded to the Royal Flying Corps in July 1916. For his service in France he was awarded the DSO. After the war Leigh – Mallory was granted a permanent commission in the Royal Air Force and, as a squadron leader, he joined the School of Army Co – operation which he later commanded for three years. After serving as an instructor at the Army Staff College, and service at the Air Ministry and overseas, he was appointed to command 12 Group Fighter Command in 1937.

With 11 Group being on the Channel coast, its forward airfields separated from German occupied France by but a thin strip of water, Park's squadrons were more favourably placed to intercept the incoming enemy formations than Leigh – Mallory's pilots in 12 Group. Whilst Park's exhausted pilots fought the enemy daily, the 12 Group squadrons, particularly those of the Duxford sector which were within striking distance of the battle zone, became frustrated that the 11 Group controllers did not call on them to reinforce their hard pressed comrades. Park's tactics were to break up the bombers before they could reach and inflict damage on their targets, and generally to shoot down as many enemy machines as possible. As the pressure of attacks on 11 Group's airfields increased, Park was forced to call upon Leigh – Mallory to protect his airfields whilst his fighter squadrons were in action. As we have seen, on August 26th Park had called for 12 Group to protect Debden in Essex, but before the fighters could arrive the airfield was severely damaged by German bombs. Park demanded to know why the 12 Group units were not in position when the Luftwaffe arrived over their target. Leigh – Mallory's reply was that he had been asked to respond too late by the 11 Group commander. This incident brought the two commanders' dislike of each other to a head, and into the open.

On August 30th, 1940, Squadron Leader Douglas Bader waited impatiently at the 12 Group coastal aerodrome of Coltishall, for the call to reinforce Park's fighters. He was deeply resentful that his squadron, No.242, was forced to play a secondary role to the 11 Group units. Bader received orders to proceed with his squadron to Duxford from where No.242 Squadron was scrambled and intercepted a large formation of enemy aircraft north of London. Bader's Hurricane pilots subsequently claimed the destruction of twelve enemy aircraft and a further five probably destroyed. The squadron received a signal from Leigh – Mallory: "Heartfelt congratulations on a first class show. Well done 242." Further messages of congratulations were also received from the Chief of the Air Staff and the Under Secretary of State for Air. Squadron Leader Bader spoke to his Air Officer Commanding stating that he could have inflicted far greater losses on the enemy given a number of squadrons under his command as opposed to a "penny packet" force consisting of just one squadron of twelve, or less, aircraft as used by 11 Group. Bader elaborated and explained his belief that given several squadrons, based at Duxford, a wing could be scrambled, form up over the airfield, and arrive over the battle zone in force to attack the enemy in numbers and hopefully on relatively equal terms. In Leigh – Mallory, who recognised at last the opportunity for his command to play a greater part in the struggle, Bader's tactics found an important ally. Enthusiastically supporting a tactic totally opposed to that endorsed by Dowding and employed by Park, both protagonists argued that even though the wing may take time to form up and arrive over the battle area, it was better to attack and destroy the enemy in large numbers on their way home than harry the formations in small numbers to less effect as they approached a target. Park believed that the wing would take too long to take off, form up and arrive over the battle area to take advantage of the brief warning of an incoming raid which radar allowed his controllers. Events were to prove him right.

On September 6th, No.611 "County of Lancashire" Squadron arrived at Fowlmere to take No.19 Squadron's place in the Duxford sector whilst the unit exchanged, with relief, its cannon armed Spitfires for standard eight machine gun armed Mk Ia's. Most of these aircraft had been drawn from Operational Training Units, and were somewhat worn, but Flight Sergeant Unwin's new mount, P9546, "QV – H", had been delivered from Hendon having initially been allocated to No.257 "Burma" Squadron which had formed and worked up on Spitfires prior to a switch to Hurricanes. On the same day Squadron Leader Lane was informed that, until further notice, No.19 Squadron would fly as part of a wing led by Squadron Leader Bader. The wing would comprise Bader's No.242 Squadron, No.19 Squadron and the Duxford based Czechs of No.310 Squadron. Bader's Hurricanes moved to operate out of Duxford, whilst No.19 Squadron remained at nearby Fowlmere. During the morning Squadron Leader Lane led his Spitfires on a patrol of North Weald and Hornchurch airfields in conjunction with the other wing squadrons; no enemy aircraft were sighted. In the afternoon Flight Lieutenant Clouston led No.19 Squadron on a second wing patrol but again the enemy were not met.

The major turning point in the Battle of Britain occurred on Saturday, September 7th, 1940. Fighter Command's airfields in the south of England had taken a pounding in the last few weeks of fighting. Although none had been rendered non – operational, given but a few more attacks they certainly would be; Fighter Command was on its knees. As soon as major fighter airfields ceased to remain operational control of the air would rapidly shift to the Luftwaffe, making an invasion possible. During the afternoon, Reichsmarschall Göring stood on the cliffs at Cap Blank Nez with his chiefs, watching huge formations of bombers. and fighters roar overhead bound for England. Following several night raids on Berlin by Bomber Command, Göring had broadcast to the Reich that he had now taken personal command of the Luftwaffe's air assault on England. As Fighter Command's controllers anxiously monitored the progress of the approaching enemy formation, which was easily the largest to have so far attacked England, Dowding assumed that the sector airfields were yet again the target. He knew that this huge attack could well deliver the telling blow. At 4.17 pm eleven squadrons scrambled and by 4.30 pm every squadron in the London area was airborne, twenty – one in total. East of Sheppey the defenders encountered the enemy, almost a thousand enemy aircraft flying in a formation stepped up one and a half miles high and occupying eight hundred square miles of sky. As the formation ponderously and deliberately flew along the Thames Estuary, without the usual separation into smaller groups each to attack a different target, it became obvious to Fighter Command that the airfields were to be spared: the target was London.

The British fighters were urgently vectored towards Thames Haven and Tilbury, and Londoners witnessed combat on a scale which had never before been seen in the history of aerial warfare. Through sheer weight of numbers the German force reached its target and huge fires were started in dockland and the East End, which pressed the fire fighters to the full. On "Black Saturday" the Duxford Wing were patrolling North Weald and were vectored towards the enemy. At 4.45 pm the wing was ordered south and, approaching its patrol line, about fifteen miles north of the Thames, anti – aircraft fire was sighted bursting around a formation of twenty bombers escorted by fifty fighters which were heading westwards at 15,000 feet. The eight Spitfires of No.19 Squadron, led by Squadron Leader Lane, were the last to attack the formation and were in a tactically poor position to do so, being 5,000 feet lower than the enemy. As the squadron desperately struggled to gain height, an Me110D of Stab II/ZG2, which was already being attacked by Flying Officer Holderness of No.1 Squadron and Pilot Officer Janough of No.310 Squadron, dived in front of the Spitfires. Squadron Leader Lane led "A" Flight in pursuit of the enemy machine and later reported:

"An Me 110 dived in front of me and I led "A" Flight after it. Two Hurricanes were also attacking it. I fired a short burst at it, the other aircraft attacking at the same time. The crew of two baled out, one parachute failing to open. The E/A crashed one mile east of Hornchurch and one of the crew landed nearby and was seen to be taken prisoner".

The Me110, "A2 + NH", crashed at Park Corner Farm, Hacton Lane, Hornchurch, at 5.10 pm. Actually the pilot, Leutnant Schunemann, who was also the Gruppe Technical Officer, baled out too low and was killed. His gunner, Unteroffizier Mescheder fell to his death at Franks Cottages, St Mary's Lane, Cranham, as his parachute failed.

After this engagement Squadron Leader Lane, Sergeant Jennings and Flight Lieutenant Lawson returned to base, being unable to re – locate the main combat.

After breaking away from "A" Flight's attack on Schunemann's aircraft, Pilot Officer Cunningham, Red 3, blacked out and lost the squadron. Recovering, he climbed in an easterly direction and saw a squadron of Hurricanes which he joined and flew south east with. At 5.20 pm over east Kent, south of Sheppey, a formation of twenty plus He111 bombers were sighted at 15,000 feet. The formation with which Cunningham now flew attacked the enemy in a front quarter attack, but the bombers turned east and the attack was therefore delivered from the rear. As Cunningham's Spitfire hurtled through the Heinkels he did not fire as the enemy formation broke up, but he subsequently singled out one machine and fired a burst of four or five seconds at it from astern. The Heinkel caught fire and started losing height. The Spitfire pilot attacked again from below. The bomber lost height rapidly thereafter and was last seen ten miles inland from Deal. Climbing again, Pilot Officer Cunningham attacked a solitary vic of three further Heinkels travelling eastwards. Selecting the leader as his target, he fired only to find after a short burst that his ammunition was expended.

Following the attack on the Me110, Flight Sergeant Unwin found himself and Spitfire P9546 down to 4,000 feet and he had also lost the rest of No.19 Squadron. Climbing to 25,000 feet he saw a Hurricane squadron "going somewhere in a hurry" and followed them. Suddenly three separate formations of about thirty aircraft each, with escorts of a similar number, appeared. The Hurricanes attacked the bombers and "Grumpy" found himself surrounded by Me109s. Fighting a running battle high in the sky between Ramsgate and west London, he decided that attack was the best form of defence:

> "The usual fight ensued during which I definitely hit at least five of them but only two were definitely shot down, both in flames. I then climbed for a breather and shadowed the third enemy formation when I saw yet a fourth arriving. By this time two of the other three formations had turned north and the other went straight on in a north westerly direction. The leading formation turned east and I was at 25,000' and above them. As there did not seem to be any of their escorts left, I dived on the rear vic of the bombers and gave them the rest of my ammunition, about fifty rounds in each gun, and at about 450 to 50 yards range. The aircraft wobbled but carried on and I returned home."

Pilot Officer Dolezal had also become detached from the squadron and, joining with another unit, attacked and shot down an Me110 which he saw crash into the sea off Margate. By the time Flight Lieutenant Clouston's "B" Flight had climbed to the height of the raiders they were out of range. Clouston and Flight Sergeant Steere returned to Fowlmere with the fabric covering over their gun ports intact.

All of No.19 Squadron's Spitfires returned to G1 without loss, but both Nos.242 and 310 Squadrons had been bounced by the German fighter escort as they climbed to attack the bombers. Bader himself had been shot up and his Hurricane, P3061, was badly damaged. Sub – Lieutenant Dickie Cork, also of No.242 Squadron, was slightly injured, but the pilots were to wait in vain for the return of Pilot Officer Benzie. The Czechs had lost two aircraft: V7437, which Sergeant Koukal had managed to abandon although he was grievously burned, and V6643, which Pilot Officer Goth force landed at Whitman's Farm following combat over Southend. Although the Duxford Wing had claimed the destruction of eleven enemy machines in total, for Squadron Leader Bader the Wing's first meeting with the enemy was a disappointment. The wing had been called upon too late by the 11 Group controllers and were, therefore, unable to attack from a favourable position. Caught by the fighter escort on the climb, Bader later wrote "it was windy work, let there be no mistake."

As a result of the raid on the capital, 1,800 Londoners were killed or seriously injured. As the fires in London illuminated the night sky, the Luftwaffe continued to rain down bombs in a nocturnal attack which lasted from 8.10 pm to 4.30 am the following morning. The Blitz had begun. The resiliant inhabitants of the capital proclaimed "London can take it", and won the admiration of the free world. For Fighter Command Göring's tactical blunder was a miracle. Keith Park later wrote

"It was burning all down the river. It was a horrid sight. But I looked down and said: "Thank God for that", because I knew that the Nazis had switched their attack from our fighter stations thinking they were knocked out. They weren't, but they were pretty groggy."

In the fighting on "Black Saturday" Fighter Command had lost a further twenty eight aircraft. The raid on London cost the Luftwaffe forty.

During Monday September 9th, the next action in which the Duxford Wing took part, one main attack took place on London during the early evening when three hundred German aircraft crossed the coast between North Foreland and Dover. At 6 pm the wing was again patrolling North Weald and sighted a large formation of 130 plus enemy bombers and fighters flying north west. The squadron, being led by Flight Lieutenant Clouston, was put into line astern and climbed to 23,000 feet preparatory to an attack on seven Me110s which were also climbing in a similar formation. As the Spitfires were about to attack, two Me109s cut across in front of them. Clouston opened fire on the enemy fighters, the first bursting into flames and the second gliding down in "apparent distress." Having used all his ammunition in this attack Clouston returned to Fowlmere, but the squadron, still in line astern, went on to attack their intended target. Pilot Officer Burgoyne, as Blue 2, remained with Blue Leader, Flight Lieutenant Clouston, and did not take part in the main attack, firing only a short opportune burst at a passing Me 109 which Clouston reported as having seen "in a spiral dive, apparently out of control." Blue 3, Flight Sergeant Harry Steere, claimed an Me 110 as "highly probable":

> "I was line astern and, cutting across in front of Blue Leader and Blue 3, I closed with an Me 110 which was in line astern with six others. I closed, giving a full deflection shot, and saw my tracers going home. I closed to within fifty yards and was forced to break underneath him — he was slipping inwards in a very peculiar attitude. I then came round again and chased another 110 half way across the Channel, but was unable to catch him. I turned around when the guns on the French coast looked uncomfortably close."

Steere's first victim was confirmed by Flight Lieutenant Clouston who added to the combat report that he had seen the 110 go down in a "left hand spiral which appeared to be completely out of control."

Flight Lieutenant Lawson claimed an Me 110 destroyed:

> "I sighted an Me 110 to my starboard and approximately 2,000' below me. I turned to starboard and dived onto his tail, getting in a short burst at 300 yards. Then ensued a really enjoyable dogfight which ended by my hitting his starboard engine causing it to stop. He then started losing height and pieces fell away from his starboard wing. He continued to go down in a slow spiral turn and when at about 500' two Hurricanes and a Spitfire followed him. He finally crashed in a field five miles east of Biggin Hill."

Sub-Lieutenant "Admiral" Blake followed the main formation out to sea and attacked a straggling Heinkel. As he broke away the bomber was in flames and sinking inexorably towards the sea. Blake's life was saved by his armoured windscreen which stopped a bullet from the Heinkel's rear gunner. [1]

Pilot Officer Cunningham, having broken formation to chase the fleeting Me 110s, latched onto the tail of an Me 109:

> "I found a stray Me 109 with a yellow nose passing to the right and in front of me. I took up position on his tail and fired two very long bursts until he was flaming and some parts of his engine flew out. I broke off the attack as it was evident that the aircraft was destroyed. As long as I had him under observation the pilot made no attempt to jump. My Spitfire received a bullet hole in the port mainspar."

Flying Officer Frank Brinsden attacked two Me 109s with a deflection shot but observed no result. He then spotted two

---

[1]   This is now in the Battle of Britain Museum, Hendon.

Hurricanes attacking an He111 and joined in, making several attacks from dead astern until his ammunition was exhausted. By that time the Heinkel was down to just 1,000 feet with both engines stopped and flaps and undercarriage lowered. When Brinsden last saw the bomber it was gliding down in an easterly direction to make a forced landing south of Detling.

Opening his "score" as a fighter pilot was Pilot Officer Arthur Vokes, who had joined No.19 Squadron on June 23rd, fresh from an Operational Training Unit:

"I was Number Two in Yellow Section, led by Flying Officer Brinsden, climbing to attack Me 109s. I saw six Do 215s below and dived down on the nearest one. He was flying south and by the time I attacked him was separated from the others with his wheels down. I fired all my ammunition into him and saw bits coming off. Just before breaking away I experienced a heavy bump from below which I think was AA fire. Subsequently another Spitfire attacked the Dornier so I returned home as my ammunition had run out."

Sergeant David Cox shot down an Me109 in flames during a dogfight, but his Spitfire was hit in both the wings and airscrew.

Apart from the minor damage caused to machines flown by Cunningham, Cox, Vokes and Blake, No.19 Squadron had acquitted itself well against the enemy. The pilots claimed seven enemy aircraft destroyed, one probably destroyed, and one damaged. Bader's No.242 Squadron claimed eleven destroyed, but had lost Sergeant Sclanders who had been killed. No.310 Squadron had done less well, but two of their three "missing" pilots later turned up. Pilot Officer Rypl crash landed, and Flight Lieutenant Gordon Sinclair and fellow Englishman, Flying Officer John Boulton, had collided over Croydon. In the biggest mid – air collision of the Battle of Britain the two Hurricanes and an Me110 from 9/ZG76 fell from the sky over Woodmanstern, Surrey, and crashed to the ground within a few hundred yards of each other. Sinclair baled out, but Boulton was killed when his machine crashed. From the Me110 Leutnant Ostermüncher fell without his parachute opening and his gunner, Gefreiter Zimmermann, was found dead in the burnt out wreckage. In total the wing had claimed twenty enemy aircraft destroyed for the loss of four Hurricanes. The statistics were looking good, and in the summer of 1940 loss statistics were of great importance. Squadron Leader Bader spoke again ·with Air Vice – Marshal Leigh – Mallory, requesting that even more fighters be absorbed into his "Big Wing".

Two days later (September 11th) the Luftwaffe launched a single major attack in the late afternoon. Two hundred and fifty aircraft crossed the Kent coast and of these about thirty raiders reached London. Flying his usual aircraft, P9386 "QV – K", Squadron Leader Lane was leading an all Spitfire wing over London. It consisted of

Nos.19, 611 and 74 Squadrons. Having sighted anti–aircraft shell bursts south of Gravesend at 4.15 pm, Squadron Leader Lane observed a large formation of enemy bombers and fighters flying north at 20,000 feet. He recorded the following notes in his log book:

> "Party over London, 19 leading 611 and 74 Squadrons. Sighted a big bunch of Huns south of the river and got in a lovely head on attack into leading Heinkels. We broke them up and picked on a small bunch of six with two Me 110s as escort. I found myself entirely alone with these lads so proceeded to have a bit of sport. Got one of the Me 110s on fire, whereupon another left his charges and ran for home! Played with He 111s for a bit and finally got one in both engines. Never had so much fun before."

Sergeant Jennings, flying Spitfire P9391, singled out a Heinkel during the wing's head on attack. Seeing the bomber's starboard engine burning he attacked again. The enemy machine went down out of control, but as "so much tracer was whizzing past I was unable to stay and watch him crash." Jennings then spotted a formation of fifteen Me110s of 9/ZG26. The rearmost machine, "3U + LT", was flown by Oberleutnant Junghans. This aircraft Jennings attacked next:

> "This one fell back from the rest of the formation with smoke pouring out of his starboard engine. I did another attack from above and behind and he crashed in a wood, south of the Ashford railway line between Sittingbourne and Maidstone. I didn't see anyone jump by parachute. I then chased eleven Me 110s out to sea, finished my rounds without any visible result, and returned home."

The Messerschmitt 110 shot down by Jennings crashed at Barnes Cote, Harvel. Both crewmen were killed, the gunner, Gefriete Paul Eckert, remains listed as "missing" to this day.

Other No.19 Squadron pilots were also successful. Flight Lieutenant Lawson claimed an He111 destroyed, Sergeant Roden and Flying Officer Haines an Me110 each, Sergeant Cox a probable Do215 and Pilot Officer Dolezal an Me109. Flight Sergeant Unwin claimed an He111 probably destroyed, and a Do215 as damaged:

> "I was Red Four with Squadron Leader Lane. I sighted a large enemy formation on our starboard side and below. We attacked in line astern. I attacked an He 111 and fired a 7 – 8 second burst at fifty yards range. Bits came off both engines and the aircraft went into a steep spiral. I did not see him crash as I immediately attacked a Do 215. I opened fire from below at one hundred yards closing to fifty. I fired all my rounds into him but did not see any result owing to the fact that my windscreen and engine were shot up by fire from his bottom gunner. My engine was running badly as I dived away and was pouring out glycol smoke. I switched off and forced landed with my wheels down. No damage was caused to my aircraft during landing, the site of which being one mile north of Brentwood, near searchlight site EC 11."

George Unwin recalls:

"I attacked a Dornier over London in P9546 and was stupid enough to be shot down by the gunner they carried in the dustbin below the fuselage. I landed in a field near Brentwood in Essex and was taken to RAF North Weald by the army. With the aid of a fitter plus spares "QV – H" was repaired and I flew it back to Duxford on September 13th. One bullet had penetrated the bullet proof windscreen; as this could not be repaired on the station P9546 was flown away to a Maintenance Unit."

In the desperate days of 1940 when both aircraft and pilots were commodities in desperately short supply, Flight Sergeant Unwin's handling of his damaged Spitfire was highly commended. The squadron diary recorded that he had made a "wizard forced landing with undercarriage down!!!"

Two other No.19 Squadron Spitfires were damaged in the combat, N3046, in which Pilot Officer Dolezal returned to Fowlmere slightly wounded in the leg, and X4059 which Flying Officer Haines crashed on landing due to bullets having punctured both tyres. Sergeant Shepherd of No.611 Squadron abandoned his Spitfire Mk II, P7298, over Croydon. This subsequently crashed into Nos.49 and 51 Hartland Way, Shirley. Tragically, blazing fuel from the crashed machine poured into an Anderson shelter in the garden and killed two people sheltering there. The pilot, whose parachute was in flames, fell dead at Court Wood Lane. Sergeant Sandy Levenson's Spitfire, P7321, was severely damaged by a Heinkel's return fire and crashed at Pendall Court, Bletchingley. Fortunately Levenson, who was later to lose his life in action flying a Stirling bomber, was unhurt. No 74 Squadron suffered no casualties.

The following day No.19 Squadron received eight replacement Spitfires, all Mk IIs and badly needed as were the three new operational pilots who reported the same day. These were Sergeants Lloyd and Charnock, and Pilot Officer Jones.

The afternoon of Saturday, September 14th, saw Flight Lieutenant Clouston leading No.19 Squadron over the London area in a now common wing patrol. No enemy aircraft were sighted, but the Czech Sergeant Marek inexplicably dived out of formation and crashed near Hordon – on – the – Hill, Orsett, and was killed. The cause of the accident is believed to have been a black out due to an oxygen system failure. The unfortunate pilot had called Pilot Officer Hradil, the only other pilot in the formation with a VHF radio set, and told his fellow countryman that he had no oxygen.

Later the same day the Wing patrolled again over Kent and the Channel, almost as far as France, but still did not contact the enemy. The squadron diarist records "the enemy saving up for "Der Tag" evidently". How right he was for "Der Tag" was to come the following day, Sunday, September 15th. So intense and decisive was the fighting that this day is now recognised as the climax to the Battle of Britain and celebrated each year as "Battle of Britain Day".

Dawn on the great day found most of southern England shrouded in grey mist, but as the sun climbed higher the mist rapidly evaporated. By 8 am visibility was excellent. The fine weather heralded the onslaught which Fighter Command was anticipating. Before 11 am German reconnaissance aircraft probed the Straits of Dover and the east coast of Kent. From first light onwards standing patrols of Spitfires and Hurricanes had been up over the coast from Harwich to Land's End. Each sector station kept one squadron at readiness to take off at a moment's notice. At 10.50 am the British radar stations reported an enemy formation massing south – east of Boulogne and five minutes later all of 11 Group's squadrons were at readiness. At 11.33 am an enemy formation crossed the coast between Dover and Folkestone, being followed three minutes later by two further hostile formations which crossed the coast between Dover and South Foreland. The enemy flew a zig – zag course and their progress was being plotted and monitered by the Observer Corps. First they flew in a northerly direction, but all formations turned south before reaching the north coast of Kent. The raiders then flew westwards towards Maidstone and upon reaching this the enemy spread out to make for London. The selected targets were the gasworks and other industrial locations. To meet this attack twenty of Park's squadrons were in the air and were reinforced at mid – day by the Duxford Wing, which now comprised two Spitfire and three Hurricane squadrons. Squadron Leader Bader and his formation were instructed to patrol the Canterbury – Gravesend area to intercept a group of raiders before they reached London. The air over east Kent and London was now a colossal battlefield with fighters and bombers locked in mortal combat. As Big Ben struck noon, the wing attacked a force of Do17s escorted by Me109s over London.

Twenty – four Do17s of KG76 were at 16,000 feet over Brixton at 12.09 pm. One of the Dorniers, "F1 + DT", was flown by Feldwebel Wilhelm Raab, a veteran of the campaigns in Poland and France as well as a number of sorties over England. Raab's bomber was attacked by British fighter pilots including Sergeant Tyrer of No.46 Squadron, Flight Lieutenant Rimmer of No.229 Squadron, and Flight Lieutenant Brothers together with Pilot Officer Mortimer of No.257 Squadron. As the Dornier dived and made a dash for some cloud cover the Hurricanes of Flight Lieutenant Powell – Sheddon and Pilot Officer Tamblyn of Bader's No.242 Squadron attacked. Squadron Leader Lane saw the Dornier and fired at its starboard engine, unaware of the attack being delivered by the two Hurricane pilots. Seeing the other fighters, Lane realised that he had "jumped the queue". Following the Hurricanes he took his turn to fire, but was unable to tell whether hits on Raab's aircraft were caused by his own fire or that of Powell – Sheddon or Tamblyn. Raab reached the protective billowing cumulus cloud, but his aircraft was seriously damaged and the rear gunner had been killed. Descending at about 100 feet per minute the Dornier slid out of the bottom of the cloud. Immediately British fighters attacked once more. As bullets ripped into the stricken aircraft the aileron and elevator wires were severed. Raab ordered his crew to bail out and after they had tumbled into space he followed them. He was captured and spent the rest of the war in captivity. At 12.30pm Brian Lane saw the pilotless Dornier narrowly miss a house and explode on impact at Under River, south of Sevenoaks in Kent.

The Dorniers of KG76 suffered at the hands of Fighter Command, six of them being shot down and crashing on English soil. One of these, possibly the most famous German casualty of the Battle of Britain, had been attacked by numerous fighters before breaking up and crashing on the forecourt of Victoria station. By this time, as a result of the London bombing, feelings were running very high amongst the civilian population and when the Dornier's wounded pilot, Oberleutnant Zehbe, landed by parachute at Kennington he was roughly handled by a civilian mob.

Flight Lieutenant Lawson probably destroyed a Dornier, and Sub – Lieutenant Blake damaged another. Other No.19 Squadron pilots fought KG76's fighter escort, amongst which were the Me109E's of 3/JG53. At 12.10 pm, near Westerham, Kent, Flight Sergeant Unwin engaged JG53's Staffel Kapitän, Oberleutnant Haase, in a dogfight:

"I was Red Three with Flight Lieutenant Lawson. We sighted the enemy aircraft which were flying in vics of three. The escorts dived singly onto us and I engaged an Me 109 with a yellow nose. I gave one burst of six seconds and it burst into flames. The pilot baled out and the enemy aircraft crashed between Redhill and Westerham."

Haase's aircraft crashed at Mullard Wood near Biggin Hill. The pilot was killed as his parachute failed to open.

As the Messerschmitts dived on No.19 Squadron, Sergeant David Cox climbed and flew south. A few minutes later he found six Me109s of 2/JG27 flying in the same direction. Simultaneously the Germans saw the Spitfire and Green 3 attacked. Getting on the tail of one Messerschmitt, Cox's target immediately half – rolled and dived away. Four of the fighters then broke off and continued south, no doubt running low on fuel, but Green 3 then found the sixth machine attacking him head – on. Cox's assailant, Unteroffizier Walburger, pulled up and roared above the Spitfire. Cox climbed

and turned sharply, coming up underneath Walburger, and opened
fire. The Messerschmitt then commenced a flat glide which
developed into a steep dive. Sergeant Cox followed his victim
through cloud and when he emerged he could see a fire below
which was the wreckage of Walburger's fighter. The aircraft had
crashed at Lodge Wood near Uckfield, and the pilot was captured
unhurt.

Such was the ferocity of Fighter Command's attack on the
raiders that the hundred Dorniers of the main formation were
broken up before their targets were reached. The enemy
subsequently bombed at random across southern England. Two
bombs fell on Buckingham Palace and now it could be shown that
the King and Queen were in the fight alongside the commoners of
the East End. Bombs also fell at Crystal Palace, Clapham Common,
Anerley, Norbury, Upper Tooting, Wandsworth, Thornton Heath,
Battersea and Chelsea.

Back at Fowlmere, the returning No.19 Squadron pilots
completed their combat reports. Further to the individual combats
previously described, Pilot Officer Cunningham shared the
destruction of an Me110, Flight Lieutenant Clouston destroyed
another, Flying Officer Haines destroyed an Me109, and Flight
Sergeant Steere claimed one as probably destroyed. The wing had
done well. The only casualty was Flight Lieutenant Eric Ball from
No.242, who had been shot down but was safe. With the Luftwaffe
chiefs insisting to their aircrews that Fighter Command was down to
its "last fifty Spitfires", the sight of the Duxford Wing joining the
combat over London must surely have seriously affected the enemy's
moral. The battle had already embroiled twenty 11 Group squadrons
and one from 10 Group when the wing joined combat. At last
Fighter Command engaged the enemy in numbers capable of
inflicting substantial losses. Visiting the 11 Group operations room
at Uxbridge, the Prime Minister had enquired of Air Vice – Marshal
Park the number of fighters held back in reserve; Park replied that
there were none.

The first mass attack had hardly been dispersed before the radar
screens indicated further enemy formations assembling in the Pas de
Calais. Between 2.10 and 2.34 pm eight or more formations of
German bombers and their escort crossed the English coastline
between Rye and Dover heading for London. If the numbers of the
British fighters engaged in the morning's fighting caused anxiety to
the Luftwaffe airmen then the thirty – one squadrons in action that
afternoon would cause more serious consternation amongst their
number. Unfortunately the Duxford Wing was once more scrambled
too late. Squadron Leader Bader led his five squadrons of fighters
through a gap in the cloud over London and saw the enemy, about

forty aircraft, but they were at least 4,000 feet above the Wing. With throttles wide open the little fighters struggled to obtain height before engaging the enemy, but whilst on the climb the Me109 fighter escort plunged like an angry swarm onto the Hurricanes and Spitfires. "Break up!" Bader yelled, the Wing scattered, and the sky immediately became an arena of fighting, cutting, thrusting aircraft. Squadron Leader Lane was leading No.19 Squadron and wrote in his log book:

"Party. 242 leading Wing. Ran into the whole Luftwaffe over London. Wave after wave of bombers covered by several hundred fighters. Waded into escort as per arrangement and picked out a 109. Had one hell of a dogfight and finally he went into a cloud inverted and obviously crashed as he appeared out of control."

His combat report provides greater detail:

"I was leading 19 Squadron on Wing patrol. At approximately 1440 hrs AA fire was sighted to the south and at the same time a formation of about thirty Do 215s was seen. I climbed up astern of the enemy aircraft to engage the fighter escort which could be seen above the bombers at about 30,000'. Three Me 109s dived on our formation and I turned to starboard. A loose dogfight ensued with more Me 109s coming down. I could not get near to any enemy aircraft so I climbed up and engaged a formation of Me 110s without result. I then sighted ten Me 109s just above me and I attacked one of them. I got on his tail and fired several bursts of about two seconds. The enemy aircraft was taking violent evasive action and made for cloud level. I managed to get in another burst of about five seconds before it flicked over inverted and entered cloud in a shallow dive, apparently out of control. I then flew south and attacked two further formations of about thirty Do 215s from astern and head on. The enemy aircraft did not appear to like head on attack as they jumped about a bit as I passed through. I observed no result from these attacks. Fire from rear of the enemy aircraft was opened at 1,000 yards. Me 110s opened fire at similar range and appeared to have no idea of deflection shooting."

Flight Sergeant Unwin was again flying as Red 3 in Squadron Leader Lane's section. He sighted "thousands of 109s" and when the Wing was bounced George singled out one enemy machine and delivered a three second burst at close range. The target half rolled and dived steeply into the clouds pursued by Spitfire X4179. At 6,000 feet Unwin lost his prey when his windscreen froze up. Climbing to 25,000 feet a "Rotte" of two further Me109s appeared above him, flying in a southerly direction. He gave chase and caught both at Lydd. The first one he fired at burst into flames and went down vertically. Seconds later the other Messerschmitt caught fire and crashed in the sea.

As the Messerschmitts rained down on No.19 Squadron, Flying Officer Alan Haines picked out an enemy fighter of 3/LG2 flown by Unteroffizier Klick. As a result of Haines's attack the enemy

153

aircraft's radiator was badly damaged. Klick turned his aircraft for home, but he crash landed and was taken prisoner at Shellness at 2.45 pm. Haines later successfully engaged an Me110 and claimed both of these machines as destroyed.

In his combat report, Sub – Lieutenant Blake noted the number of enemy aircraft engaged over London as "innumerable". Blake dived on a group of six Dorniers which had become detached from the main formation. As he singled out his target the "Admiral" noticed some Me109s above him. He attacked one of them with two bursts of fire, the second of which found the mark and the enemy aircraft burst into flames. Blake then found a stray He111 of 1/KG26 which was also being attacked by Squadron Leader Eric McNab of No.1 Squadron (RCAF), Pilot Officer Baker of No.91 Squadron, Pilot Officers Mortimer and Cochrane of No.257 Squadron, and Sergeant Prchal of No.310. Blake was only able to deliver one brief attack on the bomber as his Spitfire, R6991, had been hit and was smoking badly. Blake left the Heinkel to its fate and headed for Rochford Airfield where he made a safe forced landing. Upon terra firma he was informed that the Heinkel had crashed in the mud off the Thames Estuary. The bomber had force landed below the high water mark at Alspens Head, Foulness, at 3 pm. The crew were all taken prisoner.

"B" Flight of No.19 Squadron managed to engage six Dornier 17s, one of which was claimed as destroyed by Flight Lieutenant Clouston. Pilot Officer Vokes and Flight Sergeant Steere chased one of the Dorniers which was destroyed by Steere, who also described in his combat report that the number of enemy aircraft engaged were "Countless":

"I was Blue 2 and we were in the rear of the Wing formation. The fight was developing as we approached. Six Do 17s approached about 3,000' below and to the left, having apparently broken through the combat. I followed Blue 1 into the attack and singled out one on the right. I closed from 350 to 50 yards, giving several bursts. Several lumps flew off it and the port engine caught fire – the crew baled out and the Do 17 waffled into the clouds, black smoke spreading rapidly. Three bombs were jettisoned before the aircraft was abandoned. This was all seen by Plt. Off. Vokes who was coming up in the rear."

Having witnessed Steere shooting down the Dornier, Vokes returned to the mêlée of twisting, turning and diving aircraft. He later reported:

"I climbed up into the fray again and was surprised by an Me 110 from astern. Tracer flashed past the starboard wing, one bullet going through the mainspar. I climbed steeply and after two or three turns ended up on his tail. I gave him everything I had, closing from 200 to 50 yards range. His starboard engine was streaming black smoke and he dived steeply until by the time he reached the cloud he seemed out of control."

Sergeant Roden's Spitfire, P9431, was hit in the glycol tank during combat with the Me109s. Roden crash landed back at Fowlmere and was slightly injured. One No.19 Squadron pilot who would not return to Fowlmere that day was Sergeant Jack Potter. Presumably having pursued an enemy aircraft across the Channel towards France, he was shot down in Spitfire X4070. Wounded, and with his aircraft seriously damaged, Potter ditched in the sea near to the French coastline and was taken prisoner of war.

As the tattered remnants of the Luftwaffe force retreated south, harried constantly by Fighter Command, fires were burning in Woolwich, Barking, Stepney, Stratford Gasworks, West Ham, Penge and at a petrol depot at West Ham Park.

With the threat to London now over, 27 Heinkels attacking Portland were dealt with by six Spitfires. Later six squadrons and accurate anti-aircraft fire frustrated an intended raid on the Spitfire factory at Woolston by Me110s of a precision bombing unit. The thwarted raid marked an end to the day fighting on September 15th.

Fighter Command had claimed the destruction of 185 enemy machines, of which the Duxford Wing claimed 52 destroyed and 8 probables. The No.19 Squadron tally was twelve destroyed, four probables, one damaged, and three shared. Post war research has indicated the actual figure of German aircraft destroyed to be nearer fifty eight, with a further twenty three returning to base with dead or wounded crew members and bearing the scars of combat damage. Against this number Fighter Command lost twenty eight aircraft destroyed. When the figures were released to the public they were a tremendous morale booster. Few in England now doubted that the tide of battle had turned in favour of the hard pressed and exhausted defenders.

With summer passing into autumn, and because Göring's arrogant boasts of conquering England by aerial attack had not been realised, the German High Command had to make an urgent decision regarding the future of Operation Sealion. On Tuesday, September 17th, British Intelligence intercepted a German signal ordering the dispersal of invasion facilities; Hitler had postponed the proposed invasion of Great Britain indefinitely.

On the same day, No.19 Squadron patrolled London with the wing, but no enemy formations were encountered. The squadron diary reports that "Flight Sergeant Unwin was today awarded the DFM. Good Show! Ten Huns to his credit."

The following day (September 18th) the Luftwaffe launched three major assaults on London and its environs. Fighter Command's performance on September 15th may well have shown the Germans that Britain was far from beaten, but the daylight attacks were to continue for some days yet. The enemy were now pursuing a new tactic – a smaller number of bombers protected by many fighters. However, at 4.30 pm the Duxford Wing was scrambled to patrol Hornchurch at 20,000 feet. Bader climbed his fighters above the cloud layer at that altitude and seeing anti – aircraft shells bursting above the cloud he led Nos.242, 310, 302 and 19 Squadrons below. Sensibly, the Spitfires of No.611 Squadron were left as top cover above the cloud layer. The wing subsequently sighted two formations of enemy aircraft, about forty in all, flying along the Thames near Gravesend. It was what Bader had been waiting for – the number of British fighters outnumbered the enemy. As Bader's pack of fighters pounced on the enemy bombers, the Ju88s of Stab III/KG77, who were without fighter escort, were broken up. Red Section of No.19 Squadron, consisting of Flight Lieutenant Lawson, Pilot Officer Cunningham and Sergeant Lloyd, attacked the Ju88 of Major Klehs, the Gruppen Kommandeur, and promptly shot it down. The Junkers, "3Z + ED", crashed at Eastry Mill, near Sandwich. Klehs and Oberleutnant Lauth were killed, but Feldwebel Himsel and Feldwebel Pröbst baled out and were captured. In the attack, Lawson's Spitfire, X4170, was hit in the glycol tank. His aircraft streaming white smoke, Lawson executed a hasty forced landing at Eastchurch airfield on the Isle of Sheppey. Flight Sergeant Steere attacked an He111, which was already receiving the attention of other British fighters:

"I was Blue 2 and we closed with the bombers. I saw four Heinkels below and slightly ahead. I dived and closed with one; another fighter then broke over him on completing a beam attack. I closed with the bomber and he disappeared through the clouds after I had fired a burst of about 5 secs. I followed through the clouds and saw him hit the water and sink at the mouth of the Thames. I climbed through the clouds in a southerly direction and saw a Ju 88 streaking down. I closed with it and gave a burst of 2 or 3 seconds at about 30 degrees deflection. His starboard engine burst into flames and he disappeared vertically through the clouds. I saw two or three Spitfires above me and they had evidently had an attack at the E/A. Flg. Off. Haines was one of the Spitfires and had fired a burst at it. E/A would crash near the south coast of the Thames, probably close to the Isle of Sheppey."

With both engines ablaze the Ju88 had crashed at Mocketts Farm on the Isle of Sheppey. Feldwebel Damshen was killed, Oberfeldwebel Semerau and Unteroffizier Treutmann were reported missing, and Unteroffizier Eggert baled out and was captured. Badly wounded he died in the Royal Naval hospital at Chatham six days later. Sergeant Plzak also attacked a Ju88, "3Z + DT", which crashed with both engines on fire, breaking up on impact at Cooling Court, Cooling. Unteroffiziers Burkant and Glaeseker both baled out and were captured unhurt. The two other crew men, Unteroffizier Kurz and Gefreiterr Kuhn were killed. Flying Officer Haines claimed to have probably destroyed an Me109, Pilot Officer Dolezal claimed an He111 destroyed, and Flight Sergeant Unwin an Me110.

Back at Duxford and Fowlmere the wing pilots were jubilant. Without casualties the wing squadrons had claimed the destruction of around thirty enemy machines, six probables and two damaged. In reality the Luftwaffe lost only eighteen aircraft altogether in action over England that day. The problem of over claiming was understandable for in the confusion of battle, with events happening so quickly, a pilot would attack, note the result, and make a claim accordingly. However, possibly unknown to him, other pilots may have been attacking the same target simultaneously, and would also make individual claims. This situation was no doubt more pronounced with the numbers of British fighters in action that day against KG77. Furthermore, the German loss records, which are remarkably accurate, do not detail the loss of any He111s or Me110s on this day. It can only be assumed that, in the heat of the moment, the No.19 Squadron pilots claiming to have engaged those types must have wrongly identified their victims. Certainly in reports submitted by Fighter Command pilots combat with Heinkel 113s was often mentioned. It is now known that this type was never used in action.

However, the claims made in good faith by the wing were accepted and were a morale booster. Bader's adjutant, Peter MacDonald, happened to be a Member of Parliament and through his connections managed to speak to Churchill regarding the "Big Wing" theory and the essence of scrambling the wing in good time. The claims of September 18th certainly made the people who mattered sit up and take note. Not all the wing's pilots were happy with Bader's tactics, as Frank Brinsden recalls:

"I often felt a bit cheated in the Battle of Britain in so much as, for various reasons, I was late off the ground and too late to take part in whatever was going on, or having a day off when the squadron got into combat, or arrived with the squadron over the battle zone to find all had gone home. I put this down to the tactics of our 12 Group commander and the ponderous progression of the Bader Wing. Our traditional vics of three aircraft proved too restrictive, but when these eventually gave way to the more nippy finger four formations we had a new found efficiency and independence. Then the constraints of Bader's mass formation. Disaster, in my opinion, a retrograde step. Nothing was achieved by arriving en masse because the wing disintegrated almost immediately battle was joined. In fact time, and therefore advantage, was lost during assembly and this compounded the effects of belated scramble orders. These observations on tactics are, of course, in retrospect but I do recall at the time feeling some unease or dissatisfaction at No.19 Squadron's inability to do better."

However, ask any pilot who flew with the wing and invariably you will receive a different answer; David Cox:

"It is possible that a number of actions during which 19 Squadron was at a height disadvantage could have been more successful had 11 Group given us earlier information. I have always been of the opinion that 11 Group tried to hog the Battle of Britain. At the same time I think that Bader's Wing of five squadrons took too long to form up. Three squadrons was quite enough."

George Unwin makes some interesting observations:

"Quite simply the wing was a huge success from our point of view at Duxford in that not only did we destroy more enemy aircraft, but the casualties amongst the three Hurricane squadrons were greatly reduced. From a morale point of view the wing was important for its effect on the enemy who had been told that Fighter Command was licked. On the other hand, large wings of five squadrons were out of the question when operating from the aerodromes around London. You just could not get them in position in time to intercept. We at Duxford and Fowlmere, only three miles apart, had forty – fifty miles to cover before arriving over the London area and this was sufficient for us to form up. I have always thought that the so called row between the 11 and 12 Group commanders was pointless. They were both right in the given circumstances under which they were operating, which were totally different, 11 Group being unable to operate wings due to being too close to the battle area, and 12 Group able to form up beforehand and arrive in the combat area en masse."

No.616 "South Yorkshire" Squadron had already been in action earlier in the Battle of Britain whilst flying as one of Park's 11 Group squadrons. The unit suffered heavy casualties. On one sortie on August 26th the squadron had been attacked by the Me109s of JG51 over Dungeness. No.616 Squadron lost seven Spitfires, two pilots were killed and two were wounded. A few days later No.616 Squadron was pulled out of the line, but on September 18th, whilst based at Kirton – in – Lindsey, Squadron Leader Billy Burton announced that his squadron was once more operational. As from the next day No.616 Squadron was to fly daily to Fowlmere and be included as the sixth squadron in the Bader Wing.

The next few days saw the wing patrolling the London area, but with nothing to report. On September 22nd Red Section were on patrol over Duxford and missed a Do17 which popped out of cloud and bombed Fowlmere. Ten bombs were dropped on "B" Flight's dispersal and one Spitfire, X4351, was destroyed. Red Section arrived and chased the Dornier back into cloud, but lost it in the all enveloping mists.

At 6.15 pm on September 23rd, the wing again patrolled without event. As the other wing squadrons returned to base, Squadron Leader Lane continued on patrol over Duxford with No.19 Squadron to protect the landing fighters against a similar attack to that suffered the previous day. One enemy aircraft was sighted very high up which promptly dived flat out in a south easterly direction. The aircraft was thought to be an Me109 on reconnaissance duties. The same day saw the awards of DFCs to both Flying Officer Haines and Pilot Officer Cunningham, both now "aces".

Further uneventful patrols were carried out during the next three days. On September 25th, No.19 Squadron had received a number of new Spitfire Mk II fighters with Dowty Rotol Constant Speed airscrews, Koffman cartridge engine starters, and a more powerful Merlin engine than was fitted to the Mk Ia.

Friday, September 27th, was again to be a day of heavy fighting. Throughout the day Generalfeldmarschall Kesselring launched three major attacks on London and the south – east, with a lesser raid on Filton. The first raid consisted of one hundred fighters and eighty bombers, but Fighter Command halted the enemy's progress over the Maidstone and Tunbridge area, although some raiders did reach London. The second raid crossed the coast between Dover and Lympne at 12 pm, and consisted of three hundred aircraft, the majority of which were fighters. Fighter Command engaged over Kent and East Sussex and the enemy were turned back. As from 11.45 that morning, No.19 Squadron had been on patrol over the London area and at about 12.15 pm intercepted a formation of some twenty bombers and "innumerable" fighters over Canterbury. As Squadron Leader Lane's take off had been delayed, Flight Lieutenant Lawson led the squadron into an attack on the Me109s. At this point a further formation of Messerschmitts pounced on the squadron from above. Squadron Leader Lane had by this time joined the wing and attempted to thwart the second German formation's attack on his comrades. After firing two short bursts his Spitfire became uncontrollable. As he skidded away, desperately struggling to bring his mount under control and contemplating taking to his parachute, he had to use all his strength on the aircraft's "stick" to level out at 3,000 feet. The offending Spitfire, one of the squadron's new Mk IIs, was found to have a misshaped rudder and a wrongly adjusted trim tab which prevented one elevator functioning correctly. After his exertions, and due to his low height, Lane was no longer in a position to continue with the fight and returned to Fowlmere.

South of the Thames Estuary the remainder of No.19 Squadron set about the German fighters. Sergeant Jennings, in his usual Spitfire, X4474, "QV – I", submitted the following combat report:

> "I was Yellow Two in Luton Squadron. We attacked a large formation of yellow nosed Me 109s, our height being practically the same, at 20,000'. I attacked the leading Me 109 of a section of five. I fired one burst, saw him

turn to starboard with white smoke coming from his engine. I followed him down and saw thick black smoke coming from the engine in place of the previous white smoke. I couldn't see the flames owing to the density of the black smoke. As I followed him down I saw tracers pouring past me, and found the other four Me 109s in line astern coming down after me. I turned to starboard and dived away. I pulled up and saw a Spitfire or Hurricane in flames, spinning down. The pilot jumped and I followed him down to the ground. He landed OK, in a clearing near a big wood."

Flight Sergeant Unwin, Yellow Section Leader, had led his section against a pair of Me109s but, as the attack was delivered, the Spitfires were split up by an attack from above. Yellow Leader engaged a Messerschmitt in a prolonged dogfight of around ten minutes, during which time the enemy fighter neared the French coast. Unwin closed to fifty yards and fired a burst of seven seconds into his target which was now flying straight and level. Nothing seemed to happen as a result of his fire, so he gave a second burst with similar result. Moving to one side, Flight Sergeant Unwin fired a thirty degree deflection shot. The Messerschmitt stalled and span into the sea. He noted on his combat report "the Me 109s must now be very heavily armoured."

Flight Lieutenant Lawson had also destroyed an Me109, as had Flying Officer Parrott, Sergeant Plzak, and Flight Sergeant Steere, whilst Sub – Lieutenant Blake had shot down two. The successes were not without loss. Pilot Officer Eric Burgoyne's Spitfire, X4352, fell victim to the Me109s. The twenty five year old pilot crashed and was killed at Coldred. Sergeant David Cox was also shot down.

"I had jumped into the nearest Spitfire, X4237, "QV – L", as mine would not start. This aircraft was nearly always flown by Sergeant Plzak, the 6'6" Czech who had dubbed me "Little Boy". To save time I buckled on his parachute which was in the cockpit – more of that later!

"19 Squadron took off just before noon and we were the top cover of the Duxford Wing. It was in the Dover area when a large number of Me 109s attacked us from above. After some hectic moments avoiding being shot down, I found myself more or less on my own between Ashford and Folkestone. I then saw towards Folkestone a Hurricane being attacked by four 109s. Before I could give any assistance, which was my intention having got within a few hundred yards of the scrap, the Hurricane went down in a vertical dive inland. This was a 242 Squadron Hurricane flown by Pilot Officer Michael G. Homer DFC who crashed near Sittingbourne and was killed.

"The four Me 109s then turned their attention to me. They knew their stuff as two got above me and two below. Naturally I had some hectic moments of turning this way and that as they came at me in attacks from all directions. I remember doing quite a lot of firing of my guns, but I think it was more in the hope of frightening them or raising my morale than in any real hope of shooting anything down."

"All of a sudden there was a loud bang in the cockpit and for a second or two I was dazed. When I became normal again there was a lot of smoke about and my Spitfire was in a steep dive. I grabbed the control column and went up in a steep climb. As I lost flying speed I opened the hood, turned the aircraft over, undid my straps and fell out, quickly pulling the rip cord of my parachute. When the canopy opened it gave me a severe jolt, and several days later a lot of bruises showed on my chest and shoulders. Remember that the parachute harness was fitted for a man of 6'6" – I was lucky not to fall out of it!"

"As I floated down a 109 came and had a look at me and then flew off. It was then that I felt a lot of pain in my right leg and saw lots of holes in my flying boots out of which blood was oozing.

"Ground observers say that I took about fifteen minutes to come down as I was so high up – I know that it was jolly cold up there when I came out of the aeroplane. I landed in the corner of a ploughed field near a farm at Walsford near Ashford. Two farm hands carried me into the farmhouse. By this time I was feeling rather rough and must have looked it as the farmer handed me a bottle of whisky of which I took a large swig. I was later taken to hospital at Walsford where a surgeon from Folkestone Hospital extracted several large pieces of cannon shell from just below my knee cap down into my ankle. I was in hospital about six weeks and off flying until December 1940. By coincidence, the next time I was shot down was on Friday, June 27th, 1941, again in a Spitfire coded "QV – L"."

"Pilot Officer Eric Burgoyne, who was killed in the action, is buried in the churchyard at Burghfield. I have visited the grave which is in a quiet spot underneath a large oak tree. He joined 19 Squadron on the same day as myself in May 1940, along with Sergeant Roden and Pilot Officer Sutherland; I am the only survivor of the four."

The No.19 Squadron diary records that the claims of seven enemy aircraft confirmed as destroyed and one probable signified their best day so far, despite the loss of Burgoyne killed and Cox wounded. In the heaviest day of fighting for some time the Luftwaffe lost a total of fifty six aircraft destroyed and ten damaged, of which at least nineteen were Me109s. Therefore, the No.19 Squadron claims on this day are believed to be particularly accurate in respect of attributing kills to individual pilots.

As September drew to a close the Battle of Britain entered its final phase in which the entire nature of the German day raids had changed. Only the fast and versatile Ju88 bombers generally ventured over England in daylight, the slower He111s and Do17s being transferred increasingly to nocturnal bombing sorties. The majority of raiders now became high flying single and twin engined fighter bombers. Although many of these aircraft reached their targets the number of bombs dropped was so small that little damage was achieved and, due to the high altitude from which the raiders bombed, accuracy was minimal. The bombing of London became indiscriminate and with the Luftwaffe's switch to making major attacks at night Fighter Command at last received some little respite.

On October 3rd, Air Vice – Marshal Leigh – Mallory visited Duxford and Fowlmere to discuss tactics against the new fighter formations being encountered and the prospect of night interception patrols. The cannon armed Spitfire appeared back on the scene. On October 5th, Pilot Officer Vokes returned from the Air Fighting Development Unit at Northolt with a new Spitfire, R6889, allocated to No.19 Squadron for thorough testing. The cannon's feed mechanism had a booster coil fitted which helped to push each new cartridge in as the spring within the magazine ran down. The feed shute had a wider sweep and went through one of the wing struts. Over the next few days Vokes tested the new Spitfire on the ranges at Sutton Bridge. On October 9th he suffered a stoppage due to "G", but later the same day he sortied again and wrote in his log book "No stoppages, target bounced up into the air." During this time the squadron were also engaged on further wing patrols, but without event.

At 4.15 pm on Tuesday, October 29th, No.19 Squadron was on patrol with the wing above Kent. Anti – aircraft fire was sighted, but as Squadron Leader Bader's radio was not working the wing was unable to orchestrate an attack on whatever the gunners' targets were. Some of the Spitfire pilots noticed seven Me109s flying above the squadron, but no attack was made. Spitfire P7423, however, failed to return to Fowlmere. Sub – Lieutenant Blake was apparently acting as weaver at the rear of the squadron's formation and it is believed that one or more of the Messerschmitts sighted by the squadron picked off Blake in a surprise attack. P7423 crashed at 5.15 pm at Oak Lodge, London Road, Chelmsford. The twenty three year old nautic was buried in St Mary's churchyard, Slough. The squadron diary records that "it is a great loss to the squadron as he was well liked by all as well as being a pilot of exceptional ability." Wallace Cunningham recalls:

"I remember the "Admiral" particularly well as he was very popular. I recall that up until he was killed he was messing officer at Fowlmere and ran his personal account and the mess account together. I do not think it had been settled by the time I was shot down over Holland and taken prisoner a year later!"

"Jock" Cunningham also relates a story regarding one of No.19 Squadron's able Czech pilots:

"Some six of the Czechs had to gain a working knowledge of English. What they learnt was influenced by their squadron associates. I remember one of them, Sergeant Plzak, sitting writing to his girlfriend in Cambridge and asking me, "Jock, what is difference between beautiful and bloody fool?" It was long afterwards that we received a telephone call from that girlfriend and had to tell her that Plzak was dead."

On Thursday, October 31st, 1940, the Battle of Britain officially came to its close. The bombing of Britain was now only conducted under cover of darkness with the German Kampfgeschwadern unable to wreak havoc in daylight hours due to the peril facing them from Dowding's fighters. Thanks to the relentless efforts of Britain's young pilots, Göring's aspirations of gaining aerial supremacy over Britain as a prelude to invasion came to nothing. Although, as Wellington said of Waterloo, "It was a damn near run thing." Churchill captured the admiration of the world for Fighter Command with just one inspiring sentence:

"Never in the field of human conflict was so much owed by so many to so few."

Amongst the pilots, hardened veterans and professionals though they were despite the majority being mere youngsters in their late teens or early twenties, the significance of the conflict in which they were fighting had not sunk in. Frank Brinsden:

"I do not believe that many of us at squadron pilot level realized that we were engaged in a full scale battle, nor how important the outcome would be if lost. Again in retrospect, intelligence briefing was sadly lacking."

George Unwin:

"At the time I felt nothing out of the ordinary. I had been trained for the job and luckily had a lot of experience. I was always most disappointed if the squadron got into a scrap when I was off duty, and this applied to all of the pilots I knew. It was only after the event that I began to realise how serious defeat would have been – but then, without being big–headed, we never even considered being beaten, it just was not possible in our eyes, this simply was our outlook. As we lost pilots and aircraft replacements were forthcoming. We were never much below full strength. Of course the new pilots were inexperienced, but so were the German replacements, and it was clear at the end of 1940 that these pilots had not the stomach for a scrap with a Spitfire."

That Germany was unable to secure aerial supremacy in order to invade Britain showed the world that Hitler's military might could be defeated. Following Hitler's successes in Poland and western Europe, many feared him invincible. The handful of Hurricane and Spitfire pilots had challenged and defeated that myth. As Churchill said, "It is not the end, it is not even the beginning of the end, but it is the end of the beginning." Britain still stood alone, but proud, and Fighter Command had laid the foundation stone for every allied military success that was to follow until the German High Command signed an unconditional surrender at Luneberg Heath in May 1945. Make no mistake, without victory in the Battle of Britain there would have been no other battles.

For Dowding and Park victory was to have a bitter postscript. In the winter of 1940 both men were summoned to a meeting at the Air Ministry. The two commanders were accused of having reacted too cautiously towards enemy attack by committing only small numbers of fighters against them. Leigh – Mallory gave his case on "big wings", and Squadron Leader Douglas Bader, the most junior officer present, corroborated these theories. Bader also stated that more independence should be given to formation leaders in the air regarding the height and when and where to engage the enemy, as opposed to being rigidly bound to orders from the ground controlling station. As a result of the meeting Dowding received a telephone call at Stanmore soon after instructing him to clear his desk within twenty four hours. The Air Council had no further work to offer him. Park was sent from 11 Group to Training Command. Leigh – Mallory was immediately elevated to command 11 Group. In an exercise conducted later Leigh – Mallory's 11 Group operated a wing formation in response to a simulated attack similar to those experienced during the Battle of Britain. It proved to be a shambles and confirmed the practicality of Park's tactics. However, Leigh – Mallory was not to be prevented from eventually taking over Dowding's former position as Fighter Command's Commander – in – Chief.

Sadly, Lord Dowding himself was to die in 1970 having been accorded no form of public tribute in London. Fortunately this sorry state of affairs has since been rectified, albeit belatedly, and on October 28th, 1988, the Queen Mother, wartime Queen of England, unveiled a statue of the Fighter Command's former Commander – in – Chief outside the church of St Clement Danes, the Royal Air Force's "own" church in the Strand.

CHAPTER FOUR

The onset of winter, and the fact that Fighter Command had remained a force to be reckoned with despite the summer and autumn's onslaught, saw an end to mass bombing of the British Isles by day. Whilst the Kampfgeschwader ventured virtually unchallenged over England under cover of darkness, the German fighters continued with their sweeps over the south of England by day and clashes between them and Fighter Command were just as fierce as during the summer. Many German historians even argue, with good reasoning, that the Battle of Britain was not actually won until May 1941. May marked not only the worst ever attack on London, but also the end of concentrated night bombing as a result of the toll taken of intruders by improved British night fighter defences.

November 1940 saw No.19 Squadron continuing much as it had in October, flying numerous wing patrols over London and the south. At 10.30 am on Tuesday, November 5th, the wing was on patrol. No.19 Squadron was being led by Flight Lieutenant Lawson, whose radio later became defective and his place as leader was taken by Flight Sergeant Harry Steere. Between 9.34 and 10.45 am fifty German fighters crossed the coast at Dungeness, some then flying towards Sheppey and some to Biggin Hill. Ten of these intruders, Me109s of II and III Gruppe, JG26, were sighted by No.19 Squadron between Dover and Deal. Flight Sergeant Steere led his formation in pursuit of the enemy. In the ensuing combat Sergeant Charnock claimed a certainty, and Flight Lieutenant "Farmer" Lawson claimed a probable.

Between 2.27 and 4.20 pm on the same day, forty two enemy aircraft crossed the coast at Ramsgate, continued inland as far as Tilbury and Hornchurch, and turned back. Further smaller formations followed, but these did not penetrate as far inland. The Duxford Wing was scrambled to intercept the Me109s of JG26. As the wing patrolled between Canterbury and Dover, the Hurricanes of No.310 Squadron were "bounced" by the Messerschmitts. Five Hurricanes were hit in the attack. Sergeants Jiroudek and Puda baled out and three others crashed on landing due to the damage sustained by their machines. Bader's No.242 Squadron engaged the enemy. After a long chase from high altitude Flight Lieutenant McKnight severely damaged the Me109 flown by Feldwebel Scheidt, who waggled his wings as a sign of surrender. As McKnight flew alongside the cockpit canopy blew off and Scheidt baled out. His fighter crashed at Birchington, thus denying

McKnight the prospect of having been responsible for the capture of an enemy machine. Scheidt's fighter had also been attacked by No.19 Squadron's Flying Officer Haines, who was credited jointly with its destruction. Sergeant Charnock destroyed an enemy fighter, as did Flight Lieutenant Lawson. Lawson was flying the cannon armed Spitfire, R6889, and attacked an Me109. He later reported that it "literally fell to pieces." Pilot Officer Vokes wrote in his log book, "Sgt. Charnock got a cert, Farmer blew another to bits with the cannon, its first success since July. No stoppages". Hauptmann Rolf Pingel, Gruppenkommandeur of I/JG26, selected Spitfire P7545 as his target and proceeded to attack, setting the British fighter alight. The Czech Pilot Officer Hradil crashed in flames and was killed near Southend Pier, Essex. Flight Sergeant Unwin claimed to have destroyed a "Heinkel 113", being recorded in the squadron diary as being "the first of this type shot down by Duxford". In the process his Spitfire, P7427, was severely damaged. Hauptmann Gerhard Schoepfel of III/JG26 claimed two Spitfires as destroyed, one of these possibly being Unwin's. Two Hurricanes of No.242 Squadron were also lost. Pilot Officer Hart was killed by Hauptmann Johannes Seifert, and Sub – Lieutenant Gardner crash landed at Rochford due to a damaged fuel tank.

The following day Flying Officer Frank Brinsden was promoted to Flight Lieutenant and posted as a flight commander to No.303 "Kosciouzko" Squadron, the top scoring Polish unit in the Battle of Britain. The Poles had earned a reputation of being remarkable fighters and extremely aggressive. The No.19 Squadron diarist recorded his fears that the Poles would turn even Brinsden's hair "prematurely grey!"

On Friday, November 8th, German fighter sweeps again met with fierce opposition. A number of Fighter Command's squadrons engaged the enemy. Squadron Leader Lane led No.19 Squadron in a wing patrol of the Canterbury area. Bernard Jennings relates events:

"We were over Canterbury and I was flying as Sandy Lane's Number Two. We were told that a party was going on above us which we could not see as the sky was covered by a layer of 8/10ths thinnish cloud. Sandy put us into a climb, and as we were nearing the cloud base an Me109 dived out of the cloud a short distance in front of us, followed by a Hurricane firing his guns even closer, in fact over the top of Sandy and myself. Sandy's engine was hit, packed up and he lost height. As his Number Two, and because there were obviously some unfriendly people about, I stayed with him.

"Once we were clear of trouble I called up Sandy and suggested that he held his gliding course and I would go ahead and find somewhere for him to land. I said "Waggle your wings if you hear me." He did so and I dived away only to find the airfield at Eastchurch bombed and unusable. However, there was a small strip clear of bomb craters. I flew back up to Sandy and asked him to follow me. He did, and taking one look at the state of the airfield rightly decided to land with wheels up."

"He crash landed his aeroplane OK, but, as I circled low over him, I saw Sandy in the cockpit but not moving. I looked round the airfield until I saw an air raid shelter which I beat up until two airmen poked their heads out of the entrance. I pointed towards Sandy and then circled him and saw the airmen go behind the shelter to get into a truck. I circled Sandy again and saw him getting out of his aircraft, holding his face with one hand and waving to me with the other. I waited until the truck had picked him up, then I returned to base.

"I told everybody that he was safe and told his wife that I would fetch him the next day in the Magister. We got a message through to Eastchurch to that effect. Early the next morning I flew the Magister to Hornchurch and after some argument with sector control managed to get permission to go to Eastchurch. After circling low over the airfield a truck brought Sandy to the small strip which I had seen the previous day. I landed, but, as Sandy walked towards me, I burst out laughing as he had a puffed up nose. In order to keep an eye on the squadron following him, Sandy Lane used to fly with his shoulder straps very loose. He forgot to tighten them before his crash landing and hit his face on the gunsight."

Squadron Leader Lane recorded the following of the incident in his log book:

"Sighted Me 109s over Canterbury and turned to give chase. Hurricane squadron chased us and the leader put a burst into my engine!! Apparently the CO of one of the North Weald squadrons. Force landed at Eastchurch OK. Jennings escorted me down and refused to leave me. Damn good of him."

Over the next few days Squadron Leader Lane led No.19 Squadron and the Wittering Wing, consisting of Nos.1 and 266 Squadrons. On November 14th the squadron diary recorded "Last patrol with Wittering Wing; nearly last patrol with any Wing! Ajax leader led his squadron straight into us from the sun as we climbed to meet them. Created quite a shambles".

At 9.45 am on Friday, November 15th, No.19 Squadron was detailed to patrol a convoy twenty miles east of Harwich with No.242 Squadron . The two squadrons were unable to find the convoy that they were to protect, only discovering three or four very small craft moving in line abreast. Information was received of three "bandits" approaching England from a north westerly direction at 25,000 feet. Leaving the Hurricanes to continue searching for the convoy, Squadron Leader Lane climbed No.19 Squadron to investigate. Soon two condensation plumes were spotted at 35,000 feet, fifteen to twenty miles apart, and the squadron split up into flights to give chase. Yellow Section of "A" Flight, led by Flight

Sergeant Unwin, manoeuvred to cut off the line of retreat of "B" Flight's quarry, and Blue Section broke away to attack the rearmost aircraft. Squadron Leader Lane led Red Section, comprising Pilot Officers Vokes and Cunningham, after the leading German and climbed south to get between the enemy aircraft and the sun. After a chase up the Thames Estuary lasting twenty minutes, described by Lane as a "Cook's tour", the Messerschmitts were sighted. Their quarry turned east and dived. Lane ordered the section into line astern and opened fire at 800 feet. A cowling flew off the Me110 as his bullets struck their target and a stream of coolant gushed from the port engine. Cunningham then set the German's starboard engine alight. The enemy aircraft then climbed and Lane delivered a further attack from the starboard quarter, the telling blow. The enemy machine, "4N + BH", crashed into the Thames Estuary in the middle of a convoy near Southend. Unteroffizier Boschen was killed, but the pilot, Oberleutnant Heinz Vejakob, baled out and was captured. The other Spitfires caught and destroyed "4N + DH", which also plunged into the Thames Estuary. The crew, Feldwebel Kaiser and Gefreiter Sande remain posted "missing".

After the action, Arthur Vokes wrote home to his parents in Erdington, Birmingham:

"Dear Mother and Pop,

Feeling very excited. This morning three of us shot down an Me 110 into the Thames Estuary after a thrilling chase from Felixstowe – North Sea – London – Buckingham – Southend. We eventually set him on fire and he crashed near a convoy with an enormous splash. The pilot baled out and had a long dip. Yesterday we did four hours flying and nothing happened, so it was good to have some fun today. "A" Flight is ripping after "B". I fly with the C.O. and Jock.
It's a glorious day so we may have some more fun yet. Many thanks to you both for a topping leave. I am sorry that it was so short, but I should have hated missing this morning."

Wallace Cunningham recalled an unusual incident during Red Section's attack on Veyakob's Me110:

"I was tucked in behind Brian Lane and diving after the fleeing Me 110 fighter bomber. Because of our high speed Brian was struggling to get his sights on the target – I was almost jostling him off to get a chance. Before we eventually destroyed the enemy aircraft, after letting the pilot bale out, I had my armoured glass windscreen shattered. Not, I worked out later, by the enemy, but from Brian's empty cartridge cases!"

Returning from the engagement, Sergeant Roden landed in bad visibility in a field and struck a tree on the leeward boundary. His

Spitfire, P7420, was written off and the unfortunate pilot was killed.

On November 16th confirmation was received of Flight Lieutenant Lawson's DFC. Over the next few days, despite constant convoy protection sorties, the enemy were not met. At 2.30 pm on Friday, November 29th, five Me109s of I/JG26 were sighted above No.19 Squadron and attempted to attack the rearmost section of Spitfires. The attack was broken up and the squadron engaged the enemy between Southend and the Kent coast, chasing them back over the Channel. Flight Sergeant Steere destroyed an Me109 east of Ramsgate:

"I was Green Leader carrying out rear search. I observed four Me 109s closing on us. I called out to Freedom Leader and turned towrds them. Three of them overshot me and I closed behind one of these. I gave one a burst of about seven seconds at 3/400 yards – he half rolled and spiralled downwards. I followed and saw him go into the sea about eight miles east of Ramsgate."

Flying Officer Haines also claimed an Me109 destroyed and Flight Sergeant Unwin together with Sergeant Fulford shared a third. In fact two JG26 machines failed to return: Feldwebel Wolfgang Kaminsky, whose aircraft crashed into the Channel, and Unteroffizier Heinz Wolf who belly landed his damaged fighter at Udimore in Sussex and was captured.

In a different action, the Luftwaffe lost its leading "ace", Major Helmut Wick, Gruppenkommandeur of JG2, who crashed into the sea off the Isle of Wight after his formation engaged the Spitfires of No.609 "West Riding" Squadron over the Solent. It is believed that Flight Lieutenant John Dundas DFC shot down Helmut Wick, but was in turn killed by Wick's wingman, Rudi Pflanz.

The end of November saw such poor weather that flying came to a full stop as far as No.19 Squadron was concerned. This situation persisted throughout December, during which there was very little operational or practice flying. The highlight of the month occured on Boxing Day when George Unwin was promoted to Warrant Officer and received a bar to his DFM. January 1941 brought with it more poor weather, although patrols were conducted with the wing. On January 13th Pilot Officer Howard – Williams crashed on landing after a wing patrol, but was fortunately unhurt. On January 16th, Flight Lieutenants Lawson and Cunningham flew with Pilot Officer Vokes on a security patrol for the King and Queen who visited Duxford to award the two former pilots with their DFCs. Two days later "A" Flight provided a further security patrol for their Monarchs who visited Mildenhall. Five minutes after landing a Dornier approached but was fortunately driven off by anti – aircraft fire. Foggy conditions continued into February, although on February 13th Sergeant Jennings intercepted a Do17 over a convoy and chased it sixty miles out to sea before losing the bomber in cloud. Squadron Leader Lane had flown Hurricane L1565 on February 2nd and engaged Flight Lieutenant Petre in a practice dogfight. The Hurricane was fitted with a new gyroscopic gunsight, as opposed to the reflector type standard in both aircraft at that time. Lane recorded in his log book, "Sight excellent. I wish I could get one for myself". February 25th saw a German night intruder follow a Hurricane into Duxford and bomb the flarepath. Luckily its bombs missed by a narrow margin. On March 1st a vapour trail was sighted during a practice wing sweep. Yellow Section gave chase but made no contact.

On March 9th, Flying Officer Cunningham was promoted and made commander of "B" Flight. A flight commander's vacancy also came the way of Peter Howard – Williams, but to take up this post he was sent to join a new Spitfire squadron, No.118, at Filton. Other postings by this time had included the squadron's senior NCO pilots, Harry Steere and George Unwin. Both had been posted on instructors courses having been told that they were too old to be fighter pilots; George Unwin was twenty eight during the Battle of Britain, and Harry Steere was twenty six. Having been together since their ab initio flying training, the pair were later to join forces in February 1942 as Central Flying School instructors. Both were commissioned and were to receive the DFC and DSO respectively in addition to their DFMs. They went on to night intruder operations in Mosquitos later in the war, but neither were to increase their "score". Harry Steere, a married man with a young son, did not survive the conflict. At 2 am on June 9th, 1944, just three days after the Allied invasion of Normandy, Steere's No.627 Squadron Mosquito was shot down over France and crashed in a field at Orgeres, near St. Erblon. In spite of an order by the Germans for the crew to be buried at the crash site, both Flight Lieutenant Steere and his navigator, Flying Officer "Windy" Gale, were buried in the presence of nearly all the village's inhabitants in the local cemetery.

During the winter of 1940 the night blitz on British cities was in full progress. On the night of November 15th, 449 German bombers dropped 400 tonnes of high explosive on Coventry, devastating the city centre and causing some 1,350 casualties. During that month the Luftwaffe's Kampfgeschwader flew around 6,000 sorties. Despite the poor weather, 1,200 sorties were flown in February 1941. So unsophisticated were Britain's night defences at this time that the German bombers were virtually free to roam at will over the British Isles. As a desperate defensive measure British day fighter squadrons were often pressed into the night fighter role. The Spitfires and Hurricanes were fitted with no radar or other gadget to assist them in this task. All the pilot could rely upon to guide him to an interception was his eyesight and the ground controller's metallic voice in his earphones. On nights when the sky wa s filled with British fighters, called "Fighter Nights", the Spitfires and Hurricanes would enter their patrol area over London via a "gate" in the searchlight beams, before patrolling at pre – determined heights so as to minimise the risk of collision with a friendly aircraft.

As from March 1941 the squadron flew an increasing number of these night patrols, but without success. On the night of April 8th Arthur Vokes wrote in his log book in red ink; "Night patrol. Two bandits, one bogey and one friendly very close according to ops". Squadron Leader Lane and his pilots not only flew the daily routine of convoy protection sorties, standing patrols and practice flights, but most nights would also find them airborne seeking the enemy. Again in red ink, Arthur Vokes wrote in his log book on April 16th; "Fighter Night! Zero hour 2 a.m. over London. Heavy raid on docks, hundreds of incendiaries. Nine aircraft at 500' intervals. No E/A chased".

The weather increasingly improved as May approached and on May 7th the squadron, led by Flight Lieutenant Cunningham, took off with No.310 Squadron's Hurricanes to reinforce 11 Group if required. The squadron patrolled Manston and Dover without event.

On the night of May 10th, the Luftwaffe launched its biggest ever night attack on London during which five hundred aircraft unloaded seven hundred tonnes of bombs onto their target. The raid also coincided with a full moon spring tide which meant that the fire – fighters' water supply was severely restricted. By the end of the night's bombing over one thousand Londoners were dead and another two thousand were injured. The pilots of No.19 Squadron patrolled over London on that terrible night, but saw no sign of the enemy. Some Spitfire pilots were, however, able to exact revenge upon the attackers. Whilst returning to West Malling with airscrew pitch control problems, Flying Officer Roger Boulding of No.74 Squadron sighted an He111 which he attacked and shot down. The bomber, "A1 + JN" of 5/KG53, crashed at Church Road, Ashford.

The bombing of London a few nights later was to be the Luftwaffe's last major attack on the British Isles. As the technology required for the cat and mouse art of night fighting improved, so did the toll of raiders shot down increase. For example, in January 1941 only three bombers were destroyed by night fighters; in May the same year ninety six were claimed.

The air war was also changing by day. Following the defensive fighting during the summer of 1940, Fighter Command were now in a position to take the fight to the enemy in daylight. The first raid was carried out in January and comprised a small number of bombers escorted by a number of fighters. Little opposition was met, but this was not so on the next occasion. The tactical thinking was that these small formations of bombers should attack strategic targets, particularly in northern France, and cause sufficient damage so that the Luftwaffe fighters could not ignore them. Drawn into battle against superior numbers of fighters, under conditions dictated by the attackers and therefore favourable to them, the enemy would enter a war of attrition. These operations were known as "Circus" sorties. At this time Hitler also turned his military ambitions eastwards, towards Germany's ideological enemy, Stalin's Soviet Russia. Instead of a resumed daylight offensive against Britain, many Luftwaffe units left the Channel coast to re – fit in Germany prior to the scheduled invasion of Russia in June 1941.

On May 21st, No.19 Squadron flew to West Malling with Nos.310 and 266 Squadrons to take part in a "Circus" which also involved a number of other fighter squadrons. The task allocated to Nos 19, 310 and 266 Squadrons was to patrol the south east coast area at 20,000 feet to protect the bombers from attack should the Germans be so bold as to pursue the Blenheims as far as the English coast. The Luftwaffe proved not as ambitious as anticipated and No.19 Squadron's patrol time passed without incident. However, the operation as a whole was considered a great success.

June 1941 was to be Squadron Leader Lane's last month with No.19 Squadron. On June 4th he led Nos.19 and 266 Squadron on a sweep of south east England and the Thames Estuary area. For reasons unknown Green Leader of No.266 Squadron crashed into the sea. The following night Brian Lane took off at 1.00 am for a patrol, but was recalled ten minutes later in preparation for a "Fighter Night" over Birmingham. The operation did not materialise as the German attack failed to develop. The night of June 14th again saw Lane on a nocturnal patrol, but apart from seeing an enemy aircraft crash in flames, the patrol was uneventful.

On the morning of June 15th, Squadron Leader Roy Dutton DFC and bar, having previously commanded No.452 (Australian) Squadron at Kirton – in – Lindsey, arrived to take command of No.19 Squadron. Squadron Leader Lane, who had flown operational duties since the outbreak of war, was posted on a staff appointment to 12 Group Head Quarters. For the squadron, 1941 was to continue with many "Circus" operations and fighter sweeps. Brian Lane's posting to 12 Group was really at the time of the turning point for both the air war in western Europe and for Fighter Command. "Their finest hour" was over, and during that time Squadron Leader Lane had led his pilots with distinction.

CHAPTER FIVE

Having left No.19 Squadron, Squadron Leader Lane reported to 12 Group H.Q. at Watnall for staff duties on June 20th, 1941. Away from his beloved Spitfires and fellow fighter pilots, he was to remain there until November 11th, when he left on a troop ship bound for a further staff appointment overseas. He arrived at the Desert Air Force H.Q. on January 28th, 1942, but four months later he made the long sea voyage back to England. Now he could fight the enemy from the cockpit of a Spitfire again instead of from behind a desk. In the thirteen months that Brian Lane had spent away from operations the war had changed a great deal and the tide was at last turning in favour of Britain and her allies.

By 1942 the Luftwaffe's forces on the Channel coast were somewhat depleted since Hitler's Wehrmacht had executed "Operation Barbarossa", the invasion of Soviet Russia, on June 22nd, 1941. Germany's resources were stretched in maintaining their territorial conquests in western Europe and gaining new territories from Russia in the east. The majority of the Channel based fighter and bomber units had been sent east for the Russian campaign. Only JG2, commanded by Hauptmann Wilhelm Balthasar, and JG26, commanded by Oberstleutnant Adolf Galland, remained in France. The intensive bombing of British cities during the night blitz, having reached its zenith in May 1941, was also over when Squadron Leader Lane returned to England.

On Sunday, December 7th, 1941, Japanese aircraft inflicted severe damage on the American fleet at Pearl Harbour in an undeclared act of war. At last the sleeping giant awoke, unable to continue pretending that events in the rest of the world were of not of its concern. As the Russian army suffered horrendous casualties, the western Allies were put under pressure from Stalin to increase offensive operations against the enemy to relieve the burden borne by his people. As from July 1941 the Royal Air Force had stepped up the tempo of its daylight fighter and bomber offensive. The Luftwaffe were now fighting against superior numbers of enemy aircraft, but were enjoying the benefits exercised by Fighter Command during the Battle of Britain. It was now the Hurricane and Spitfire pilots who flew to battle contending with two sea crossings. More importantly, it was now the RAF who would lose pilots and machines if shot down or forced down due to mechanical failure. The Luftwaffe, as had the RAF in the Battle of Britain, were fighting over home ground and their pilots could return to fly again. Following fierce fighting throughout the summer and autumn of 1941 the Royal Air Force halted their offensive in November and planned for a fresh assault the following spring. Since the attack on Pearl Harbour, American troops and military hardware had commenced arriving in England in increasing numbers. On August 17th, 1942, General Ira Eaker led the 8th Air Force's B17 Flying Fortress bombers on an attack of the Rouen – Sotteville marshalling yards so signalling the start of the American daylight bomber offensive. By night Bomber Command pounded the enemy heartlands, the German people reaping a terrifying whirlwind for the horrors of mass bombing which their leaders had unleashed.

Further pressure from Soviet Russia led to the Allies launching the ill – conceived "Operation Jubilee", the landing of a large number of troops for a major raid on the French port of Dieppe. The raid failed and losses were high.

The biggest impact on the air war in western Europe since Brian Lane had last flown on operations was the arrival of a new German fighter. In late 1941 an unfamiliar silhouette puzzled Allied fighter pilots. It displayed a radial engine, square wings and a more tapering fuselage than the Me109. The performance of the new fighter was stunning, being much faster and more stable than the Me109, and it was armed with a mixture of both cannon and machine guns. Following sketches provided by pilots who had fought the new German machine, it was first thought that the new encounter was a force of Curtis Hawk radial engined, mono – plane fighters captured from the French. However, this aircraft was in no way capable of matching, let alone bettering, the performance of the Spitfire Mk V which was Fighter Command's mainstay at that time. To the German pilots the new fighter was known as "Die Wurger", or "Butcher Bird". It was the Focke Wulf FW190. For the first time Spitfire pilots had cause to doubt that their Spitfires were superior, or at least as good as anything the enemy could throw at them, and morale suffered accordingly.

On June 23rd, 1941, the Focke Wulf FW190s of 7/JG2 engaged the Spitfire Vs of the Exeter based Polish Wing who were returning from a raid on Luftwaffe airfields in northern France. In the ensuing combat, Oberleutnant Arnim Faber claimed to have destroyed a Spitfire, but he then became disorientated. Making the navigational error of mistaking the Bristol Channel for the English Channel, and being short of fuel, he landed at the first available airfield after landfall. No doubt Faber was horrified to discover that he had actually landed at Pembrey in South Wales – and undoubtedly his arrival caused as much surprise amongst that station's personnel! Faber's mistake had delivered to Britain a completely intact FW190A – 3, which the experts at Farnborough and the Air Fighting Development Unit lost no time in evaluating.

Comparing its performance against the Spitfire Mk V, the subsequent results were in the FW190's favour in virtually every respect.

Desperate measures were needed to restore the balance and work continued with great urgency to produce a more powerful Spitfire which would be capable of taking on the "Butcher Bird" on equal terms. The resulting fighter was the Spitfire Mk IX, which was basically a Mk V airframe married with a Merlin 61 engine which developed three hundred horse power more than the Mk V's Merlin 46. Comparative trials between the Mk IX and the FW190 were conducted and it was discovered that at heights up to 25,000 feet the new Spitfire was superior in speed and manoeuvrability. Any differences in performance at lesser altitudes were minimal. No.64 Squadron received the first Spitfire Mk IX s in July 1942 and as more units began re–equipping with the improved Spitfire the balance of air power, and morale, shifted again in Fighter Command's favour.

The scene had changed, therefore, by September 16th, 1942, when Squadron Leader Lane reported for his Spitfire refresher course at No.61 Operational Training Unit. The unit had formed at Heston on July 1st, 1941, and had moved to Rednal in north Shropshire on April 15th the following year. Rednal's satellite station was at Montford Bridge, and it was there that Brian Lane found himself living and flying for the next few weeks. The accomodation at the airfield was spartan to say the least, consisting of a few primitive Nissen huts which were notoriously cold. Flying in Shropshire skies, safe from enemy attack, Squadron Leader Lane familiarised himself with the improved marques of his old mount, and no doubt noted with satisfaction that following No.19 Squadron's trials and tribulations with the Spitfire Ib, the 20 mm Hispano Suiza cannon was now a standard feature of Spitfire's armament. The unit's instructors were experienced pilots on rest from the rigours and danger of operational flying. It was their task to teach new pilots to become competent with the Spitfire fighter, and to pass on tips and instruction regarding current combat conditions. By the completion of his course, in early December, 1942, Squadron Leader Lane had flown a total of thirty hours and forty minutes. Twenty–six hours and fifty minutes had been on Spitfires, one hour ten minutes in a Tiger Moth, and one hour in a Hurricane.

Before he left Montford Bridge, Brian was to meet on old No.19 Squadron friend in a country pub in Cheshire. This was Frank Brinsden, who was on a night fighter conversion course. Since Fowlmere days the New Zealander had served with No.303 (Polish) Squadron, No.485 (New Zealand) Squadron, the staff of the

Merchant Ship Fighter Unit, and had commanded No.3 Aircraft Delivery Flight. Later posted as a flight commander to No.25 Squadron at Church Fenton, flying De Havilland Mosquitos, Brinsden was to regret that the squadron had persuaded Group H.Q. to allow them to fly night intruder sorties. He was shot down on the night of Bomber Command's famous raid on the V1 sites at Peenemünde and he finished up in the sea off Sylt. He consequently became a prisoner of war and was never to see Brian Lane again.

Squadron Leader Lane reported to No.167 "Gold Coast" Squadron on December 9th, 1942, as a supernumery squadron leader. He was to gain practical experience of current combat conditions prior to being given command of his own squadron.

Delighted though she no doubt was to have her young husband back from overseas, Eileen Lane must have been most anxious the day Brian travelled to his new squadron at Ludham, between Norwich and the Norfolk coast. Being the wife of a fighting man was not easy, particularly when the husband was aircrew. Every hour couples were separated the wife would not know if her husband's feet were safely on terra firma, or whether he was engaged in a fight for his life. How wartime wives must have dreaded the sound of the postman's footsteps, heralding arrival of the curt official telgram which began "Deeply regret to inform you that...."

No.167 Squadron had formed at Scorton, Yorkshire, on April 6th, 1942, and was a Dutch unit with an English commanding officer, Squadron Leader D.S. Edwards, who was formerly of No.611 Squadron. Scorton was near Brompton – on – Swale, which the unit's diary records as a "queer village". Apparently the village churchyard boasted the burial place of one Henry Jenkins who had supposedly died at the ripe, and appropriate, old age of one hundred and sixty seven years! On April 17th the new squadron received its aircraft, Spitfire Mk VBs, which arrived from Acklington in Northumbria. A number of the squadron's personnel were British and amongst them were several other former members of No.611 Squadron. One of the flight commanders, Flight Lieutenant Tony Whitehouse, was previously an NCO pilot and Battle of Britain veteran with No.501 "County of Gloucester" Squadron. On May 24th, No.167 Squadron pilots fought their first combat with the enemy and engaged a Ju88 near Acklington. Seven days later the squadron moved to Castletown in Scotland. On September 16th, the Dutch Prince Bernhardt was scheduled to inspect the squadron. His Spitfire was expected to land at 2.40 pm in formation with that of Wing Commander Ian "Widge" Gleed's, but unfortunately Prince Bernhardt's aircraft ran off the runway and tipped on to its nose in boggy ground. The following month No.167 Squadron moved south, to Ludham, where they relieved No.610 "County of Chester" Squadron. On October 26th permission was granted for Dutch pilots to fly "Rhubarbs" which were low level strafing attacks by two or four aircraft against targets of opportunity in occupied Europe. The pilots concerned must have been elated at the prospect of hitting back at the enemy who had occupied and oppressed their homeland for over two years. Two days later Queen Wilhelmina of Holland summoned Flying Officer Jan Leendert Plesman to award him for escaping from Holland. Due to the poor winter weather, no operations had been flown, and it was still a new and inexperienced squadron which greeted Squadron Leader Lane.

At this time the squadron was equipped with a mixture of Spitfire Mk VB and Mk VC. The Spitfire Mk VC, which had been in production since October 1941, was an interesting aeroplane and was fitted with the new "C" – type universal wing designed to carry two 20 mm cannon and four Browning machine guns in each. Due to the stress imposed by the extra weight, the airframe was considerably strengthened. To cope with the extra weight of the Mk VC airframe the new Merlin 61 engine was required. When the new engine was fitted it lengthened the fuselage by nine inches. The two speed engine, with a second supercharger, required another radiator to cool its water supply. This gave the Spitfire a fully symmetrical appearance for the first time. The resultant aeroplane became the "stop gap" Mk IX, introduced to combat the FW190.

Brian Lane's first flight with No.167 Squadron was in a Spitfire VB, "3W – H", and was a local familiarisation flight of just thirty minutes duration on the morning of Sunday, December 13th, 1942. His last was to be on the afternoon of that same day.

At 3.10 pm, on a cold winter's afternoon, four Spitfires roared skywards from Ludham. Squadron Leader Lane flew VC AR612 "3W – U", Flying Officer J.L. Plesman flew VB "3W – P", Pilot Officer H.P.J. Heukensfeld – Jansen flew VC "3W – R", and Pilot Officer W.G. Evans was in VB "3W – Y". Squadron Leader Lane led his section over the North Sea towards the Dutch coast on a "Rhubarb". The pilots' intention was to strafe the main Rotterdam to Antwerp railway line between Moerdyk and Bergen Op Zoom which was just over the coast beyond a system of large islands and estuaries. As the Spitfires bobbed along, low and in line abreast, light was already fading and visibility decreased to eight or ten miles. The Dutch coast was crossed at 3.50 pm between Voorne and Goeree. The small formation followed the Haring Vliet water inland to the Hollandseh Deep Estuary at zero feet, skimming the wave tops at several hundred miles per hour. As the Spitfires flashed past Helleveotsluis surprised German flak gunners managed to loose off intense tracer at their fleeting targets, as did those at Willemstad,

Moerdyk bridge, and on the northern shore of the Hollandseh Deep. On reaching Moerdyk bridge the section turned south and flew inland some ten miles, following the railway line to Roosendaal, where Blue 4, Pilot Officer Huekensfeldt – Jansen, became detached from the section in poor light. He returned to Ludham alone. Squadron Leader Lane and his two wingmen continued along the railway line, no doubt giving the Dutch hope as they zoomed overhead, but they were unable to find any suitable targets. Lane turned the section towards base, flying out of Holland over the Ooster Scheldt, still at zero feet.

Over the estuary, two miles south of Zierikee on the island of Schouwen, two FW190s appeared in pursuit of the Spitfires and at the same height. Blue 3, Flying Officer Plesman, sighted the enemy first, but was unable to contact Blue 1 as Squadron Leader Lane's radio was defective. With the enemy fighters bearing down on the Spitfires, Plesman opened his throttle and drew alongside Blue 1, drawing Lane 's attention to the enemy. By this time the enemy fighters were within firing range and at three hundred yards they opened fire on Blue 1 and Blue 2. Squadron Leader Lane immediately took evasive action by breaking to the right, and Pilot Officer Evans broke left. Plesman climbed 2,000 feet to the right to obtain a tactically superior position from which to attack the enemy and dived onto the leading German fighter. Plesman fired a two second burst in a head on attack. The Spitfire and "Die Wurger" twisted and turned, and in a split second had passed without collision. Blue 2 had climbed into some cloud cover and whilst doing so had got in two long bursts at an FW190 at long range, but without result. Pilot Officer Plesman disengaged his attack as Squadron Leader Lane had disappeared. Craning his neck round and searching the darkening sky, he spotted his leader pursuing an enemy fighter. This was the first time Brian Lane had seen an FW190, and he lost no time in getting on the tail of one of the German fighters. He chased it inland in a south easterly direction, just south west of Zierikee. As Lane appeared to be in control of the situation Plesman decided instead to assist Pilot Officer Evans. By the time he reached the Englishman, Blue 2's assailant had been shaken off. With the sky suddenly empty of any other aircraft Plesman and Evans searched for their leader, without success, and set course for Ludham where both landed at 5 pm.

The last moments of Brian Lane's life will forever remain a mystery. Having pursued the enemy aircraft inland it would appear that somehow the tables were turned. Possibly due to Lane being relatively short on fuel he may have been forced to break off his attack prematurely and head for home, or he may have been out manoeuvred by a more skilful adversary. What ever happened,

Oberleutnant Walter Leonhardt of the 6th Staffel, JG1, chased Squadron Leader Lane's Spitfire west across the North Sea. As the Spitfire pilot ran for home the two enemies chased the dusk across a slate grey sea, one young man trying to kill another. At 4.34 pm the German pilot claimed to have shot down a Spitfire, which crashed into the sea twenty miles west of Schouwen Island. German Naval flak gunners had claimed to have destroyed a Spitfire at 4.20 pm, near Stellendam on Goeree Island, but AR612 was the only Spitfire lost by Fighter Command that day. Therefore it was undoubtedly Squadron Leader Lane that Leonhardt had sent to a watery grave in the freezing North Sea.

Hope for his return to Ludham eventually gave way to a reluctant acceptance that Squadron Leader Lane was either a prisoner or, more likely when the geographical area of the combat was taken into account and the temperature of the freezing waters, that he was dead. For Eileen Lane the postman's dreaded foot steps came; the telegram reported her twenty – five year old husband "missing" – no one had seen him crash, so there could be hope that he was still alive. Sadly, no news was to come that Brian was a prisoner and finally the Air Ministry wrote to the effect that, as nothing further had been heard of him, Squadron Leader Lane must now be presumed dead. Mrs Lane was herself to die prematurely, of cancer in 1967, never knowing the fate of her husband and never having received his body to bury. Neither Squadron Leader B.J.E. Lane DFC, or Spitfire AR612, were ever seen again. Their only grave was the sea, shared with the souls of thousands of aircrew from both sides who had suffered a similar fate. Squadron Leader Lane is remembered on panel sixty – five of the Runnymede Memorial, the Commonwealth's tribute to those aircrew with no known grave.

So died a young man of enormous potential, both as a human being and as a fighter pilot, killed on his first sortie after having returned to operations. Had the time on staff duties made him lose the edge, or had he just been plain unlucky? As an indication of Brian Lane's good standing, the following are some tributes paid by his former No.19 Squadron comrades:

Wing Commander George Unwin:

"I flew with Brian Lane for a year, and we were in complete accord in the air. He was an officer and I was an NCO, so we did therefore not associate off duty. However, despite our difference in rank we were good friends. My very last flight with No.19 Squadron, prior to taking up instructor duties in Training Command, was formation aerobatics with Brian leading and my very great friend Harry Steere making up the third. Brian Lane was a first class pilot and leader. He was firstly my flight commander, and then the squadron

C.O. He was completely unflappable and instilled confidence in all who flew with him. It was a sad loss when he was killed."

Wing Commander Bernard Jennings:

"Brian Lane was a highly respected squadron commander, a pilot's pilot and an efficient leader respected highly even by us regular NCO pilots."

Wing Commander David Cox:

"He was in my opinion one of the finest squadron commanders I served under, not only as a fighter leader, but also as a man. He was always kind and considerate, and had time for everyone, however lowly their rank. I can illustrate his kindness and consideration by relating something he did for me. I joined No.19 Squadron on May 13th, 1940, but owing to my lack of flying experience on Spitfires I was not allowed to operate with the squadron over Dunkirk. My job was to ferry spare aircraft to Hornchurch or test them after service. On May 28th, after testing a Spitfire for radio trouble, I was preparing to land but found the undercarriage would not go fully down, sticking half way. After trying unsuccessfully for some time to rectify the situation, which included turning the aircraft on its back to try and take the weight off the pins, I had to land with the undercarriage stuck half way. The engineering officer later put the aircraft in the hanger, jacked it up and the undercarriage worked perfectly. The result was that Squadron Leader Pinkham endorsed my log book as follows:

"On August 10th, 1940, Sergeant Cox was charged at Duxford with damaging one of his Majesty's aircraft, namely a Spitfire, through landing with the undercarriage uncompletely lowered. The station C.O. Duxford directed that he be admonished and ordered me to make this entry".

"I deeply resented this and in a way the incident soured my attitude towards the RAF. During February 1941, when things were quiet, I went to Brian Lane, who was then our C.O., and told him how unjust I felt the endorsement to be as I had done my best to get the undercarriage down. He said that he would look into the matter. I heard from the squadron adjutant that Squadron Leader Lane had taken the matter up at Group H.Q. and had even made a formal visit. The result came several months later, when "Cancelled" was written in red ink across the endorsement. Brian also added below it:

"Entry made in error. No disciplinary action was taken, as accident was not attributable to pilot".

"It appears that he had discovered there had been similar accidents, caused by an air lock which had been removed by the shock of the landing, hence the reason why the undercarriage worked perfectly in the hanger.

"If Brian Lane had not been lost in such a useless action I am sure that he would have been one of the great fighter leaders of the war, quite possibly equal to Douglas Bader and Johnnie Johnson – certainly he was one of the first having led a wing of Spitfires over Dunkirk. Someone in Fighter Command surely made a blunder in posting him to No.167 Squadron, which specialised in low level ground attacks, during which flak was intense and luck played a major part in who was shot down. Brian Lane's exceptional skills as both a fighter pilot and leader were obviously useless in such a role. He should have gone to a squadron operating wing sweeps. His experience would have been very useful in the summer of 1942 when Fighter Command were having a difficult time with the advent of the Focke Wulf 190."

Wing Commander Peter Howard – Williams:

"I well remember Brian Lane. When I left No.19 Squadron to join 118 at Filton, he wrote "Good luck" above his final signature in my log book. I have it in front of me as I write this. He was a most pleasant man, and very supportive at all times – he certainly stood up for his pilots.

"Time can be a hazy thing, but I seem to remember that he fitted two mirrors to the sides of his Spitfire and streamlined them in, to improve his rearwards vision during combat. A wingless Air Commodore visited Duxford and told Brian to take them off. Brian apparently replied "Well you fly the bloody thing then!" Personally I was shot at far more often than I shot at others during the war, and got a nasty cannon shell explode in my cockpit just behind the seat on one occasion. The armour plate had saved me. Pilots like Brian Lane were exceptional."

Wing Commander Frank Brinsden:

"How pleased I am that Brian Lane is to receive public exposure and recognition at last. Being the commander of a squadron based on the fringe of the Battle of Britain area, he was prevented from showing his skills and therefore did not excite the acclaim afforded to the commanders of squadrons based in the southern counties. Brian always used a silver cigarette case without affectation. He was always so much more sophisticated than the rest of us. His fine old black Armstrong Siddeley car was always highly polished, whereas our old Standards, Fords etcetera were battered and in need of loving care and attention."

Group Captain Gordon Sinclair:

"He was a very quiet person, rather intellectual, and always in the background was the fact of his blind father. In his quiet way he was a very compelling leader, particularly since he was an excellent pilot. We became friends very soon after he came to Duxford, so close that he married Eileen Ellison – quietly and without fuss – to whom I had introduced him! I remember he had a delightful sense of humour and was quick to laugh – he smiled easily. I have thought about Brian frequently since those days."

Flight Lieutenant Noel MacGregor:

"I well remember my respected former C.O., who was courteously unassuming and a great leader at all times."

For Oberleutnant Walter Leonhardt, Brian Lane's death represented the fourth victory bar on his Focke Wulf FW190's rudder, just as the deaths of a number of young Germans represented another statistic in Squadron Leader Lane's "score". Leonhardt was to claim one more victory before his own death in action. On February 2nd, 1943, during combat with American Liberator bombers, Walter Leonhardt was shot down sixty miles north west of Texel, and the German pilot joined Brian Lane in the North Sea. Perhaps that fact illustrates how futile war is, and emphasises at what terrible cost of young lives freedom was won.

APPENDIX I

SERVICE RECORD OF
SQUADRON LEADER 37859 BRIAN JAMES EDWARD LANE D.F.C.

Accepted for Short Service Commission in the RAF	– 1936
Air Service Training, Hamble	22.03.36 – 13.05.36
No.11 Flying Training School, Wittering	03.06.36 – 08.01.37
No.66 (Fighter) Squadron, Duxford	08.01.37 – 22.03.37
No.213 (Fighter) Squadron, Northolt	01.04.37 – 30.06.37
No.213 (Fighter) Squadron, Church Fenton	01.07.37 – 18.05.38
No.213 (Fighter) Squadron, Wittering	18.05.38 – 11.09.39
Flying accident, Miles Magister L8136	11.11.38
No.19 (Fighter) Squadron, Duxford. Promoted to Flight Lieutenant and & 'A' Flight commander	11.09.39 – 20.10.39
No.19 (Fighter) Squadron, Catterick	20.10.39 – 27.10.39
No.19 (Fighter) Squadron, Duxford	27.10.39 – 17.04.40
No.19 (Fighter) Squadron, Horsham	17.04.40 – 16.05.40
No.19 (Fighter) Squadron, Duxford	16.05.40 – 25.05.40
No.19 (Fighter) Squadron, Hornchurch	25.05.40 – 04.06.40
Claimed one Ju87 and one Me109 probable, one Me109 confirmed destroyed over Dunkirk	26.05.40
Claimed one Me110 destroyed over Dunkirk	01.06.40
No.19 (Fighter) Squadron, Duxford	04.06.40 – 20.06.41
Awarded Distinguished Flying Cross	31.07.40
Claimed one Me110 destroyed over Thames Estuary	24.08.40
Promoted to Squadron Leader, officer commanding No.19 Squadron	05.09.40
Claimed one Me110 destroyed over North Weald	07.09.40
Claimed one Me110 destroyed and an He111 damaged over Gravesend	11.09.40
Claimed one Me109 probable over London	15.09.40
Shot down by Hurricane, force landed at Eastchurch airfield	08.11.40
Awarded share in Me110 destroyed	15.11.40
H.Q. 12 Group, Watnall	20.06.41 – 10.11.41
Air H.Q. Western Desert	28.01.42 – 13.02.42
H.Q. Middle East	13.02.42 – 25.06.42
No.61 Operational Training Unit, Montford Bridge	16.09.42 – 07.12.42
No.167 'Gold Coast' (Dutch) Squadron, Ludham	07.12.42

Killed in action twenty miles west of Schouen Island, off Dutch coast, in Spitfire AR612, by Oberleutnant Leonhardt, 2/JG 1. Body never recovered, remembered on Runnymede Memorial, panel 65.   13.12.42

APPENDIX II

AIRCRAFT AND PILOT LOSSES SUSTAINED BY NO.19 SQUADRON DURING THE PERIOD SEPTEMBER 3RD 1939 TO JUNE 20TH 1941

06.10.39	K9854	Flown by P/O G.E. Ball, collided with K9821, flown by F/O W.G. Clouston, latter forced landed at Newmarket race course. Both pilots uninjured.
06.10.39	K9821	See above.
24.01.40	K9811	Crashed in forced landing near Clare, Suffolk.
29.02.40	K9809	Dived into ground on take off from Duxford whilst on night flying exercise. P/O H.A. Trenchard killed.
31.03.40	K9858	Crashed on take off from Horsham St. Faith, the pilot, F/O D.R.S. Bader, having ommitted to select correct airscrew setting. Pilot uninjured.
26.05.40	N3200	S/L G.D. Stephenson shot down in combat near Dunkirk, made forced landing on beach and taken prisoner.
26.05.40	N3237	P/O P.V. Watson shot down in combat near Dunkirk. Pilot baled out but was never seen again.
26.05.40	L3198	F/O G.E. Ball, aircraft damaged and pilot slightly wounded in combat with Bf109s near Dunkirk.
26.05.40	P9305	Sgt C.A. Irwin shot down and killed over the Channel, pilot's body never recovered.
26.05.40	L1031	Damaged in combat with Bf109s near Dunkirk. P/O M.D. Lyne wounded in leg and forced landed on Walmer Beach.
01.06.40	K9836	Sgt J.A. Potter shot down in combat with Bf109s near Dunkirk. Pilot ditched in Channel and returned via boat.
19.06.40	L1032	Hit by return fire from He111 near Bury St Edmunds at 0100 hrs. Spitfire exploded, pilot F/O G.W. Petre baled out badly burned. Enemy aircraft also destroyed, believed to be the first Spitfire nocturnal victory.
13.07.40	R6688	Sgt R.R.G. Birch crashed near Duxford and was killed during dogfight practice with F/Sgt H. Steere.
28.07.40	R6627	Sgt H.A.C. Roden crashed on landing at Fowlmere following combat with Ju88, pilot uninjured.
16.08.40	R6904	Sgt H.A.C. Roden – Damaged in combat with Bf110s off Harwich, pilot uninjured.
31.08.40	X4231	F/O J.B.Coward shot down during attack on Do17s. Cannon shell exploded in cockpit, severing lower right leg. Pilot baled out and survived.
31.08.40	R6958	F/O F.N.Brinsden shot down in combat with Bf109s over the Thames Estuary. Baled out unhurt.

31.08.40	R6912	Flaps damaged in combat with Bf109s, crashed on landing ay Fowlmere, P/O R.A.C. Aeberhardt killed.
05.09.40	P9422	S/L P.C. Pinkham shot down, believed by return cross fire from Do17s over Thames Estuary and/or possibly hit by Bf109. Pilot, wounded, baled out too low and killed.
05.09.40	N3286	Returned to Fowlmere severely damaged following combat with Bf109s over Hornchurch. P/O W.J. Lawson unhurt.
05.09.40	P9391	Damaged in combat with Bf109s over Thames Estuary, P/O E. Burgoyne unhurt.
09.09.40	P9431	Damaged in combat over North Weald, Sub – Lt A.G. Blake unhurt. Note: the shattered windscreen from this aircraft can be seen at the Battle of Britain Museum, Hendon.
09.09.40	P9546	Received bullet through port mainspar during combat with Bf109s over London, P/O W. Cunningham unhurt.
11.09.40	N3046	Damaged in combat with Bf109s over London, F/O F. Dolezal (Czech) wounded in leg.
11.09.40	P9546	F/Sgt G.C. Unwin shot down by return fire from Do215. Pilot unhurt and executed a wheels down forced landing near Brentwood, Essex. One enemy round penetrated the armoured windscreen and was in the pilot's possession for many years.
11.09.40	X4059	Damaged in combat with Bf109 over London, F/O L.A. Haines unhurt.
14.09.40	R6625	Sgt F. Marek (Czech) dived into the ground and killed at Horndon – on – the – Hill, believed as a result of oxygen failure.
15.09.40	R6991	Damaged in combat over the Channel, Sub – Lt A.G. Blake unhurt.
15.09.40	X4070	Shot down near French coast after chasing enemy aircraft across the Channel. Sgt J.A. Potter wounded and taken prisoner.
15.09.40	P9431	Damaged during combat with Bf109s over the Channel, Sgt H.A.C. Roden slightly wounded.
18.09.40	N3265	Force landed as a result of engine failure during routine patrol. Pilot P/O F. Hradil unhurt.
18.09.40	X4170	Damaged in combat over the Thames Estuary, P/O W.J. Lawson forced landed at Eastchurch Airfield.
22.09.40	X4351	Destroyed during attack on Fowlmere.
27.09.40	X4352	Shot down near Canterbury by Bf109, P/O E. Burgoyne killed.
27.09.40	X4237	Shot down by Bf109s near Canterbury, Sgt D.G.S.R. Cox baled out, wounded in foot.
29.10.40	P7423	Shot down by Bf109s in surprise attack over London. Sub – Lt A.G. Blake killed.

29.10.40	P7379	Sgt A.N. McGregor force landed at Rochford out of fuel.
05.11.40	R6889	Damaged in combat with Bf109s near Rochford, P/O W.J.Lawson unhurt.
05.11.40	P7545	Shot down in flames by Bf109 and crashed near Southend Pier. P/O F. Hradil (Czech) killed.
05.11.40	P7427	Damaged in combat with Bf109s near Rochford, F/Sgt G.C. Unwin unhurt.
08.11.40	P7377	Shot down by a Hurricane which dived out of cloud in pursuit of a Bf109. S/L B.J.E. Lane forced landed at Eastchurch Airfield and received minor facial injuries.
15.11.40	P7420	Sgt H.A.C. Roden killed whilst making a forced landing near Boxford, Sussex, when aircraft hit a tree.
12.01.41	P7318	P/O P.I. Howard – Williams crashed on landing at Fowlmere after wing sweep, pilot unhurt.
20.02.41	P7430	Sgt H.W. Charnock crashed on take off from Fowlmere, pilot unhurt.
22.02.41	P7535	Dived into ground after take off. Sgt Johnson killed.
25.02.41	P7421	Forced landed after wing sweep, Sgt Brown unhurt.
24.03.41	P7379	Damaged in mid – air collision with P7429 during practice flight. Sgt H.W. Charnock forced landed unhurt at Fowlmere.
24.03.41	P7429	Collided with above aircraft at 5,000 ft. P/O Anderson baled out unhurt.
21.04.41	P7617	Believed crashed at Claxton, Norfolk, circumstances not known.

NOTE: Squadron Leader B.J.E. Lane left No.19 Squadron on 20.06.41. The next aircraft loss following that on 21.04.41 occured on 23.06.41 when a Spitfire was damaged in combat with Bf109s off Le Touquet. As from that time No.19 Squadron became involved in flying the early offensive fighter sweeps and "Circus" daylight bomber escort sorties, harrassing the enemy in northern France and the Low Countries. The squadron was in regular combat with the enemy and their losses, and claims, increased. However, as that period of No.19 Squadron's history is beyond the period covered by this book, they are not included here.

APPENDIX III

COMBAT CLAIMS MADE BY NO.19 SQUADRON PILOTS DURING THE PERIOD SEPTEMBER 3RD 1939 TO JUNE 20TH 1941

11.05.40	F/L W.G. Clouston F/O G.W. Petre F/S H. Steere	Ju88 destroyed. 1340 hrs, 10 miles east of East Dudgeon.
26.05.40	S/L G.D. Stephenson	Ju87 destroyed Dunkirk area.
26.05.40	P/O M.D. Lyne	Ju87 destroyed Dunkirk area.
26.05.40	F/O F.N. Brinsden	Ju87 destroyed Dunkirk area.
26.05.40	Sgt J.A. Potter	Bf109 destroyed Dunkirk area.
26.05.40	F/L W.G. Clouston	2 Ju87s destroyed Dunkirk area.
26.05.40	F/S H. Steere	Ju87 destroyed Dunkirk area.
26.05.40	F/O G.E. Ball	Bf109 destroyed Dunkirk area.
26.05.40	F/O G.L. Sinclair	Bf109 destroyed Dunkirk area.
26.05.40	F/L B.J.E. Lane	1 Ju87 & 1 Bf109 probable, 0913 hrs, Dunkirk area.
26.05.40	F/L B.J.E. Lane	1 Bf109 destroyed, 1600 hrs, Dunkirk area.
27.05.40	F/L W.G. Clouston	1 Do215 destroyed, French coast.
27.05.40	F/S H. Steere	1 Do215 destroyed, French coast.
27.05.40	F/L W.G. Clouston F/O G.W. Petre F/S G.C. Unwin	1 Hs126 destroyed inland of Dunkirk.
28.05.40	F/S G.C. Unwin	1 Bf109 destroyed, Dunkirk area.
28.05.40	F/S H. Steere	1 Bf109 destroyed, Dunkirk area.
01.06.40	P/O H.C. Baker	1 Bf110 destroyed, Dunkirk area.
01.06.40	F/L W.G. Clouston	1 Bf109 destroyed, Dunkirk area.
01.06.40	F/L W.G. Clouston F/S H. Steere	1 Bf109 destroyed, 0540 hrs, French coast.
01.06.40	P/O L.A. Haines	1 Bf109 destroyed, Dunkirk area.
01.06.40	Sgt B.J. Jennings	2 Bf110s destroyed, Dunkirk area.
01.06.40	P/O G.L. Sinclair	2 Bf110s & 1 Do17 destroyed, Dunkirk area.
01.06.40	F/S G.C. Unwin	1 Bf110 destroyed, Dunkirk area.
01.06.40	F/S H. Steere	1 Do215 destroyed, Dunkirk area.
01.06.40	F/L B.J.E. Lane	1 Bf110 destroyed, 0540 hrs, 2 miles NE of Dunkirk.
19.06.40	F/O G.W.Petre	1 He111 destroyed. This aircraft was "5J+AM" of 4/KG4 which crashed at Six Mile Bottom, Cambridgeshire at

		0115 hrs. Believed to be the Spitfire's first nocturnal victory.
19.06.40	F/O G.E. Ball	1 He111 destroyed. "5J + FP of 6/KG4, crashed inton the sea off Margate, Kent, at 0215 hrs.
16.08.40	Sgt J.A. Potter	1 Bf110 destroyed 35 miles east of Harwich.
16.08.40	F/S G.C. Unwin	1 Bf110 destroyed as above
16.08.40	P/O W. Cunningham	1 Bf110 destroyed as above
19.08.40	F/O L.A. Haines F/S H. Steere Sgt D.G.S.R. Cox	Claimed as a Bf110 destroyed, but believed by Cox to be a Do17 as third crew member seen to bale out.
24.08.40	F/L B.J.E. Lane	1 Bf110 destroyed, 1610 hrs, mouth of Thames Estuary.
24.08.40	Sgt B.J. Jennings	2 Bf110s destroyed, Thames Estuary.
31.08.40	F/L W.G. Clouston P/O E. Burgoyne	1 Bf110 destroyed south of Colchester.
31.08.40	Sgt D.G.S.R. Cox	1 Bf110 destroyed, 0900 hrs south of Colchester. Aircraft "3U + HS" of II/ZG76, Oblt Bergen & Uffz Becker missing.
03.09.40	F/O L.A. Haines	1 Bf110 destroyed.
03.09.40	F/S G.C. Unwin	1 Bf110 destroyed.
05.09.40	F/O L.A. Haines	1 Bf109 destroyed, 1005 hrs. Aircraft "9 +" of 1/JG54, crashed at 6 Hardy Street, Maidstone, the pilot, Uffz Hotzelmann baled out unhurt.
05.09.40	Sgt Plzak	1 Bf109 destroyed south of London.
07.09.40	P/O W. Cunningham	1 He111 destroyed, 1720 hrs, east Kent, south of Sheppey.
07.09.40	F/O F. Dolezal	1 Bf110 destroyed, Thames Estuary.
07.09.40	S/L B.J.E. Lane	1 Bf110 destroyed, 1710 hrs, over North Weald. Aircraft "A2 + NH" of Stab II/ZG2. Lt K.Schunemann and Uffz H.Mescheder both baled out too low and were killed. Also attacked by Hurricane of 1 and 310 Squadrons.
07.09.40	F/S G.C. Unwin	2 Bf109s destroyed, 1730 – 1750 hrs, between Ramsgate & west London.
09.09.40	Sub – Lt A.G. Blake	1 He111 destroyed south of London.
09.09.40	Sgt D.G.S.R. Cox	1 Bf109 destroyed south of London.
09.09.40	F/L W.G. Clouston	1 Bf109 destroyed south of London.
09.09.40	P/O W.J. Lawson	1 Bf110 destroyed, 1750 hrs, London area.

09.09.40	P/O W. Cunningham	1 Bf109 destroyed, 1745 hrs, over London.
09.09.40	F/S H. Steere	1 Bf110 probable, 1800 hrs, south of London.
09.09.40	P/O A.F. Vokes	1 Do215 damaged, over north London.
09.09.40	F/O F.N. Brinsden	½ He111 probable, south of Test.
11.09.40	Sgt B.J. Jennings	1 Bf110 destroyed & 1 probable He111, 1615 hrs, Gravesend. The Bf110 crashed at Barnes Cote, Harvel, and was "3U + LT" of 9/ZG26. Oblt J. Junghans killed. Gefr P. Eckert remains missing to this day.
11.09.40	F/O L.A. Haines	1 Bf110 destroyed east of London.
11.09.40	Sgt H.A.C. Roden	1 Bf110 destroyed east of London.
11.09.40	P/O W.J. Lawson	1 He111 destroyed east of London.
11.09.40	F/S G.C. Unwin	1 He111 probable, 1 Do215 damaged, 1600 hrs over east London.
11.09.40	S/L B.J.E. Lane	2 Bf110s destroyed, 1615 hrs over Gravesend.
15.09.40	S/L B.J.E. Lane	1 Bf109 probable, 1450 hrs, London area.
15.09.40	F/L W.G.Clouston	1 Bf110 destroyed over Detling.
15.09.40	P/O W. Cunningham	1 Bf109 destroyed, 1450 hrs over London. Aircraft of 7/JG51, pilot, Lt K Bildau baled out and captured.
15.09.40	F/O L.A. Haines	1 Bf110 & 1 Bf109 destroyed. Latter aircraft "2 +" if 3/LG2, crash landed at Shellness, 1445 hrs, Uffz A. Klick captured unhurt.
15.09.40	F/S H. Steere	1 Bf109 destroyed, 1220 hrs, south of London.
15.09.40	F/S H. Steere	1 Do17 destroyed, 1450 hrs, above cloud over London.
15.09.40	Sgt D.G.S.R. Cox	1 Bf109 destroyed, 1215 – 1230 hrs, 5 miles south of Tunbridge Wells. Believed to have been "5 +" of 2/JG27. Forced landed near Uckfield, pilot, Uffz A. Walburger captured.
15.09.40	F/S G.C. Unwin	1 Bf109 destroyed, 1210 hrs, near Westerham, Kent. Believed to have been an aircraft if 3/JG53, crashed at Mullard Wood, Biggin Hill. Pilot Oblt J. Haase, killed as parachute failed.
15.09.40	F/S G.C. Unwin	2 Bf109s destroyed, 1440 – 1455 hrs,

189

15.09.40	P/O/ A.F. Vokes	1 Bf110 probable, 1440 hrs over north London.
15.09.40	Sub – Lt A.G. Blake	1 Bf109 destroyed & 1 He111 destroyed, 1430 hrs, London area. Latter aircraft "1H + IH" of 1/KG26 which forced landed below high water at Foulness. Crew captured. Also attacked by fighters of 1, 41, 257, and 310 Squadrons.
18.09.40	F/L W.G. Clouston P/O W. Cunningham P/O W.J. Lawson Sgt D.E. Lloyd	1 Ju88 destroyed, 1725 hrs, London area. Aircraft "3Z + ED" of Stab III/KG77, crashed at Eastry Mill, near Sandwich, Kent. Major M. Klehs and Oblt F. Lauth killed, Fw F. Himsel and Fw F. Probst baled out and captured.
18.09.40	F/O L.A. Haines F/S H.Steere	1 Ju88 destroyed, mouth of Thames Estuary. Aircraft "3Z + ES" of 8/KG77, crashed on Isle of Sheppey at 1700 hrs. Fw H. Damschen killed, Oberfw W. Semerau and Uffz H. Treutmann missing, Uffz K. Eggert captured but died of wounds.
18.09.40	F/O F. Dolezal	1 He111 destroyed.
18.09.40	Sgt S. Plzak	1 He111 destroyed.
18.09.40	Sgt G.C. Unwin	1 Bf110 destroyed.
18.09.40	F/S H. Steere	1 He111 destroyed, shared with Spitfires of 66 Squadron, mouth of Thames Estuary.
27.09.40	Sub – Lt A.G. Blake	2 Bf109s destroyed over the Channel.
27.09.40	P/O W.J. Lawson	1 Bf109 destroyed 10 miles off Cap Gris Nez, French Coast.
27.09.40	F/O D.T. Parrott	1 Bf109 destroyed off Folkestone.
27.09.40	Sgt S. Plzak	1 Bf109 destroyed
27.09.40	F/S H. Steere	1 Bf109 destroyed, 1215 hrs, Deal area.
27.09.40	F/S G.C. Unwin	1 Bf109 destroyed 1215 hrs, SE Kent.
27.09.40	Sgt B.J. Jennings	1 Bf109 destroyed, 1215 hrs, south of Thames Estuary.
05.11.40	F/S G.C. Unwin	1 Bf109 destroyed.
05.11.40	F/O L.A. Haines	½ Bf109 destroyed. Aircraft "White 12 +" of 1/JG26. Crashed into garden at Albion Road, Birchington. Fw E Scheidt captured. Victory shared with

05.11.40	F/L W.J. Lawson	F/O W.L. McNight of 242 Squadron.

05.11.40   F/L W.J. Lawson

05.11.40   Sgt H.W. Charnock

15.11.40   S/L B.J.E. Lane
           P/O W. Cunningham
           P/O A.F. Vokes

15.11.40   F/O L.A. Haines

28.11.40   F/O L.A. Haines

28.11.40   F/S H. Steere

28.11.40   F/S G.C. Unwin
           Sgt D. Fulford

F/O W.L. McNight of 242 Squadron.
1 Bf109 destroyed.
1 Bf109 destroyed.
1 Bf110 destroyed, 1100 hrs, Southend. Believed to have been aircraft "4N + DH" of 1(F)/22, crashed into Thames Estuary. Crew Fw O. Kaiser and Gefr H.v.d. Sande missing.
1 Bf110 destroyed. Believed to have been "4N + BH" of 1(F)/22, Lt H. von Jakob captured, Uffz J. Boschen killed.
1 Bf109 destroyed.
1 Bf109 destroyed, 1600 hrs, 5 miles east of Ramesgate.
1 Bf109 destroyed.

NOTE: The next victory claimed by No.19 Squadron was a Bf109 destroyed by Flight Lieutenant W.J. Lawson near Lille on 27.06.41 As Squadron Leader B.J.E. Lane DFC left No.19 Squadron on 20.06.41, that victory and the three others claimed during 1941, are beyond the period covered by this book.

Index to RAF personnel

Aeberhardt P/O   123;132,5.

Ball P/O G.E.   101,2.

Bader F/O D.   104,5;123;141,2,5,7;
                        150,2,3,6,7,8;162,4;
                        181.

Baker P/O   154.

Banham F/Lt A.J.   101

Benzie P/O   145

Birch Sgt.   123

Blake Sub – Lt G.A.   119;123,4;131,7;146,7;
                        151,4;160,2.

Boulding F/O R.   171

Boulton F/O J.   147

Bowring P/O J.H.   101

Boyd Sgt T.   101

Brinsden P/O F.N.   101,5,7;110,2,8;128;
                        131,4;146,7;157;
                        163,6;175;181.

Brothers F/Lt   150

Bruce Sgt A.   101

Burgoyne P/O   132,4,8;146;160,1.

Burton S/L   158

Carpenter P/O   137

Charnock Sgt   149;165,6.

Clouston F/O W.   101,2,5,6;112,7;
                       124,6;133,4;
                       142,4,5,6,9;154.

Cochran P/O   154

Coleman Sgt J.A.   101

Cork Sub – Lt R.   145

Coward F/O J.   133,4.

Cox Sgt D.   114,5;126,7;130,3,
                       134,5;147,8;151,8;
                       160,1,9;180.

Cozens S/L H.I.   101,3,4.

Cunningham P/O W.   123,4,8,9;131;144,6,7;
                       152,6,9;162,8,9;171.

Dolezal P/O   133;144,8,9;157.

Dowding ACM H.   102;124;141;164.

Dundas F/Lt J.   169

Dutton S/L R.   172

Edwards S/L   176

Evans P/O W.G. — 177,8
Fulford Sgt — 169
Furst Sgt — 137
Gardner Sub – Lt — 166
Groth P/O — 145
Gunning Sgt P.S. — 101
Haines P/O L.A. — 101;113;130,6,8;148, 149;152,3,6,9;166,9.
Hart P/O — 166
Heukensfeld P/O H.P.J. — 177,8.
Homer P/O G. — 165

Hood S/L R. — 112,3.
Howard F/O J.B. — 101
Howard – Williams P/O P. — 109;119;123;169; 170;181.
Hradil P/O — 133;149;166
Janough P/O — 143
Jennings Sgt — 110,2;128;131,2,3, 137;143,8;159;167, 169;180.
Jiroudek Sgt — 165
Jones P/O — 149
King – Clark P/O — 118
Koukal Sgt — 145
Lane Mrs. E. — 118;176,9.
Lawson P/O — 117;137;143,6,8; 151,6,9;165,6,9.
Learoyd F/Lt R.A.B. — 97
Leigh – Mallory AVM T. — 106;137,9;140,1,7; 162,4.
Levenson Sgt — 149
Little Cpt — 113
Llewellyn P/O A.J.A. — 101
Lloyd Sgt — 149;156.
Lyne P/O M.D. — 101,3,4,8;110.
MacGregor F/Lt N. — 181
Marek Sgt — 133;149.
Marples P/O L. — 101
Maude S. — 98
Matheson F/O G.C. — 101,4.
McKnight F/Lt — 165
McNab S/L E. — 154
Mermagen S/L — 102,5.
Mortimer P/O — 150,4.
O'Brien S/L — 118

Pace F/O T.G. — 101,5.
Park AVM K. — 126;131;140,1,2,5; 152,8;164.
Parrott P/O P. — 132;160.
Petre P/O G.W. — 101,2,6;110,2,7,8,9; 170
Phillips Sgt P.B. — 98
Pinkham S/L P. — 113,9;120,1,2,5,6,7; 130,3.
Plesman F/O J.L. — 177,8.
Plzak Sgt — 133,8;156;160,2.
Potter Sgt J.H. — 101,7;112;128,9;155
Powell – Sheddon F/Lt — 150,151.
Prchal Sgt — 154
Puda Sgt — 165
Quintin Brand AVM Sir C. — 140
Rimmer F/Lt — 150
Robinson F/O A.I. — 101
Roden Sgt — 124,8;131;148;155; 161,8.
Rypl P/O — 147
Sclanders Sgt — 147
Scott – Malden P/O D. — 115
Shepherd Sgt — 149
Sinclair P/O G.L. — 101;110,8;132;147; 181.
Steere F/Sgt H. — 101,2,6;112,5,7; 123;130;144,6;152, 154,6;160,5,9;170,9
Stephenson S/L G. — 104,7,8,9;113;121.
Sutherland P/O — 122;161.
Tamblyn P/O — 150,1.
Tofts F/Sgt — 126
Trenchard P/O — 103
Tyrer Sgt — 150
Unwin F/Sgt G.C. — 101,2,5;111,2;128, 129;133,7;142,4,8,9; 153,4,5,7,8;160,3,6, 168,9;170,9.
Vokes P/O A. — 127;137;147;154; 162,6,8,9;171.
Watson P/O — 106,8,9.
Whitehouse F/Lt T. — 176
Withall F/Lt L.C. — 101
Woodhall Gp Capt — 118;135.
Wray J. — 97,8.

192